# THE NEW NURSE MANAGER

## A Guide to Management Development

**Donna Richards Sheridan, R.N., M.S., M.B.A.**
Management Development Coordinator
Editor, *Stanford Nurse*

**Jean Eppinger Bronstein, R.N., M.S.**
Assistant Director of Nursing,
Adult Critical Care

**Duane D. Walker, R.N., M.S., F.A.A.N.**
Associate Administrator/Director of Nursing

Stanford University Hospital
Stanford, California

AN ASPEN PUBLICATION®
Aspen Publishers, Inc.
Rockville, Maryland
Royal Tunbridge Wells
1984

Library of Congress Cataloging in Publication Data

Sheridan, Donna Richards.
The new nurse manager.

"An Aspen publication."
Includes bibliographies and index.
1. Nursing service administration. I. Bronstein, Jean Eppinger.
II. Walker, Duane D. III. Title.
RT89.S53     1984     362.1'73'068     84-6324
ISBN: 0-89443-594-9

Publisher: John R. Marozsan
Associate Publisher: Jack W. Knowles, Jr.
Editorial Director: N. Darlene Como
Executive Managing Editor: Margot G. Raphael
Managing Editor: M. Eileen Higgins
Editorial Services: Jane Coyle
Printing and Manufacturing: Debbie Collins

Library of Congress Catalog Card Number: 84-6324
ISBN: 0-89443-594-9

*Printed in the United States of America*

4  5

*To the Nursing Managers*
at Stanford University Hospital
Stanford, California

and

- To my husband, Jim,
  and my four daughters,
  Barbra, Nicole, Lauren, and Rachel
  —Donna

- To my husband, Gary,
  and my two sons,
  Greg and Chad

  –Jean

- To Donna and Jean
  for the exhilarating experience
  of working with them
  —Duane

Continuing Education credits can be obtained using this book. For information, contact Donna Sheridan, c/o Stanford Nursing, Stanford University Medical Center, Stanford, CA 94305.

# Table of Contents

# Foreword

It is a pleasure to write the Foreword for *The New Nurse Manager* for at least two reasons. First, I have a long-standing respect for one of its authors, Mr. Duane D. Walker, Associate Hospital Director and Director of Nursing at Stanford. It is always a treat when such an excellent nurse manager shares his knowledge with the rest of the nursing management community. Second, because I believe that this book serves a very useful purpose: it is designed for the education of the new nurse manager (whose prototype is still the head nurse). The authors, unlike many, never forget the purpose of their book: helping the *novice* manager. One gets a feeling that all three authors must be intimately involved in the education of many such managers. Their sensitivity to the problems of the new manager is evident throughout the work.

Two special features of this book stand out. First, it is designed for one's first exposure to the management perspective. It contains many examples of pragmatic problems that might occur on the nursing unit. The examples are simple—but not to the brand-new manager. They are also typical—and, therefore, especially valuable to the new manager. The authors convert management principles to practical application in the nursing care environment.

The exercises concluding each chapter represent the second outstanding feature of this book. Much of the reader's learning (probably the largest portion) is achieved by doing these exercises, specially designed for the new nurse manager. They are diverse in kind, ranging from case studies to tests to research questions concerning one's own organization. For example, the nurse manager is asked, "Who is your director of nursing?" "How can you change a policy?" The exercises are highly directive and force managers either to apply what they have just learned, to learn more about the workings of their own institutions, or to learn more concerning the general theme of the chapter.

The exercises often add new material not addressed in the preceding chapters. They are not an afterthought; indeed, they constitute the major work of the book

ix

and should not be skipped if the book is to have its major impact on the learner. They make the book an excellent one for the manager-learner who learns best by doing. (The "workbook" approach might work well with groups of new managers learning together under the guidance of an instructor.)

In one way, this book is written at a more fundamental level than is the norm in books for the beginning manager. This is the only book, for example, that forces head nurses to:

- find out and write down the names of their institutions' presidents and vice presidents
- identify and work through three current problems on their own nursing units
- calculate the FTE employees allotted to their own units
- specify an institution's policies for electrical safety
- analyze how float pools are assigned in their own institutions.

This level of knowledge is frequently taken for granted in management books and, consequently, remains unstated. Much of the content of this book, therefore, may not be found elsewhere. (Other texts may give principles, but they offer no specifics that tie their content to the reader's home institution.)

This book makes no assumptions concerning the reader's prior managerial know-how. The authors write with the realization that basic elements must be understood by the novice manager before he or she is ready to move on to a more sophisticated overview of management. Many of us who write nursing management texts have been away from the entry management position so long that we tend to forget these concerns. This book does not make that error and consequently should appeal to the new manager who steps into the role with little preparation.

A major strength of this book is that it facilitates the new manager's knowledge of his or her organization and how it runs and also introduces the nurse manager to the utility of various conceptual models of management. Most chapters evolve from one or more such models, usually such well known ones as management by objectives, Maslow's hierarchy of needs, and Blake and Mouton's managerial grid. The authors then apply these models to the problems or goals of the individual nursing unit.

Tone is always important in a management book, and one is always interested in the managerial philosophy underlying such a book. I, for one, was pleased to find a strong commitment to management. Nowhere is the management function underplayed or subjugated to clinical care goals. The role that the manager plays *as manager* in improving clinical care is clear. The difference between management of staff and clinical management of a patient case load is stressed throughout. This book is for managers who take pride in being managers.

In summary, this book is highly directive. Each chapter begins with clearly specified behavioral objectives, moves through content, and ends with a large assortment of learning activities. It presents solutions and strategies; it seldom dwells on subtleties of interpretation. It is clearly a "how to" book for new managers who need all the help they can get, providing direction, answers, and paths to follow. It will be especially valuable for the action-oriented manager who learns by doing.

The greatest charm of this volume is its ability to zero in on the everyday problems of the new manager. It treats these problems with sensitivity and interest and looks at "old problems" (repeated by every generation of new managers) in ways that make the solutions of those problems new, exciting, and challenging. *The New Nurse Manager* is a must for the formative library of any new nurse manager.

*Barbara J. Stevens*, R.N., PH.D., F.A.A.N.
Director, Division of Health Services,
Sciences and Education
Chairman, Department of Nursing Education
Teachers College, Columbia University

# Preface

"Being a first level supervisor is one of the most difficult, demanding, and challenging jobs in any organization. Buried in an organizational web, this person must be adroit at administering a unit and at perceiving which, among all the daily tasks delegated downward, are the most important to accomplish," says Sasser and Leonard in a recent Harvard Business Review article (1980, p. 113). They compare the performance of a first line manager to walking a circus high wire— both require skillful balancing when forces pull in a variety of directions. First-level managers need to harmonize often conflicting management and work force demands and may lose their sense of identity in performing this precarious balancing act. Yet the goals of the entire organization are dependent upon the success of the performance of first line managers.

In health care this first line manager, called the head nurse or clinical coordinator, has responsibility 24 hours a day, seven days a week for the quality of nursing care given to a specific patient population. "The head nurse's responsibilities may be enough to tax the physical, intellectual, and emotional resources of any individual. The head nurse should be a master in interacting with people and should possess excellent communication skills, maturity, and good physical health," says Rotkovitch (1983). This country's 7,000 hospitals spend 1.6 billion dollars annually on head nurses. We need to ask how much of this money is wasted if nursing directors and assistants do not promote growth and development for head nurses as first-line nursing managers (Rotkovitch, 1983).

Nursing management is growing more complex in several ways. Today's nurse manager must work within a negotiated-order model rather than rely upon hierarchical authority. This nurse must negotiate with many other power groups in achieving her nursing service ends. This calls for a more sophisticated form of management than was the case when nursing retained control of many other services and departments (Stevens, 1979).

Stevens, an authority in nursing management development, emphasizes the need to develop the nurse manager so that this nurse leader can synthesize the disciplines of nursing and management to better achieve nursing ends. Stevens recommends that the nurse manager's development include a clear definition of expectations, orientation to the realities of today's management, and a coaching process to accompany the orientation.

"Middle managers face difficult and complex responsibilities. Their ability to manage is crucial to good, cost-effective patient care—and too important to be developed through trial-and-error, on-the-job training," says Stetler (1980). And Zander (1981) concurs:

> Relying on experience to educate nurse managers is a tenuous proposition because it assumes that the nurse manager will be able to have intellectual and emotional objectivity about the highly personal function of management. Without the necessary objectivity, a nurse manager is too busy and often too overwhelmed to learn from either mistakes or successes. Learning by hands-on experience without the background of theory and the input of knowledgeable administrators as teachers is just as restricting as book knowledge without practical application of the principles to be learned.

The need for effective management development strategies cannot be overemphasized, agree Lanigan and Miller (1981), and developing a program that can be offered in a climate conducive to growth will contribute to the new manager's successful transition. Their conclusion is based on a series of interviews with nurse managers, where feelings of "not knowing enough" or "not knowing what I don't know" were found to be common among new managers. The experiences described by the interviewees suggested that any management development intervention should be designed to address at least three basic needs: belonging, gaining knowledge, and mastering skills. To meet these needs, Miller and Lanigan suggest regular coaching sessions with the new manager's supervisor and working with experienced coworkers for additional coaching, modeling, and emotional support. The need for developing a support network for new managers was also clearly indicated. "The feeling of isolation and loneliness seems to come shortly after the new manager begins and lasts until a supporting network of relationships is established" (p. 22).

A written survey conducted by Sheridan and Bronstein (1981) asked head nurses about their preparation for the role. What was effective in this preparation?

What was lacking? How could it be improved? All but one of the fifteen respondents believed that additional knowledge and skills were necessary for the new role. In an open-ended question, head nurse respondents themselves asked for information on communication, problem solving, systems, counseling, budget, goal setting, evaluation, and assertiveness. Learning methods suggested by respondents included mentoring by peers and/or supervisor, coaching sessions with a supervisor, self-study, a checklist for self-assessment, an overview of job responsibilities, and an understanding of the "pecking order," both formal (according to the organizational charts) and informal (who *really* has the power).

In searching for a methodology to meet the unique and complex learning needs of the new head nurse, we reviewed then current resources. Although our organization had recently begun to offer intensive seminars on two levels for management development, an additional self-study/coaching tool for new nurse managers seemed to be needed and desired. Such a tool would:

- integrate management theory with nursing by using examples common to the experience of the new head nurse
- help new head nurses learn about and begin to fit into their new organizational culture, whether at a new level, in a new organization, or both
- structure a series of developmental coaching sessions with a new supervisor
- provide a basic knowledge of management and management skills, then a means to adapt them to a variety of clinical and cultural settings
- be useful to new nurse managers and their supervisors and be easy (maybe even fun) to use.

Needless to say, it was difficult to find this very specialized tool.

So, we began to develop our own tool, a series of learning modules based on a loosely defined model. Over a period of three years of intensive work—research, trial by new managers, feedback, and revisions—we have written this book to help develop new nurse managers. The refinement of our model, "Development of the New Nurse Manager," is the core of the book. We are grateful, through Aspen Systems, to have the opportunity to share our new nurse managers' self-study/ coaching developmental tool with the nursing community.

"Nurse managers need managerial expertise in order to expand into the new roles required of them for the future multiorganizational health care systems," says Barbara Brown (1983). Spicer (1984) adds:

> The challenge to Nursing Administrators to provide management development will continue. If the challenge is not met, managers will exist within the illusions that surround their roles, these illusions decrease and inhibit their ability to function effectively. If the nurse manager's role is

not effective, nursing administrators will fall behind in the continuous struggle to optimize the patient care delivery system.

*The New Nurse Manager* offers nurse administrators an efficient, effective tool to develop that $1.6 billion head nurse resource while optimizing patient care in a variety of unique settings. If offers head nurses and future head nurses a tool for self-development in nursing management.

*Donna Richards Sheridan*
*Jean Eppinger Bronstein*
*Duane D. Walker*

---

## REFERENCES

Brown, B. From the editor: The nurse manager. *Nursing Administration Quarterly*, 1983, 7(2), viii–ix.

Lanigan, J., & Miller, J. Developing nurse managers. *Nursing Administration Quarterly*, 1981, 5(2), 21–24.

Rotkovitch, R. The head nurse as a first-line manager. *The Health Care Supervisor*, 1983, 1(4), 14–27.

Sasser, W.E., & Leonard, F.S. Let first-level supervisors do their job. *Harvard Business Review*, 1980, 58(2), 113–121.

Sheridan, D.R., & Bronstein, J.E. *Survey of new nurse manager needs*, Unpublished work, Stanford University Hospital, Department of Nursing, Stanford, Calif., 1981.

Spicer, J.G. Dispelling illusions with management development. *Nursing Administration Quarterly*, 1983, 7(2), 46–49.

Stetler, C. A modular approach to management development. *Journal of Nursing Administration*, Dec. 1980, 23.

Stevens, B.J. Improving nurses' managerial skills. *Nursing Outlook*, December 1979, 774–777.

Zander, K. Management training won't work . . . unless nursing administration provides it. *Nursing Administration Quarterly*, 1981, 7(2), 77–87.

# Chapter 1

# Role Transition

## OBJECTIVES

Upon completion of this chapter, including the activities, the new nurse manager will be able to:

- describe the four functions of the nurse manager using Fayol's classical framework;
- recognize your primary transitional barrier and formulate a strategy for dealing with it;
- describe your VANE filter (values, attitudes, needs, and expectations) and how it affects your perception of nursing;
- compare the doer role of the nurse clinician to the facilitator role of the nurse manager;
- contrast the job satisfactions of the staff nurse with the job satisfactions of the nurse manager;
- develop a plan for a new peer support system;
- set up a peer network to meet learning needs and to learn organizational norms; and
- describe perceived learning needs for your new head nurse role.

# DEVELOPMENT OF THE NEW NURSE MANAGER™ 1981

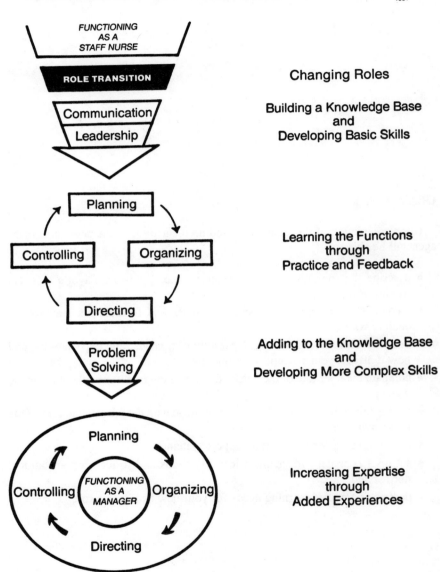

¶ As a new manager, you are about to assume a challenging new role. It may create discomfort by causing you to question your values while challenging you to reach for new heights. Whether you are promoted from within your organization or are coming to a new one, your perspectives will change substantially, affecting your expectations of staff and theirs of you. Friendships may be questioned. New skills will be needed. Redefinition of your career and life goals may be necessary.

## UNDERSTANDING ROLE TRANSITION

Understanding the transition will be helpful as you adapt to your new role. You may be thinking of how well you perform as a staff nurse—the performance appraisals you have received, the positive feedback from peers who recognize your professional expertise. Your skills may be outstanding as a clinician, but what do you know about management? Administrators frequently select the best clinician or technician for promotion to management, thereby moving that person from the position of expert to that of novice. The best clinician does not necessarily make the best manager. Besides inherent differences in the perspectives of clinician and manager, the knowledge and skills needed for each job also differ.

An important part of your role transition, therefore, is to find out what new knowledge and skills you will need. As a manager, you will be responsible for organizing and processing work and for influencing others. Henri Fayol (1949), the originator of clinical management theory, defines a manager's functions as planning, organizing, directing, and controlling. Although the managerial role may be unfamiliar, these functions are not new to you as a professional nurse. You have been planning and organizing patient care, directing staff and patients, and controlling the quality of patient service by evaluating care given and revising plans accordingly. Through these four functions you have been organizing and processing work and influencing others. These functions had to be learned when the role of staff nurse was new to you. As a new graduate, you may have awakened a physician at 3:00 a.m. with a concern for a patient. The physician may have let you know in no uncertain terms that you could have waited until morning. Another new experience you may remember is how overwhelmed you felt trying to balance your time between various patients, treatments, psychosocial patient needs, charting, and so forth. Finally you became sufficiently organized to give good patient care without what you considered to be excessive overtime. You could leave within an hour of the end of your shift. Yet your head nurse asked you why you still could not leave on time. In these two examples, both the doctor and the head nurse had expectations of you in your role as a staff nurse. These transitions of the new graduate nurse are part of reality shock.

Reality shock "is the surprise and disequilibrium experienced when a person moves from an understood, familiar culture to a new culture that has new demands and new unfamiliar meanings for familiar events" (Kramer, 1974, p. 4). As a new graduate, you had a good knowledge base and some of the skills necessary for your job as a nurse. But when thrown into the "culture of nurse" from the "culture of student," you had to meet new demands, such as increased patient assignments. Your primary goal had to change from learning about patient care to giving patient care. The way you adapted was to take on the perspective needed to perform the role of nurse—the expected culture. You also learned how to adapt familiar skills and use them in a new role. For example, when doing patient teaching, the way you learned as a student may have been useful in helping patients learn about their diseases. Your classroom theory needed grounding in experience to complete the learning process. You learned about communication, leadership, planning, and directing not only from books but from performing these functions.

You began to manage patient care as a new staff nurse. Perhaps you needed to learn and grow most in the area of management skills during your transition from student to staff nurse. You gained those skills in organizing complex patient assignments, setting priorities for conflicting patient needs, directing experienced nursing assistants, and communicating your observations to physicians.

So—what's new? The newness is the organizational position from which you will manage. By moving into management, you are now one step removed from patients. Your managing skills will be directed toward nurses and other health care staff, not specifically toward patients. The primary focus of your job is now removed from direct patient care. You may have experienced this role as a team leader in nursing.

In Exhibit 1–1, a comparison is made between how planning, organizing, directing, and controlling were manifest in your clinical role and how these skills will be adapted in your management role. Before, you planned to meet a patient's specific needs, but now you must plan to create an environment in which your staff can meet specific patient care needs. Whereas you once organized and set priorities for aspects of patient care, now you need to organize and set priorities for unit needs in a way that will facilitate patient care. Instead of directing patients, you will be directing staff, and your control responsibility will shift from individual patients to quality care for an entire patient population. Although the goal is still high-quality patient care, you must now attempt to achieve it through others. A wider range of forces will have an impact on achieving your patient care goals. No longer will you go to the bedside and administer care. Any direct patient care you give should be the exception—an emergency, a demonstration, perhaps observation or development of one of your staff.

## DISEQUILIBRIUM IN A NEW ROLE

Moving from staff nurse (the care giver) to head nurse (the director of care givers) will be a great challenge for you as a new manager. From your new position in the organization, your perceptions, your peer relationships, and your sources of

**Exhibit 1–1** Comparison of Clinician/Doer Role to Manager/Facilitator Role

|  | *Clinician-Doer* <br> *Clinical Base* | *Manager-Facilitator* <br> *Clinical/Managerial Base* |
|---|---|---|
| Plan | Plans care for patient(s) to meet specific health care needs and coordinates other health care personnel. | Plans for an environment in which clinicians can give good care. |
| Organize | Organizes and sets priorities for care delivery to meet needs of patients assigned to him/her. | Organizes unit systems, affecting both human and material resources, to support quality patient care on the unit. |
| Direct | Directs patients' care and health care team members in coordination of patient care delivery. | Directs staff for the 24-hour delivery of nursing care on the unit, including hiring, firing, coaching, and scheduling. |
| Control | Controls care plan evaluations and updates with health care team to reflect current patient needs/status. | Controls the quality of care on the unit through developing, maintaining, and measuring standards for the unit's patient population. |

job satisfaction will change. These will be major sources of surprise and disequilibrium.

## Personal Filters

Perception is the way we view the world; it occurs through a personal "filter" of sorts. Your personal filter is made up of your values, attitudes, needs, and expectations. Kelly (1980) calls this frame of reference the VANE—values, attitudes, needs, and expectations (see Figure 1–1). Outside information continually filters through each person's unique VANE. Thus several persons may have the same experience, but each will have a different perception of that experience as its particulars filter through various, unique VANEs.

Throughout life we form values, attitudes, needs, and expectations. Some of your filter is from early childhood, but many of the elements of your present VANE about nursing were developed during your professional education and experiences. While you were a staff nurse, your values, attitudes, needs, and expectations guided your clinical practice, your interpersonal relationships with peers and supervisors, and your decision making. Now some of your filter will change as you look at nursing from a new perspective, that of a manager. Values are the strongest of the filter parts because they are belief systems. Values

**Figure 1–1** Stimulus and Perception by the Organism

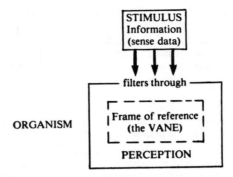

*Source:* Reprinted from *Organizational Behavior: Its Data, First Principles, and Applications* (3rd Ed.), by Joe Kelly with permission of Richard D. Irwin, Inc., © 1980.

encompass such core entities as your religion and work ethic beliefs. Values can change, but this usually requires some soul-searching. Attitudes generally address whether or not you approve of something. Attitudes can change more readily than values—sometimes merely through an increase in information. Needs are described by Atkinson (1958) as those motivators that, when activated, give off a sense of satisfaction or accomplishment. Maslow (1954) describes motivators as unmet needs. Some needs are basic in a personality, says McClelland (1961), with each managers having a primary motivating need—achievement, affiliation, or power. Individuals have expectations about outcomes based on prior experiences and knowledge. Expectations may change relatively easily.

## New Perspectives

Now you will adopt a new management perspective in nursing. You will look at the same situations, facts, and people, but through a changing filter and from a different angle.

For example, imagine you are a staff member, sitting at the nurses' station, reviewing the charts of patients assigned to you. One patient is very anxious about his scheduled angiogram and needs some time to talk. Another has frequent intravenous medications and is also on a controlled substance, necessitating special records. With staffing low, you add the cases of these two patients to yesterday's already full patient load. You plan how you will try to meet all these patients' needs that compete for your time.

Now at the same nurses' station, imagine yourself in the position of nurse manager. Two of your nurses are out sick, though you think that one is not ill but looking for a more lucrative position. The patients normally assigned to those two nurses, all with special needs, must be cared for by other staff on duty, but they already have more than enough patients. The administrator is rigidly against management providing direct patient care; yet she has been pressing you to find a way to cut back on the number of staff assigned to the unit. The new batch of interns on the unit is insecure and full of questions for your staff, and one is rather abrupt, yesterday upsetting two patients. The place, the problems, and the patients are the same whether you are a staff member or the head nurse, but the perspectives are vastly different.

The variation in perspectives is well illustrated in the poem "The Blind Men and the Elephant."

### The Blind Men and the Elephant

by John G. Saxe

It was six men of Indostan,
   To learning much inclined
Who went to see the elephant
   (Though each of them was blind.)
That each by observation
   Might satisfy his mind.

The first approached the elephant,
   And happening to fall
Against his broad and sturdy side,
   At once began to bawl:
"God bless me! but the elephant
   Is very much like a wall!"

The second, feeling of the tusk,
   Cried: "Ho! what have we here
So round, and smooth, and sharp?
   To me 'tis very clear
This wonder of an elephant
   Is very like a spear!"

The third approached the animal,
   And happening to take
The squirming trunk within his hands,
   Thus boldly up he spake:
"I see," quoth he, "the elephant
   Is very much like a snake!"

The fourth reached out his eager hand,
     And fell upon the knee:
"What most this wondrous beast is like,
     Is very plain," quoth he;
"Tis clear enough the elephant
     Is very like a tree!"

The fifth who chanced to touch the ear
     Said: "E'en the blindest man
Can tell what this resembles most:
     Deny the fact who can,
This marvel of an elephant
     Is very like a fan!"

The sixth no sooner had begun
     About the beast to grope,
Then, seizing on the swinging tail
     That fell within his scope,
"I see," quoth he, "the elephant
     Is very much like a rope!"

And so these men of Indostan
     Disputed loud and long,
Each in his own opinion
     Exceeding stiff and strong,
Though each was partly in the right,
     And all were in the wrong!

The situations you will manage in nursing will often be those with which you are already familiar. Perhaps you held an "elephant's ear" before and now hold the "trunk." The added information changes your perspective. Having had the prior experience will affect your current perception. You have held the ear and now hold the trunk; thus, your "elephant" concept has not just changed from ear to trunk but is greater than either and incorporates both ideas. Similarly, your clinical knowledge and skills give you important information that is relevant to your current position, but you must also learn new facts and skills to be a manager. Integration of clinical and management information will allow you to make management decisions based on both clinical and management needs and priorities.

You now have a broader perspective; you see two parts of the elephant. Both parts will have an impact on your decisions now. Thus, your decisions are more difficult because your underlying assumptions (values, attitudes, needs, and expectations) are changing in light of a more integrated perspective. In

Exhibit 1–1, the move from a clinical decision-making base to a broader clinical and managerial decision-making base demonstrates the change in perspective necessary in making the role transition from staff nurse to nurse manager.

An example of your broader perspective becomes clear when you are making out schedules and trying to accommodate vacation requests. The staff nurse's primary concern is to have off on the days he/she requested. The head nurse's primary concern is safe unit staffing. This does not diminish the importance of an individual staff nurse's request, nor does it suggest a lack of concern for patient care by the staff nurse; however, the differences in perspective are clear.

**Peer Changes**

Surprise and disequilibrium may also emerge when your former peers behave differently toward you. Your old friends may go off to lunch without inviting you. They may stop talking when you enter a room, and their comments about each other's performance may become guarded when you are within earshot. Most information comes through a filter; the former openness is no longer there.

Expect this dynamic, because staff nurses will go on as staff nurses, treating the head nurse like a head nurse. Since you have elected to change roles and assume that of head nurse, their behaviors toward you are directed, first, toward your new role and, second, to you as a person. Sarbin and Allen explain in role theory that certain actions and qualities are expected of people who occupy certain positions (1968). The role expectations of a head nurse are well known to staff nurses, and they respond to those expectations. Role expectations are made up of rights, privileges, duties, and obligations of a person in a specific social position in relation to people occupying other specific positions in the social structure. In other words, your role as a head nurse is only partly defined by you. Your staff's expectations and the expectations of others in the organization, to a large extent, define your role.

In deciding to become a head nurse, you have changed your role and your relationship with staff members. Even if you expect this change, it may be difficult to accept.

**New Peer Support**

To deal with feelings of isolation from former peers, you need to establish a new peer support group. This is not to say you should not maintain strong relationships with former peers. Rather, be aware that they are in staff roles with certain expectations, responsibilities, and privileges unique to their role; you are in a head nurse role with unique expectations, responsibilities, and privileges of your own. Also, certain relationships are expected between people in particular roles. For example, since you will evaluate Jane Richard, staff nurse, do not expect as free a conversation between one of Jane's peers and yourself as you might have had before. In addition, you are not free to discuss Jane with her peers; this is inappropriate in your management role. You would be risking the return to Jane of information, not from a friend but from the boss.

Look around at your new peers. If the formal orientation system for new managers does not offer meetings with head nurses, make your own appointments. Meet with several, if not all, head nurses. You will find that all are unique—as people and as managers. Find out who has expertise in what area. Find out who you can trust, who you can talk to, who listens well, who has a finger on the organization's pulse and seems to know everything that's happening. Trade information. Ask for help. Give help. Support others. Give positive feedback when one of your peers does a good job. Talk about your peers with positive specifics to other peers, to your boss, and to your staff. For example, in a staff meeting you might say, "Karen O'Day, head nurse on Medical, set up a good system for a communication book. Let's try it on our unit." Or to your boss, "John Schmidt, head nurse in Emergency Department, really helped my staff by arranging a better transport system. Now patients have better continuity of care between the Emergency Department and our unit." To a peer you might say, "Ask Greta Pearsen, head nurse on Pediatrics, to help you with your holiday schedule. She's terrific at staffing!"

Reciprocal help and support given in a positive way have a synergistic effect and are extremely contagious. Learn from and give help to your peers. Shifting to this level of peer support is not only healthy but essential to your survival as a head nurse.

### Job Satisfaction

The second major adjustment causing disequilibrium in your new role is a vague feeling of not being appreciated. This stems from the fact that you have cut off a major source of job satisfaction—patient and family feedback. Remember how good you felt when you helped a patient understand his myocardial infarction and spent time helping him plan necessary life adjustments? Remember your sense of accomplishment when an adolescent with whom you worked could administer her own insulin? Remember the thanks or smiles that made you feel you were really making a contribution?

As a manager you are no longer in touch with that direct feedback to increase job satisfaction. Your satisfaction must come from new sources. Besides the gratification that will come from new peer relationships with other head nurses, staff development can become a major source of satisfaction. Helping a new graduate work through reality shock and become a core person on your unit will be a new source of satisfaction. Encouraging a staff nurse to return to school to get a bachelor's or master's degree and helping to rearrange the schedule to make it possible will be another. Receiving good feedback about your unit or your staff from patients, doctors, or administrators will give you great pride. Job satisfaction can also come from sharing with another unit a new teaching module developed by your staff, helping someone grow into a position, or assisting someone to leave a job with self-esteem intact.

## THE ROLE OF THE NURSE MANAGER

Besides setting up new peer support systems, looking for new sources of job satisfaction, and changing your perspective from clinical to clinical/managerial, you need to define your new role. As a nurse manager in the acute care setting, your role is to direct your staff to provide good patient care systematically within the hospital's organizational framework. You provide the link between direct care givers and nursing administration. You have four major functions as a manager: planning, organizing, directing, and controlling. These four functions are the core of the *Development of the New Nurse Manager* model (see Figure 1–2).

Getting into the core of this model requires these basic skills: the ability to make a role transition, the ability to communicate effectively, and the ability to lead. Background knowledge and practical skill building in these areas are offered in the first three chapters. Chapters 4 through 7 deal with the core of the model, the four functions that describe what you do as a manager. The manager goes around and around this core function wheel on various issues simultaneously. In doing so, the manager grows and moves forward. With each circuit around the core, you will gain more skill as a manager.

The impetus keeping you moving around the model's cycle is the daily input that comes from the continued change of the environment within which you manage. The classical core functions described by Fayol (1949) are still your management functions, but now they exist in today's dynamic world. This fast-paced movement causes collisions, problems, and changes that push the manager around the core functions more rapidly and also require special skills, such as sophisticated problem solving and good negotiating abilities. These latter adaptations to today's fast pace and complex systems are covered in Chapter 8.

Each phase of the model is explained in a separate chapter. The brief description that follows will give you the overview necessary to having a sense of the whole before exploring each phase in depth.

### Role Transition

Role transition is the change process you will experience as you move from clinician to manager. As mentioned previously, perspectives change—demanding integrated clinical and management perspectives in your decision making. Also

**Figure 1–2** Model of the Development of the New Nurse Manager

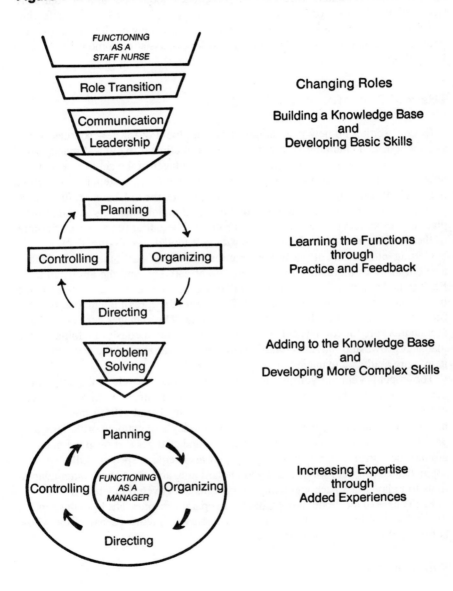

needed are new sources of peer support and job satisfaction. Awareness of the changes and a self-developmental plan for dealing with role transition will hasten and ease your transition to management.

## Communication

Communication is the manager's basic tool. You cannot function as a head nurse without being able to communicate your expectations to your staff—what needs to be done, by whom, how, when, and so forth. Communication skills, both verbal and nonverbal, written and oral, are essential for you to get along well with staff, boss, other departments, and outside the organization.

## Leadership

Leadership is your ability to influence others. As a manager, you must be able to get other people to do the organization's work, meet organizational goals, unit goals, professional goals, and personal goals. To lead in today's complex society requires that you understand your leadership style and abilities, develop any lacking management styles, and learn to use the style that is appropriate to a particular situation.

## Planning

Planning involves deciding what end you will strive to achieve before you begin. A plan is a map or guide toward that goal. Well-integrated plans take into account the manager's personal values, needs, and expectations; staff and unit needs and objectives; organization purposes; and societal influences, such as consumerism, the state of the economy, and regulatory agency requirements.

Plans may also be formulated from feedback that comes from problem solving and/or evaluative processes. Such plans are often reflected as policies and procedures, unit guidelines, or even job descriptions. Planning also requires the efficient use of time, including priority setting, learning time management skills, and using other basic tools such as calendars and schedules.

## Organizing

Organizing refers to the methodology or vehicle used to get from the plan to the goal; it is how the plan is executed. The resources available for the process should be structured to facilitate reaching the goals that have been set.

Two types of resources are available within the organization: material and human. Nurse managers facilitate organization of work (patient care) within their own units or by organizational systems through efficient use of resources. For efficient use of human resources, staffing, scheduling, and supervising skills are essential. Likewise, materials management requires skills to evaluate and use these resources, providing feedback for increased efficiency.

The nurse manager manages a particular unit—a subsystem. Of course, this unit does not function in isolation. Communication and coordination skills are needed to facilitate relations with other subsystems. The nurse manager links the top of the organization to the bottom of the organization by working with the assistant director and with unit staff. The head nurse communicates and coordinates up and down this line, sending frontline (unit) information upward and administrative policies and decisions downward. The head nurse also communicates and coordinates laterally with other units and other departments.

### Directing

A key function of nurse managers is directing personnel. A nurse manager's primary responsibility is to direct patient care through others, the nursing staff. Directing includes helping staff members progress toward their own goals while contributing to the accomplishment of the goals of the organization, the unit, and the patients.

Some directing responsibilities of a head nurse include interviewing, hiring, firing, and helping staff to develop clinical competence. An important, but less clearly defined, responsibility is enhancing motivation, job satisfaction, and productivity. Directing includes exercising skills in group dynamics, conducting meetings, team building, and group decision making.

Before addressing the staff's developmental needs, nurse managers need to assess clearly their own strengths, weaknesses, preferences, and goals for personal growth. Understanding the manager's own array of values, needs, and assumptions about people is also a prerequisite to facilitating the development of others.

### Controlling

A function that sometimes carries the negative connotation of manipulation or authoritarian management, controlling is a measure of how well you are meeting the objectives of your unit and your organization. Evaluation is an objective, measurable, and accepted means of control. When plans are developed, the goals become the evaluation criteria. These evaluation criteria must be measurable, and they should be determined in the planning stage. The criteria must also be clearly communicated, as staff cannot be expected to achieve goals they do not understand. The controlling function becomes a comparison of the plan (goal) with the actual accomplishment. This comparison is made at the end of the time allotted for a particular task. Differences between the plan and the actual outcome provide feedback for new plans.

Evaluation by the nurse manager is usually realized in four modes: quality assurance programs, program evaluations, system efficiency measurements, and performance appraisals. Feedback from these forms of evaluation provides input for future plans.

Budgeting, or financial control, is inherent in each of the four management functions. Planning may be reflected financially, in a budget. Although budgeting belongs primarily in the planning stages, in the past it has more often been an evaluative tool. In today's economy, achieving budget goals is a significant constraint and has a significant impact on all four primary management functions.

## Problem Solving

Managing change and handling conflict present management challenges that push the nurse manager through the four-function cycle over and over again. These challenges demand skills in leadership, communication, and decision making, as well as problem solving, conflict resolution, negotiating, and facilitating change. These are acquired skills at which you will become more proficient through practice, feedback, and more practice as you repeat the four functions in various situations. Problems, change, and conflict keep the four-function cycle in motion on a daily, even hourly, basis.

## Your Job Is To Manage

Leadership, communication, decision making, planning, organizing, directing, controlling, evaluating, problem solving, implementing change, and negotiating are all learned skills essential to your new role. These are the things you will do as a head nurse. If you find yourself frequently providing bedside care, you must identify and solve this problem. Some examples of why you might be at the bedside include understaffing or inappropriate staffing, not helping staff to meet their developmental needs, or poor planning resulting in management by crisis. When you are at the bedside doing your staff's job, who is doing your job? Who is managing? In order to manage, you must understand the discrete function of management and its importance in achieving quality patient care. What is your role as a manager in the organization? What skills do you have? What skills do you need to do the job? What is the planning role of a head nurse? How can you run an organized unit? How can you develop your staff? What kinds of evaluation and feedback systems will help keep your unit's standards high? What are effective problem-solving techniques and change strategies? Can you deal with conflict in a constructive manner? How can you best meet these challenges? Who will help you? What do you need to know? Where do you learn these skills? These questions are explored throughout this book to help you make your role transition.

Management is an important and valuable function in nursing. The middle management link is vital. Only through good management by the head nurse is excellent patient care possible on every unit.

# Activity 1:1

# Personal Strengths Assessment

You've been selected for this job because of your personal and professional qualities, experiences, knowledge, skills, and situational timing. Building on your personal strengths will help you in your role transition and throughout your head nurse career. First you need to be aware of your strengths.

- List the personal attributes you bring to this job: (for example: creativity, the ability to listen to people, pain assessment, and so forth)
- Ask three people who know you well what they see as your strengths. Add these to your list.
- Review and add to this list monthly during your first year as a head nurse.

_____     _____     _____
_____     _____     _____
_____     _____     _____
_____     _____     _____

- You should draw on these strengths in your role as head nurse. For three of the above listed strengths, state how each will help you as a head nurse.

| STRENGTH | USE IN HEAD NURSE ROLE |
|---|---|
| 1. _____ | _____<br>_____ |
| 2. _____ | _____<br>_____ |
| 3. _____ | _____<br>_____ |

## Activity 1:2

# Increasing Your Management Functions

Management is defined as _____.
Management is not new when you reach the head nurse role; however, your management functions increase. List examples of management tasks at each level.

| STAFF NURSE | CHARGE NURSE | HEAD NURSE |
|---|---|---|
|  |  |  |
|  |  |  |
|  |  |  |
|  |  |  |
|  |  |  |
|  |  |  |
|  |  |  |
|  |  |  |
|  |  |  |
|  |  |  |
|  |  |  |

*Note:* Job descriptions may be used to enumerate.

18

# Activity 1:3

# Head Nurse Perceived Learning Needs Assessment

Column I lists the job responsibilities of the head nurse using the "Development of the New Nurse Manager" model as a framework.

1. Describe briefly your related knowledge and/or experience(s) beside each responsibility.
2. For each responsibility, do you think your need for knowledge in this area is high, medium, or low? Put a "K" in Column III for each responsibility according to your perceived need level.
3. For each responsibility, do you think your need for experience (skill) in this area is high, medium, or low? Put an "E" in Column III for each responsibility according to your perceived need level.
4. Share this sheet in a coaching session with your boss, and together—

   - cross out any responsibilities not relevant to your new position;
   - add any responsibilities not already listed and repeat steps 1 through 3 for each; and
   - prioritize your learning needs by assigning a number to each responsibility under priority goals.

| I<br>HEAD NURSE RESPONSIBILITY | II<br>PRIOR RELATED<br>KNOWLEDGE/EXPERIENCES | III<br>NEED LEVEL | | | IV<br>Priority |
|---|---|---|---|---|---|
| | | Lo | Med | Hi | |
| **Role Transition** | | | | | |
| Assess your learning needs as head nurse and set goals. | | | | | |
| Establish peer support system. | | | | | |
| Assess your current V.A.N.E. | | | | | |
| Use management principles in your head nurse role. | | | | | |
| Contribute to the profession through education, publication, legislative activities, or research. | | | | | |
| Develop a self stress management plan. | | | | | |
| Participate on a departmental level committee. | | | | | |

## Activity 1:3 continued

| I<br>HEAD NURSE RESPONSIBILITY | II<br>PRIOR RELATED<br>KNOWLEDGE/EXPERIENCES | III NEED LEVEL | | | IV<br>PRIORITY |
|---|---|---|---|---|---|
| | | Lo | Med | Hi | |
| **Communicate** | | | | | |
| Send clear verbal messages. | | | | | |
| Send clear written messages. | | | | | |
| Maintain unit communication systems (communication book, bulletin board, etc.). | | | | | |
| Consider climate in communications. | | | | | |
| Utilize lines of authority in communications. | | | | | |
| Communicate with planned outcomes and alternatives. | | | | | |
| Maintain open communications up and down the line, interdepartmentally, intradepartmentally, and with physicians. | | | | | |
| Listen actively. | | | | | |
| Lead meetings. | | | | | |
| Set agendas. | | | | | |
| Handle crises. | | | | | |
| **Lead** | | | | | |
| Assess needed leadership styles. | | | | | |
| Use appropriate leadership styles. | | | | | |
| Recognize forces affecting leadership styles. | | | | | |
| Project a positive leader image. | | | | | |
| Delegate appropriately. | | | | | |
| Group dynamics/team building. | | | | | |
| **Plan** | | | | | |
| Develop unit plans. | | | | | |
| Give input into departmental plans. | | | | | |
| Set up a calendar. | | | | | |

## Activity 1:3 continued

| I<br>HEAD NURSE RESPONSIBILITY | II<br>PRIOR RELATED<br>KNOWLEDGE/EXPERIENCES | III<br>NEED LEVEL<br>Lo | Med | Hi | IV<br>PRIORITY |
|---|---|---|---|---|---|
| **Plan** (continued) | | | | | |
| Set weekly and daily priorities using a "to do" list. | | | | | |
| Coordinate unit plans with departmental and organizational plans. | | | | | |
| Organize | | | | | |
| Assess unit inefficiencies. | | | | | |
| Correct unit inefficiencies. | | | | | |
| Utilize organizational and management information systems. | | | | | |
| Manage in compliance with union. | | | | | |
| Coordinate unit systems. | | | | | |
| Complete unit reports. | | | | | |
| Direct | | | | | |
| Interview and hire in compliance with affirmative action and EEO laws. | | | | | |
| Direct employees. | | | | | |
| Counsel employees in line with personnel policies. | | | | | |
| Handle grievances. | | | | | |
| Consult on patient care. | | | | | |
| Develop employees to do their job well. | | | | | |
| Help employees to reach their goals. | | | | | |
| Coordinate staff activities. | | | | | |
| Control | | | | | |
| Staff using patient classification system. | | | | | |
| Maintain unit quality assurance in patient care and patient education. | | | | | |

## Activity 1:3 continued

| I<br>HEAD NURSE RESPONSIBILITY | II<br>PRIOR RELATED<br>KNOWLEDGE/EXPERIENCES | III<br>NEED LEVEL | | | IV<br>PRIORITY |
|---|---|---|---|---|---|
| | | Lo | Med | Hi | |
| **Control (continued)** | | | | | |
| Allocate and monitor resources --<br>material and human. | | | | | |
| Control unit level operating<br>budget. | | | | | |
| Give input into capital budget. | | | | | |
| Monitor unit policy and procedure<br>compliance. | | | | | |
| Set unit standards. | | | | | |
| Evaluate performance of staff. | | | | | |
| **Problem Solve** | | | | | |
| Identify problems. | | | | | |
| Generate solutions. | | | | | |
| Evaluate solutions. | | | | | |
| Manage     change. | | | | | |
| Negotiate conflicts. | | | | | |

## Activity 1:4

# Strategies for Meeting Learning Needs

1. List in Column I your top three learning needs as identified in Activity 1:3.
2. Suggest in Column II ways you might learn them in your organization. (Use this book, experts in that area, your boss, and peers for ideas.)

*Note:* You may want to redo this activity after completing the book.

*Example:*

Send clear written messages.
- Have someone critique my memos.
- Do memo exercise in Chapter 2.
- Take a writing course.
- Read and analyze good memos and copy format.

| Column I<br>Learning Need | Column II<br>Potential Learning Methods<br>In My Organization |
|---|---|
| Learning Need #1: | |
| | |
| | |
| | |
| | |
| Learning Need #2: | |
| | |
| | |
| | |
| | |
| Learning Need #3: | |
| | |
| | |
| | |
| | |

# Activity 1:5

# Goal Setting for Self-Development

*Definitions*

Goal:     The end toward which effort is directed. Needs action verb.

Objective:     Goals broken down into small units, must be specific and measurable.

Action Plan: Putting an objective on a "to do" level; tasks that make up an objective; includes time frame.

*Example*

*Sample Goal* (from a head nurse job description)

Develop, implement, and evaluate the performance appraisal process for nursing staff.

*Objective #1*

State the parameters of the job description content of unit personnel.

*Objective #2*

Counsel nursing staff regarding performance and performance problems according to Nursing Service standards.

*Action Plan* (tasks for Goal #1, Objectives 1 and 2 above)

1. Read all job descriptions of my employees by March 1.
2. Set up or review folders of each of my employees by March 1.
3. Develop an ongoing documentation system for recording anecdotal information about each employee by February 5.

*Activity*

- Select two goals from your high learning need priorities in Activity 1:3 or from your job description. Break them down into objectives.
- Formulate related tasks with time frames.

**Activity 1:5** continued

- Assign priorities to the tasks.
- Review and evaluate.

*Goal #1:* _____

_____

_____

_____

*Objectives:*

1. _____

_____

2. _____

_____

3. _____

_____

*Action Plan:* (Select from Activity 1:3 potential learning methods for tasks.)

| Task | Time Frame | Prioritize (See below) |
|---|---|---|
| 1. | | |
| | | |
| 2. | | |
| | | |
| 3. | | |
| | | |
| | | |

*Goal #2:* _____

_____

_____

_____

*Objectives:*

1 _____

_____

**Activity 1:5** continued

2. _____
   _____

3. _____
   _____

*Action Plan:* (Select from Activity 1:3 potential learning methods for tasks.)

| Task | Time Frame | Prioritize (See below) |
|------|-----------|------------------------|
| 1. | | |
| | | |
| 2. | | |
| | | |
| 3. | | |
| | | |

*Setting priorities:* Setting goals and objectives for yourself and carrying them out is an ongoing growth process. Select several to work on and review periodically to assess your growth. This may be done as a joint process with your boss for guidance. Consider your immediate needs in this job when doing this preferential rating called prioritizing.

- Go back and prioritize above Action Plan with consideration given to immediate needs.

# Activity 1:6

# Networking and Learning Plan

- Complete the matrix below to identify possible supportive individuals in your peer group.

  Look at your learning needs in Activity 1:3. Which of your peers has expertise in your learning need areas? Fill in learning needs across top of matrix, and fill in an "expert" for each need. Ask your boss and peers for names. Set up meetings with these people.

|  | L E A R N I N G    N E E D | | |
|---|---|---|---|
|  | EXAMPLE<br>Staffing | | |
| Ask your boss? | Boss will show me forms. Suggests Janet Gains, head nurse on medical unit, who does a good schedule. | | |
| Ask your peer? | Janet Gains (She suggests I meet with Barbara Lewis in staffing first.) | | |
| Ask an expert? (who) | Barbara Lewis, staffing clerk | | |

Call and schedule a meeting with Barbara Lewis and with Janet Gains. Try to meet with peers over lunch so you can informally ask about work and social norms also.

*Meetings:*

| NAME | DATE | TIME | SUBJECT |
|---|---|---|---|
|  |  |  |  |
|  |  |  |  |
|  |  |  |  |
|  |  |  |  |

# Assessing Your Values, Attitudes, Needs, and Expectations

- Circle those values, attitudes, needs, and expectations that "fit" you. Add others.

| VALUES<br>(core beliefs) | ATTITUDES<br>(prejudices) | NEEDS<br>(strong desires,<br>motivators) | EXPECTATIONS<br>(anticipated<br>results) |
|---|---|---|---|
| • Nurses should have a baccalaureate degree.<br>• Nurses are honest.<br>• Nurses are hard-working.<br>• Nurses are patient advocates.<br>• _____<br>• _____<br>• _____ | • Nurses should be female.<br>• Foreign nurses are less educated.<br>• Nurses should wear white uniforms.<br>• Doctors are difficult to work with.<br>• _____<br>• _____ | • Nurses have the responsibility to come to work on time.<br>• Coffee breaks are essential to good productivity.<br>• _____<br>• _____<br>• _____ | • Staffing should be adequate on all shifts.<br>• Staff nurses should not request overtime pay if they were socializing during work.<br>• Meetings should be productive.<br>• Staff nurses will work hard.<br>• _____<br>• _____ |

Describe your filter based on circled items above.

_____

_____

_____

_____

_____

How could these perceptions affect your decisions and actions as a head nurse?

_____

_____

_____

_____

# Activity 1:8

# A Plan To Deal with the Primary Role Transition Barrier

| | | | |
|---|---|---|---|
| **BARRIER I** | The primary barrier to your new role if you are promoted from within the organization will be related to changing levels. Do your previous peers leave you out or not take you seriously as a boss? | **BARRIER II** | Your primary barrier to your new role is that you are from outside the organization and don't "know the ropes". What are the norms? Who do you ask? |
| **STRATEGIES** | • Interview a manager who has been a staff nurse and ask about what worked for that person in changing roles.<br><br>• Meet with old friends who are staff nurses and clarify new work relationship.<br><br>• Redefine new relationship with existing nursing managers by asking them to share with you "how to succeed as a manager in this system". | **STRATEGIES** | • Call someone new each day for two weeks and introduce yourself and ask about their job.<br><br>• Volunteer to be on a department-wide committee.<br><br>• Begin a list of observed norms and add to it each day. Verify it with a peer.<br><br>• Find a secretary or receptionist who understands the system and is willing to help you. |

(OR)

Which of the two barriers above best describes your situation? After deciding, select at least one strategy to help you break that barrier or develop your own strategy.

Select:  ☐ Barrier I
        ☐ Barrier II

Strategy: _____

_____

_____

_____

_____

_____

# Activity 1:9

# Shaping Your New Role

- What you do in your job is *role enactment*. Write on the inside arrows what you would like to do in your job. Darken lines that are higher priorities for you.

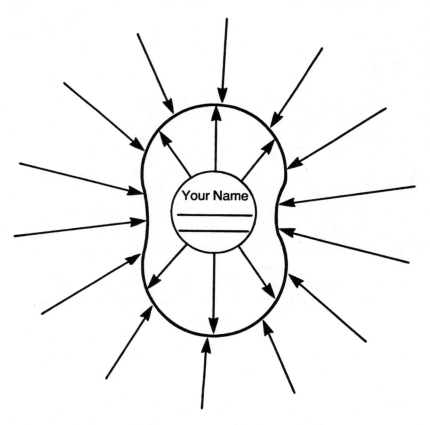

- What others expect you to do in your job is *role expectations*. Ask staff, boss, patients, physicians, and others what they expect from you as a head nurse. Put those expectations on the outside of the figure. Every head nurse job is different because the forces of the role enactment and role expectation, which actually shape the job, differ from unit to unit.

# Activity 1:10

# Stress Reducers

In your new position, your ability to deal with stress is essential. Below are ten "quickie" stress reducing techniques. Try them, then select two that work for you. Use these stress reducers two times each day this week.

1. Tighten all your muscles, hold for count of ten.
   Relax————Repeat
2. Close your eyes and visualize (image) you are somewhere that is very peaceful (e.g., the beach). Picture the setting, imagine the sounds and smells. "Stay there" for two full minutes.
3. Concentrate on your exhaling (elongate the process) for several minutes.
4. Take a walk and look at each thing you pass. Don't allow yourself to think of anything except objects you are seeing.
5. Carry a good novel and read it for five to ten minutes without interruptions.
6. Make a list of everything that is bothering you. Rip it up and throw it away.*
7. Count your breaths for several minutes while you "belly breathe" in one nostril and out the other.*
8. Take a brisk walk—stair climbing is especially aerobic.
9. Look at some aspect of your job from a humorous perspective (exaggeration of the circumstance may help you find this humor).
10. If you are with an angry person, try reducing your stress by:

   —Imaging a physical shield between you and the person, guarding you from their anger.
   —Imagine that person in a bikini.

- Check off each number as you try the technique.
- Two strategies for reducing stress that work for you are:

————————————————————————————————

————————————————————————————————

————

*Contributions 6–10 adapted from "Quick Stress Reduction for a BAD DAY," Ann Baldwin, R.N., Ph.D., Stanford University Hospital, Stanford, California (1983) (Unpublished Material).

## CASE STUDY

Consider the case of a new nurse manager who is confronted by his own values conflict. John was promoted to the position of head nurse on the unit where he had been a staff nurse for ten years. He had excellent clinical skills, had demonstrated patient-teaching skills by contributing to the development of an audiovisual educational tool, and had been the nursing representative on a hospital-wide quality assurance committee.

John had been very aware of the reputation of his head nurse who was retiring, and he had made a commitment to himself not to be like his predecessor. "I won't sit in my office if the staff are really pressed. I'm going to be helpful, visible, and let the unit know I really care."

As he steps into his new role, he is very helpful to his staff. John finds it painful to choose between writing evaluations and helping his staff. Because of this, his evaluations are overdue. He wants to be home to pack for a skiing trip at 5:30 P.M., and the unit is short staffed.

How John handles this conflict will set the tone for his style as head nurse. A staff nurse appears at his door and says, "John, you were so helpful yesterday with Mr. Jones's treatments, and we are so short today. Can I count on you to help us?" John stops a moment and remembers his commitment to himself. He hears his wife's request to be home by 5:30 P.M. He can't do it *all*. Will his staff like him if he says he can't help with patient care? Will he feel like a failure if he doesn't live up to that commitment? How important is it to finish those evaluations today? They are late already—can they wait? What will his boss say if he is late with them again? The pay raises for his employees would be still later! What should John do?

## SOLUTION TO CASE STUDY

John is experiencing role transition conflicts. His commitment to continue patient care came from his perspective as a staff nurse. Now he has a new job—that of head nurse. Patient care is to be arranged for, but not done, by the head nurse. This new perspective is causing a value conflict for John. He values good patient care and helping staff.

An unacceptable answer is for John to do patient care. His priority, as long as the patients are safe, is staff care—evaluations. John must also be responsive to the organization's policies about timely evaluations and his boss's clearly stated expectations.

It is also unacceptable to have John cancel his personal arrangements for a noncrisis situation. For personal stress management, John needs to maintain a balanced life. What John can do is show concern for staff by listening or saying, "I know you really feel pushed. I wish I could help, but I have to get these evaluations done on time. I owe it to my staff."

If the problem is serious, John could attempt to help rearrange the staffing assignment, get a float nurse, have someone come in early or stay late, or re-route or delay an admission.

## REFERENCES

Atkinson, J. W. *Motives in fantasy, action and society*. Princeton, N.J.: Van Nostrand, 1958.

Fayol, H. *General and industrial management*. London: Pitman Publishing, 1949.

Kelly, J. *Organizational behavior* (3rd ed.). Homewood, Ill.: Irwin, 1980.

Kramer, M. *Reality shock*. St. Louis: C.V. Mosby, 1974.

Kroner, K. If you're moving into management. *Nursing '80*, 1980, *11*(11), 105–114.

Maslow, A. H. *Motivation and personality*. New York: Harper, 1954.

McClelland, D. B. The two faces of power. *The achieving society*. Princeton, N.J.: Van Nostrand, 1961.

Sarbin, T. R., & Allen, V. L. Role theory. In G. Lindzey & E. Aronson (Eds.), *The handbook of social psychology*. Reading, Mass.: Addison-Wesley, 1968.

# Chapter 2

# Communication

**OBJECTIVES**

Upon completion of this chapter, including the activities, the new nurse manager will be able to:

- describe the communication model including noise and feedback loop
- explain how to use feedback loop to clarify communications
- list the major barriers to mutual interpersonal communication and describe the four-step process for decreasing barriers
- define active listening and contrast the pros and cons of using this skill
- clarify your expectations of your staff and your philosophy about how the unit will function
- evaluate your unit's telephone communication systems
- assess current written communication systems on your unit and plan needed changes
- demonstrate memo-writing skills
- plan an agenda for a meeting
- list the elements of good public speaking

# DEVELOPMENT OF THE NEW NURSE MANAGER™ © 1981

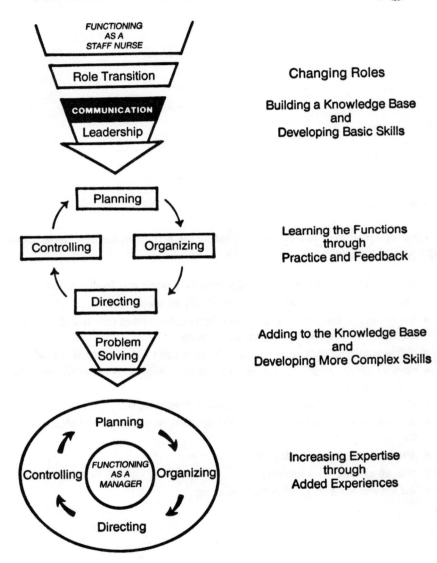

Changing Roles

Building a Knowledge Base
and
Developing Basic Skills

Learning the Functions
through
Practice and Feedback

Adding to the Knowledge Base
and
Developing More Complex Skills

Increasing Expertise
through
Added Experiences

¶ Communication is your most important management skill. If you, as a manager, cannot listen and clearly share your thoughts and expectations, you will be isolated within the organization. Communication skills depend on understanding interpersonal relations, group dynamics, and organizational systems. You must be adept at sending and receiving messages both in person and through various media in order to succeed as a manager.

## THE COMMUNICATION MODEL

Communication infiltrates every part of your position. You need good communication skills whether you are dealing with medication errors, setting budget priorities, or maintaining nursing practice standards.

This chapter will help you explore communication, assess your communication skills, and review your unit's communication systems. It will also show you how to devise continual strategies to make your communication more effective.

Communication theorists have designed a communication model that is useful as a framework through which to explore this complex and important skill. In Figure 2–1 communication is depicted as a message from the sender to the receiver. This message may be verbal or nonverbal. Messages may be sent to someone physically present or through a medium—for example, a memo. The receiver then receives the message.

Unfortunately, the receiver may not receive the message or may not receive the same message the sender intended. Interference, also called noise, often distorts the message (see Figure 2–2). Interference can have human or material origins. Material interferences are often physical and occur when senders do not speak clearly, when receivers do not hear well, or when the room is noisy or the telephone system faulty. Human interference originates in the present needs, prior experiences, and cultural values of the sender and/or receiver. Human interference may involve nonverbal messages that you send with your body, regardless of your words. Telling staff members that you have plenty of time to hear what they are saying while you stand with your hand on the door knob, ready to leave, is an example of a nonverbal message. This action gives a secondary and probably stronger message that you are ready to leave the room. Another source of human interference may be the inexactness of language. Messages differ based on the grammar, the culture, the experiences, and the technical/educational learnings of both sender and receiver.

Feedback is the best method to clarify communication and filter out the "noise" (see Figure 2-3). The receiver then "feeds back" to the sender, in his or her own words, the message that has been heard. This allows verification by the sender. Essentially, the receiver is saying, "What I heard is. . . ." The sender can thus validate whether or not the intended message was heard. If not, the sender can fine

**Figure 2–1** How Communication Travels

**Figure 2–2** How Noise Interferes between Sender and Receiver

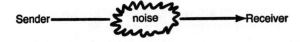

**Figure 2–3** How Feedback Can Filter Out Noise

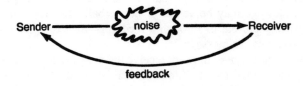

tune as necessary until the receiver understands the essence of the message. Then the receiver may become a sender by responding. This model describes an interactive communication process between two parties. The message sent is fedback through a "feedback loop," to the sender for verification.

The communication process may be used with one sender and one receiver. This process uses interpersonal skills. If the communication process is used in a small group, group dynamics skills are used. Communicating in a large organization and beyond requires additional skills in writing, speaking, and political savvy. Communication skills needed for various situations depend on the number of persons involved.

Another variable affecting communication is direction in organization. The terms *upward, downward,* and *lateral* are often used to connote direction in the organizational structure: boss, subordinate, and peer, respectively. Communication strategy needs to be planned differently, depending on organizational direction. Your communication responsibility is to take information from the hierarchical level immediately above you and share it downward, and to gather information from subordinates and share it upward. In this way you help to link the organization together from bottom to top for a good integration of ideas, efficiency in production, and high-quality control. For example, nursing administration makes a decision to institute float positions to cover last-minute variances in schedules and patient acuities (how sick the patients are). The float positions will provide hospital-wide coverage to make this an economically feasible solution to a staffing problem. You hear that information at your head nurse meeting from the assistant director of nursing. You then take the information to your staff meeting for a response.

Without the response, the communication is only one-way. Once a response is added, the communication becomes two-way. One-way communication can be extremely frustrating both to the receiver, who may need to clarify what is being heard, and to the sender, who may never know how the message was received . . . or if it was.

In the above float pool example, the staff share their concerns with you about nurses not being current in all specialty areas, from pediatrics to orthopedics to intensive care. This realistic concern needs to be shared "up-the-line" with nursing administration. By taking the information from your boss to your staff and back, you provide what Likert (1961) calls the "linking pin" function. You link the organization together from top to bottom, and vice versa (see Figure 2–4).

---

**Figure 2–4** The Overlapping Group Form of Organization

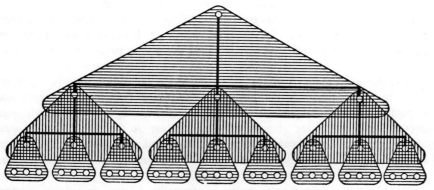

(Work groups vary in size as circumstances require although shown here as consisting of four persons.)

*Source:* Reprinted from *New Patterns of Management* by Rensis Likert with permission of McGraw-Hill Book Company, © 1961.

## INTERPERSONAL RELATIONS

Communicating on a one-to-one level means there is one sender and one receiver. When there is feedback or a response, this communication is two-way.

Rogers and Roethlisberger (1952) believe that "the major barrier to mutual interpersonal communication is our very tendency to judge, to evaluate, to approve (or disapprove) the statement of the other person." Sometimes nurse managers use this judgmental approach in response to medication errors. This communication technique has predictably poor results. Finger-pointing, with punitive statements such as "Fill out an incident report," "If you make another medication error, you will receive a written warning," is sure to elicit defensiveness and create a communication barrier between staff nurse and manager.

Rogers and Roethlisberger suggest that a gateway to communication barriers is "listening with understanding" (1952). Both parties need to understand the other's viewpoint, which gradually leads to mutual communication directed toward mutual problem solving rather than defensiveness, attack, or one party's withdrawal. Learning and positive behavioral change are likely to occur in this type of climate.

In the situation involving the medication error, a more open, trusting environment conducive to listening on both sides could have been created if the nurse manager had been willing to listen to why the error happened. For example, "It looks like Mr. Johnson had an extra dose of Valium. Can you tell me how this happened?" This would have created an opportunity to coach this nurse by mutual problem solving about why the error occurred and how to prevent future occurrences. The manager projects the accepted climate on the unit—in this case the difference between a punitive environment and a learning one.

Four steps describe the skills you need to "listen with understanding" in your interpersonal encounters as a manager (Exhibit 2–1). These steps are valuable in communication processes whether with your boss, your peers, or your subordinates.

Consider a situation in which a nurse manager would like to have a patient transferred out of the intensive care unit (ICU) but cannot obtain a private room on a specific unit as the physician ordered. The nurse manager could talk with the doctor, but a little prior "homework" might increase the productivity of this communication. The nurse must plan what is wanted and how to achieve it. For example, the nurse could determine what other beds are available, what other data may support the patient's need to leave ICU now rather than later, whether a discharge is coming up in a private room, or whether a large semiprivate room is available. With this information, the nurse manager could better present some reasons why the patient needs to leave the unit and a choice of alternatives regarding where the patient might go. This does not mean getting "hung up" on collecting volumes of data; rather, it involves thinking about a variety of alter-

**Exhibit 2–1** Four Steps to Listening with Understanding

---

1. Plan what you want and how you might achieve that result.
2. Consider the climate and environment, and make necessary adjustments.
3. Give clear messages, and encourage feedback to be sure your message is heard.
4. Be open, both verbally and nonverbally, to the responses of the other party.

---

native approaches that might produce results that will be acceptable to you and to the person with whom you will be communicating.

Again, the second step is to consider the climate and environment and make necessary adjustments. For example, if a nurse approaches you in the corridor saying: "I really need to change my schedule to have Friday off. If I change with Joan Smithson, I can work Thursday instead; and I will be able to work with Mary Friend—we like working together." Perhaps you decide to discuss this here and now. You let the nurse know her planned change is not acceptable because she is not a "strong enough" nurse to work with Mary Friend alone. If the staff nurse never realized that you perceived her skill level as not equal to Joan's, she may be hurt by your response. As her eyes fill, she becomes embarrassed. The nursing station, usually buzzing, becomes silent; a spotlight could not make you feel more on-stage. Next time, you will survey the environment and move to a more private setting before beginning what could turn into a private discussion.

The third step is exemplified next. As you leave the unit one afternoon, you put out a new needle disposal system and post the directions. The next morning you find two incident reports written by night nurses regarding needle sticks and subsequent gamma globulin shots they received during the night. Next to the incident reports is your new needle disposal system. On investigation, you discover the directions were never located; you realize the incompleteness of your communication. A demonstration by you and a reciprocal demonstration by staff would have made the introduction of this piece of equipment safer.

Being open, both verbally and nonverbally, to the responses of the other party is also an important step. For example, suppose that after several discussions with your unit clerk about the need for her to arrive by 7:00 A.M., she continues to come charging in about 7:20 A.M. She is an excellent clerk, but you really need her to cover the telephones during the 7:00 A.M. shift report. Moreover, her lateness presents a continual hardship to the nurses who take turns covering for her instead of hearing part of the report. Has she heard your message? Have you heard her response? During your next counseling session, you decide to observe each step of the communication process. You clearly state your need for her presence at 7:00 A.M. and explain why. You ask if she understands what you need, seeking feedback to verify that the message has been received. She replies that she knows how important it is for her to be there by 7:00 A.M. Then she adds, "I really try, but I can't seem to make it." At this point, instead of repeating why you need her, you decide to listen to her response. You say, "Let's go to my office and see if we can work this out." You have lowered the authoritarian barrier by reframing the situation as a problem that you both can work on together. By doing this, you open the gateway to communication. She begins to share information with you about her child-care situation and how it interferes with her 7:00 A.M. arrival. Together you explore problem-solving alternatives and eventually work out a solution acceptable to both of you.

### Active Listening

In introducing the concept of active listening, Rogers and Farson (1971) wrote: "One basic responsibility of the supervisor or manager is the development, adjustment, and integration of individual employees. He/she tries to develop employee potential, delegate responsibility, and achieve cooperation. To do so, he/she must have, among other abilities, the ability to listen intelligently and carefully to those with whom he/she works" (p. 168).

Active listening is your most essential skill. In active listening, as a manager, you have a definite responsibility in the interaction. Your role is to help employees work out their problems by trying actively to grasp the facts and feelings in what you hear. You do this by listening for the total message, both content and feeling, and by responding to whichever message is stronger. Also, you must be aware of nonverbal cues, such as hesitancy, inflections, stressed points, facial expressions, body language, and so forth.

Active listeners should avoid letting their own emotions and viewpoints interfere with their listening. Such interferences include defensiveness, opposing viewpoints, personality clashes, values, attitudes, needs, and expectations.

### Interpersonal Relations—through the Media

The same four steps of interpersonal communication also apply to relating through the media. First, plan what you want and how you might achieve that result. Second, consider the climate and environment, and make necessary adjustments. Third, try to give clear messages. Fourth, encourage feedback and be open, both verbally and nonverbally, to the responses of the other party. This happens on the telephone much as it does in person. Plan before dialing: what do I want? Have some alternatives ready to suggest to achieve that result. In considering the climate on the telephone, always tell the person you are calling what you are calling about and how much of his or her time you will need. You might call and say, "Hello John, how are you? (Pause.) I just have a quick question about the time of our next meeting." Or call the pharmacy: "Nancy, it's Barbara White from the Nursery.

Do you have about five minutes to discuss the delivery on P.M.'s of injectable medications to the nursery?'' Know when your committed time is finished, and offer alternatives. ''Nancy, this sounds more complex than I had realized. Perhaps we could set up a time to meet and work this out. Do you have some free time next week?'' Book and confirm the time, place, and purpose of the meeting. You may both decide to continue on the telephone, but problem solving is better accomplished in person.

Problem solving is least effectively accomplished by memo. However, this communication method is efficient and appropriate for one-way or simple communication. Be sure any memo you write contains who it is to and from and what it is about. Most importantly, state clearly what you want. One of a manager's most frustrating experiences is plowing through an in basket of unclear memos. When recipients finish reading your memos, will they know whether the message was just for their own information or whether they are expected to respond? If you want a response, give a reasonable deadline. Another important point is brevity. The likelihood of your memo being read is inversely related to the memo's length. Whether you communicate by telephone or by memo, remember to plan, adjust for the climate, give clear messages, and encourage feedback and responses.

## GROUP COMMUNICATION

Communicating in a group requires the same four steps as interpersonal communicating. As a nurse manager, you will need to communicate with your group regularly in staff meetings. Use an agenda for planning, and ask your staff nurses to bring you agenda items. Discuss the items, and ask the initiator to address them at the meeting. Add the contributor's name and the items to the agenda. Send out or post the agendas before meetings, and attach any information the staff nurses will need to know for the meeting. Next to each agenda item and the person who will address the item, list the intended outcome. A sample agenda is presented in Exhibit 2–2.

You may include announcements in the agenda, but they should be brief. These are essentially one-way communications, usually needing only clarification responses. One-way communications can be passed on through communication books, photocopying announcements, bulletin boards, and routing. Meetings provide an opportunity for two-way communication and group problem solving and should be used for those purposes.

Norms are an important consideration in group communication. Norms are standards of behavior developed by a group. ''Conformity to the norm is rewarded; nonconformity is punished'' (Kelly, 1980, p. 298). As a manager, be aware of the norms on your unit. Some may be helpful: ''We always start morning report on time here.'' Some may be problematic: ''New graduates are more trouble than they are worth.'' The manager needs to address the latter. Changing

**Exhibit 2–2** Sample of an Agenda

---

SUBURBAN HOSPITAL
DEPARTMENT OF NURSING
NORTH ORTHOPEDICS UNIT

Agenda for Staff Meeting on October 4

3 P.M. to 4 P.M., Conference Room 302

- Announcements. Mary Brown, Head Nurse
- Revised procedure for Bucks Traction. Review and answer any questions, Jane Brooke (procedure attached).
- Problem solving, "Streamlining Shift Report." Bring ideas for discussion; phase 1, brainstorm ideas; facilitated by Sally Brief.
- Other

---

norms can be very difficult and often requires much time and strategy by the nurse manager. Often, the first stage of change is raising awareness. Norms are not necessarily spoken; sometimes they just are. People who infringe on norms, even unspoken ones, are quickly put in their place. "So you're into pushing stretchers for aerobic exercise," might be said to a newcomer unaware that the norm on that unit is to call transport services for patients going to x-ray. What the remark really means is this: "You are breaking a norm, and if you break that one, you may break others." Breaking norms, knowingly or not, makes group members uncomfortable because norms make group life predictable. Conforming to norms is rewarded by acceptance, recognition, and positive feedback.

## Organizational Communication

How to communicate in your organization is explained in your organizational chart. Usually a chart exists for the total organization, beginning with chief executive officer (CEO) of the hospital (called the president in some hospitals) at the top. This person is not actually the top but reports to the board of directors. Under the CEO are the associate hospital administrators or vice-presidents. These administrators have department heads reporting to them. For example, one associate director might have the clinical laboratory, x-ray, physical therapy, and occupational therapy departments reporting to her. Another associate administrator might have housekeeping, materials management, and respiratory therapy departments. The associate administrator to whom nursing reports is often a dual position—associate administrator/director of nursing. All nursing departments and usually the operating room and emergency departments report to this person. The person heading each department is called a department head. Figure 2–5 shows a sample administrative organizational chart.

**Figure 2–5** A Sample Administrative Organizational Chart

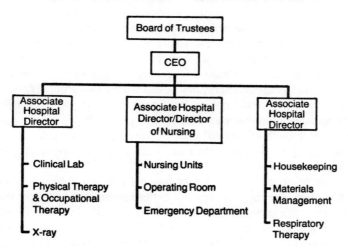

Department head levels vary with each organization, but nursing usually includes the assistant directors of nursing and sometimes the head nurses. Figure 2–6 shows a sample nursing department organizational chart. Head nurses of the units listed are responsible for the personnel on their units, including registered nurses, licensed vocational nurses, nursing assistants, and unit clerks.

**Figure 2–6** A Sample Nursing Department Organizational Chart

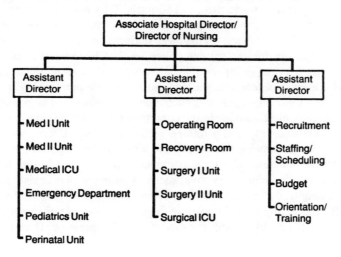

These organizational charts dictate what Fayol (1949) calls the "chain of command" and explain who manages whom. Locate your position on your organizational chart, and follow it upward; the individual above you is your boss; those below are your subordinates. Consequently, you are a member of two vertical groups on the organizational chart. In one group, with your peers, you are a member of the management team; in the other group, you are the boss. You are the person who links the communication between these two groups (Likert, 1961). As mentioned earlier, your "linking-pin" position gives you responsibility for two-way communication with each of these two groups. If you block communication either way through this formal system, communication breaks down. If you fail in your linking-pin function, the chain breaks and the dependent parts above and below you are isolated.

If, for some other reason, the system does not function to meet staff needs up and down the line, the informal system, better known as the "grapevine," will pick up the slack. Grapevines exist everywhere and serve some useful purposes, such as meeting social and support needs. For example, "Jane finished her Master's degree. Let's give her our congratulations." "John broke his leg skiing. Let's chip in and send flowers." However, like norms, the grapevine can cause problems when it is used to sabotage formal systems; for example, "If they [management] think they can float nurses where we can't function, they're crazy." The middle manager needs to be attuned to the grapevine to understand what is happening in the organization that is not getting into the formal communication system.

Interdepartmental communication (beyond nursing) is becoming more important for the head nurse as patient care becomes more complex. Nurse managers need to have input to the materials management department on monitoring equipment—capacities, warranties, and so forth. They need to have input to the clinical laboratory department to prevent one-way communications, such as a memo from the clinical laboratory manager stating a new policy of discarding all urine samples of insufficient amount. They need to have input to the security department manager regarding an unlocked door on the unit at night. The list is infinite. But even these communications should include preplanning, noting the climate, giving clear messages, and encouraging feedback and response.

Usually communication outside the department does not require prior discussion with your boss—especially routine problem solving. Inform your boss of unusual interdepartmental actions to prevent his or her being put "on the spot" if asked about the situation. Use these communications to gain insight from your supervisor about a broader perspective, such as similar problems existing on other units. For example, dietary aides will not deliver trays when overbed tables are not completely empty. Since it is impossible to guarantee completely empty overbed tables, discuss the problem with the dietary aides' supervisor. If you solve the problem, no further communication is necessary. However, if you hit an impasse, your boss may need to intervene.

Many communications will reach you that require your understanding and compliance. You have a responsibility to be knowledgeable about administrative policies and procedures, to be aware of clinical policies and procedures, and to know where to find relevant information. You are also responsible for being aware of the regulations of the Joint Commission on Accreditation of Hospitals (JCAH) and state laws that have an impact on your unit. You are responsible for making sure that your unit practices conform with current nursing research findings and any nursing practice laws in your state.

Your communication responsibilities also include being a role model as a professional nurse and a contributor to nursing through professional organizations. The latter type of communication may take the form of writing for publication, speaking about health care at a community event, or being informed of and contributing to legislative actions through position papers favoring health care.

As a new manager, begin by developing good communication with your staff. Then, when you are comfortable and have mastered the communication steps at this level, select a committee to join to contribute to your organization; learn to use good communication skills at this new level. Later, use your expertise by contributing to your profession through the nursing literature and to the larger community through public speaking on health care.

Effective communication requires continual practice, constructive feedback, and more practice. You have used many communication skills in patient care. You can adapt them for use in your new position. "Managers and professionals do their job by communicating with people . . . and improving communications is everyone's job" (Morris, 1980, p. 3).

# Activity 2:1

# Sharing Your Expectations

Communicating your expectations to your staff.

- State your philosophy of how the unit will function. (Use either example and add your own.)

  Examples:

  - Excellence in patient care
  - Primary nursing
  - _____
  - _____
  - _____
  - _____

- List six basic expectations you have of your staff. (Use any of the examples or write your own.)

  Examples:

  - I expect you to develop collegial relationships with physicians.
  - I expect you to model excellence in patient care on this unit.
  - I expect or do not expect extra supplies to be at a patient's bedside.
  - I expect overtime to be an exception.
  - I expect all patients to understand the medications they are taking.
  - I expect all nurses to take a lunch break off the unit.
  - _____
  - _____
  - _____
  - _____
  - _____
  - _____

**Activity 2:1** continued

- Plan and hold a staff meeting where you will communicate these expectations to your staff. Be sure to include all three shifts.

  ☐ Select meeting time.
  ☐ Announce meeting time to staff (in communication book, bulletin board or staff meeting).
  ☐ Send out follow-up minutes or summary of expectations.

# Evaluate Telephone Communication Systems on Your Unit

The telephone can be your most efficient management tool if used to your advantage as a manager and to the advantage of your unit. If used poorly, it wastes time and destroys attempts at organization and efficiency and hurts your public relations. Assess your unit telephone usage. Plan changes if needed.

Is your telephone answered with a brief friendly greeting and the name of your unit? _____

Who answers your telephone and is this the most cost-effective person to do it? _____.

Do all messages contain necessary information: complete name of who called, whether or not they will call back, a telephone number, and what the call regarded? _____

How are messages from calls dispersed? _____

When calls placed to physicians and other departments and calls back are pending, how are these outgoing calls recorded? _____

How are the returned calls dispersed? _____

Who makes outgoing calls on your unit? _____

   To whom? _____ For what? _____

How does a staff member who is off receive a message upon return? _____

How will your messages be taken? _____

How will you receive your messages? _____

What are your recommendations for change? (Could include a clipboard by the clerk's telephone or blackboard on wall in nursing station to record incoming messages and calls out that are waiting for a response with caller's name. Could have folder or mail slot for your messages.)

_____
_____
_____
_____
_____

# Activity 2:3

# Assess Written Communication on Your Unit

1. *Communication Book:* This is a notebook kept in the nurses' station for unit communications. It is often "tied down" so it doesn't "disappear." The advantages of a communication book are: a centralized place to look for new information, and it can increase accountability for information if reading the book is mandatory once per shift and initials are required. Disadvantages include: the communication is one-way and can be misunderstood, and messages can get lengthy or "picky."

*If You Have a Communication Book*

- Review the communication book on your unit. What is the purpose of the book?
  _____
  _____
  _____

- Does it serve that purpose [your perception and others]?
  _____
  _____
  _____

*If You Do Not Have a Communication Book*

- Would a communication book help your unit's communication between you and staff? Between shifts?
  _____
  _____

- What would be the purpose of your unit communication book? (Ask for staff input.)
  _____
  _____

2. *Routing:* This is another method of written communication. One common form of routing is to write a routing slip and attach it to the material to be routed. A

51

**Activity 2:3** continued

routing slip lists sequential names of persons to review the information. After reviewing it, that person initials the slip and forwards it to the next person. The advantages of routing are that it decreases paper—you can pass around one copy of something; and it encourages professional sharing of journal articles. The disadvantages include the fact that this process may be very slow; and sometimes the chain breaks down. To increase the effectiveness of this system, "date in and date out" can be added by each name so you can track when the process slows down. Put your own name at the bottom of the routing sheet so you will know if the item routed went to each person. Keep lists on routing sheets to less than five people whenever possible so that the process is more effective.

- Prepare two lists: professionals on unit; all unit staff.

*Sample Routing Sheet*

| From: _____ |
|---|

Date: _____

Please read, initial and forward to next person within 24 hours. Thank you.

|  | *Initial* | *Date In* | *Date Out* |
|---|---|---|---|
| • Mary Jones | _____ | _____ | _____ |
| • George Grady | _____ | _____ | _____ |
| • _____ | _____ | _____ | _____ |
| • _____ | _____ | _____ | _____ |
| • _____ | _____ | _____ | _____ |

Your name _____

- Decide when routing is feasible and when it is not feasible on your unit. Get staff input.

_____

_____

- Share use of routing slips with your staff.
  Purposes: _____
  Location of slips: _____
  Who can send: _____
  (If someone other than you initiates the material, they should place their own name at the bottom of the sheet.)

**Activity 2:3** continued

(*Note:* Journals may be routed but putting them in the staff's lounge may be more effective. Earmark especially relevant articles or attach note to cover.)

3. *Bulletin Boards:* This method of communication includes tack boards, blackboards and white marker boards. The primary advantage of these boards is the ease with which one can communicate. Simply tack up a memo or jot down a note. The disadvantages include: maintenance time—these boards quickly become cluttered and unsightly; your "one and only" copy often "disappears"; accountability for the information is random—some read it, some don't, and you don't know who has and hasn't read the information; no priority system is obvious; and all information is visible to perhaps more people than you would like to read it.

In spite of the many disadvantages, bulletin boards can be useful if their use is understood.

- Assess the use of or need for a bulletin board on your unit. (Seek staff input.)

_____

_____

You might try sectioning a bulletin board for: current notices; social; and new policies and/or procedures.

Another good use of a chalk or marker board is to have unit room numbers painted onto the board (permanently) and write in with chalk or marker the nurse for that shift or the primary nurse. This information is thus readily available to physicians, families, unit clerks, and other departments.

- Communicate the use of bulletin board(s) to your staff.
  Purpose: _____
  Who can post information: _____
  Who can remove it (perhaps unit clerk): _____

4. *Integration of Systems:* Usually one of these systems will not meet all your needs. Assess what is working and leave those systems. Consider combinations such as:

- Write in communication book, which everyone initials, that each person is responsible to read the new procedure on the bulletin board or in the procedure notebook.
- Put a note on the social section of the bulletin board announcing a holiday party and state that a sign-up sheet is being routed.
- Other: _____

_____

## Activity 2:4

# Memo Exercise (As Sender)

Memos are informal notes usually used within your organization.

- Essentials of writing a memo include:

    1. Who it is to (with title when appropriate)
    2. Who it is from (with title when appropriate)
    3. Date
    4. Topic (Re: _____ )
    5. Action desired

The "action desired" is especially important and is both annoying and bewildering to the receiver if missing. You cannot expect someone to take your desired action unless you tell him or her clearly what action you want. (Example: "For your information" or "Please check and let me know," etc.)

- Memos cover a variety of written communication needs. Using the various forms in your organization, write the following five memos:

    1. You answer the telephone and receive new patient information.
    2. Mary Smith, head nurse from another unit, sends a float RN to your unit and the RN did an outstanding job.
    3. You don't understand something on your variance report.
    4. Diet trays are coming to your unit cold.
    5. You are going on vacation from May 18 to May 22.

*After Writing*

- Check each memo for the five essentials listed above.
- Have your supervisor read and critique the memos.
- What other methods of communication might be appropriate for the above five communications?

    1. _____
    2. _____
    3. _____
    4. _____
    5. _____

## Activity 2:5

# Memo Exercise (As Receiver)

If you are spending most of your time working out of your in basket, you are working on someone else's priorities.

- Save the first twenty memos you receive. Sort these memos by priority and comment on the bottom of each memo what you should do. Remember, there are only three choices of what to do with a piece of paper: (1) throw it away, (2) act on it, (3) file it.

  Tips: The sender always keeps a copy of each memo sent so don't file what you can get elsewhere.

  For "act-on-it" memos, consider:

    1. Take to staff meeting (unit information) or head nurse meeting (peer information) or meeting with your supervisor (have files set up for each of these meetings and just drop memo into it).
    2. Posting on unit (bulletin board).
    3. Communication book—refer to memo in book, then post or copy essence of memo into book or attach copy of memo to book.
    4. Routing (saves copying but slower). Type out a list of all staff on unit/all RNs/other possible groups for routing.
    5. CC—carbon copy (1 copy for each person). Example: cc: Surgical Staff Nurses, or cc: Mary Brown. When copying, add your own message of expected action; for example, FYI (for your information), or "Get back to me," or "Please read—comment," etc.
    6. Other—write what you need to do and when you will do it on your calendar or "to do" list.
    7. Handle the matter immediately. This is best done by picking up the phone and calling someone to discuss or by setting up an appointment to discuss. This is in line with the time-saver adage: "Handle each piece of paper only once."

- Take your entire in basket for one week (all incoming written communications) to a coaching meeting with your boss. Go through each piece and discuss what to do with it. This also clarifies for you many of your boss's priorities and expectations. Repeat several times if helpful.

# Activity 2:6

# Meetings Worksheet

Meetings are when many decisions happen in large, complex organizations. Use minutes to get a historical perspective of your unit.

- Review the following meeting minutes and agendas noting content of meeting (what has been happening) and process (how it happens—type of decision making), who is present and who is absent, the type of meeting (informational or educational or problem solving). Review format of minutes, consistency—tense and titles, amount of information, and who is copied.

  ☐ Review staff meeting minutes from your unit for one year.
  ☐ Review head nurse meeting minutes for two months or longer.
  ☐ Review Assistant Director or Management or Department Head minutes if available.
  ☐ Review several of your peers' meeting agendas.
  ☐ Look at two different groups' minutes, and critique your unit's format.
  ☐ Observe one interdepartmental meeting.

- Do a sample agenda for a meeting.

_____Hospital

Unit _____ Place of Meeting _____
Time _____ Date _____
Called by _____

| Item | By | Amount of Time Needed (optional but usually makes meeting go faster) | Expected Outcome |
| --- | --- | --- | --- |
| _____ | _____ | _____ | _____ |
| _____ | _____ | _____ | _____ |

At the end of the meeting some chairpersons have a "round robin." You go around the room with each person sharing something if he or she wishes. If you do this, keep it moving. Anything leading to lengthy discussion can be added to the next agenda.

## Activity 2:7

# Committee Assessment

- List the committees in your organization in appropriate sections. State the purpose of each, a member you can contact for questions or information, and list the committee chair.

|  | Committee Name | Purpose of Committee | Contact Member | Committee Chair |
|---|---|---|---|---|
| Nursing Committees |  |  |  |  |
|  |  |  |  |  |
|  |  |  |  |  |
|  |  |  |  |  |
|  |  |  |  |  |
|  |  |  |  |  |
| Hospital Committees |  |  |  |  |
|  |  |  |  |  |
|  |  |  |  |  |
|  |  |  |  |  |
|  |  |  |  |  |
|  |  |  |  |  |
| Board of Directors |  |  |  |  |

- On which committee(s) would you like to be a member? _____

- How does this membership relate to your goals? _____

- Review above information with your boss.

# Activity 2:8

# How Do You Rate As a Listener?*

Take the following test and see how you rate as a listener. Place an "X" in the appropriate blank. When speaking interpersonally with a patient, nursing supervisor, doctor, or coworker, do you:

| Usually | Sometimes | Seldom | |
|---|---|---|---|
| ____ | ____ | ____ | (1) Prepare yourself physically by standing or sitting, facing the speaker, and making sure you can hear? |
| ____ | ____ | ____ | (2) Watch the speaker for the verbal as well as the nonverbal messages? |
| ____ | ____ | ____ | (3) Decide from the speaker's appearance and delivery whether or not what he or she has to say is worthwhile? |
| ____ | ____ | ____ | (4) Listen primarily for ideas and underlying feelings? |
| ____ | ____ | ____ | (5) Determine your own bias, if any, and try to allow for it? |
| ____ | ____ | ____ | (6) Keep your mind on what the speaker is saying? |
| ____ | ____ | ____ | (7) Interrupt immediately if you hear a statement you feel is wrong? |
| ____ | ____ | ____ | (8) Try to see the situation from the other person's point of view? |
| ____ | ____ | ____ | (9) Try to have the last word? |
| ____ | ____ | ____ | (10) Make a conscientious effort to evaluate the logic and credibility of what you hear? |

*Reprinted from *The Nurse's Communication Handbook* by Harry E. Munn with permission of Aspen Systems Corporation, © 1980.

58

**Activity 2:8** continued

## SCORING

This check list, though by no means complete, should help you measure your listening ability. Score yourself as follows: Questions 1, 2, 4, 5, 6, 8, and 10—ten points for *usually*, five points for *sometimes*, and zero points for *seldom*. Questions 3, 7, and 9—zero points for *usually*, five points for *sometimes*, and ten points for *seldom*.

If you scored below 70, your listening skills can be improved because you have developed some undesirable listening habits; 70 to 85, you listen well but can still improve; 90 or above, you are an excellent listener.

People tend to do things well when they hold positive views or "labels" about their ability to do it. You can't do it until you think you can. There is a human tendency to live up or down to labels. If you think you are a good listener, you probably are, and, because of this positive label, you make a conscientious effort to listen, to live up to your label. If you say you are a poor listener, you have turned off your listening mechanism. You must think you can do it before you attempt to do it. If you fail to try because of your fear of failure, you may never discover your hidden potential.

At a recent workshop, a nurse approached the author after taking a tape-recorded listening test and remarked, "If I hadn't done well on that test I would have been very disappointed, because I consider myself to be an excellent listener." In other words, she scored as an excellent listener, and her positive attitude toward listening played a key role in her listening effectiveness.

## CHECKLIST OF GUIDELINES TO IMPROVE LISTENING SKILLS

The following guidelines, in conjunction with the test you just took, should provide a more comprehensive basis to improve your listening skills:

1. You should prepare yourself physically by standing or facing the speaker. Making sure you can hear physically is essential for good listening. You thereby tell the sender that you are ready to listen and are able to hear the verbal messages and also see the nonverbal messages the speaker is sending. This face-to-face attention also shows that you are interested in what is being said. People tend to avoid and look away from people and things in which they are not interested. Attention and interest are synonymous. You pay attention to the things you are interested in, and you are interested in the things you pay attention to.

**Activity 2:8** continued

2. You should learn to watch for the speaker's nonverbal as well as verbal messages. Everyone sends two messages. One message is sent verbally and the other is sent nonverbally through inflection in the voice or through facial expression, bodily action, or gestures. Sixty-eight percent of all messages are sent nonverbally. The nonverbal message conveys the speaker's attitude, sincerity, and genuineness. To miss the nonverbal message is to miss half of what is being said.

3. You should not decide from the speaker's appearance or delivery that what he or she has to say is worthwhile. When you start to focus on the speaker's delivery or appearance, you become distracted from the purpose of communication, receiving the speaker's ideas! You should be more interested in what people have to say than how they say it or what they look like.

4. You should listen for ideas and underlying feelings. Again, the purpose of good communication is to be able to reflect upon and exchange ideas. For example, if I were to meet you on the street and give you a dollar and you gave me a dollar, and you then went your way and I went mine, neither of us would be better off because of the exchange. But if I gave you an idea and you gave me an idea, then both of us would be better off as a result of the exchange.

5. You should try to determine your own biases, if any, and allow for them. Communication gets blamed for many things. Whenever something doesn't go right, you might say you have a communication breakdown. But many times you don't have a communication breakdown at all. In fact, you might have a very good communication; you both know what has been said, and there is a common understanding. But you don't like what you have heard. If the nurse, physician, or surgeon could learn to recognize such differences, better relationships would be formed. You will not always agree with everyone. The trauma in such situations develops when you discover you are no longer talking about the issues, but about each other.

6. You should attempt to keep your mind on what the speaker is saying. Don't allow yourself to become distracted. Too many times people fake attention and like the little dog in the back of the car window just keep nodding their heads up and down without hearing a word of what is being said.

7. You should not interrupt immediately if you hear a statement that you feel is wrong. Indeed, if you listen closely, you may be persuaded that the statement is right. Sometimes you may fail to listen just because of this fear of something different, of the possibility that you may have to forsake some sacred position you have held for years.

**Activity 2:8** continued

8. You should try to see the situation from the other person's point of view. This doesn't mean that you always have to agree. However, there is no way that you can change other people's perceptions until you can see how they have formulated those perceptions.

9. You should not try to have the last word. Listen to what is being said and then think about it. This reflection may take some time, but you need time to think before you communicate. Sometimes, in order to solve problems, you have to walk away from the problem for a while and think about it from different points of view, and about the advantages and disadvantages of possible solutions.

10. You should make a conscientious effort to evaluate the logic and credibility of what you hear. Our mind functions at some 500 words a minute, but we normally speak at 125 words a minute. In other words, we can think four times faster than we can speak. Rather than letting our minds become bored, we can take advantage of this time differential between thinking and speaking. We can attempt to anticipate the speaker's next point, attempt to identify and evaluate supporting material, and mentally summarize what the speaker has said: What has thus far been said that I can use?

Remember, listening makes the people you are listening to feel special; sometimes it enables them to solve their own problems. Perhaps they are in the process of hearing themselves think aloud on a subject for the first time. At such times, they might just want others to listen. If you refrain from injecting yourself into the conversation, you might be able to help them resolve their own internal conflicts.

As a professional, you are paid to listen. Yet studies at the University of Minnesota, confirmed by studies at Florida and Michigan State University, showed that people forget one-third to one-half of what they hear within eight hours. [Kramer & Lewis, 1951.]

The art of listening is a skill, however, and it can be improved. You listen best when you develop a positive attitude toward listening. The first step is to become aware of the fact that listening is not a passive activity. Also, there is little correlation between intelligence and listening. You must "want" to remember

# Activity 2:9

# Active Listening Values Clarification

Active listening is essential to good employee interpersonal relations. However, Rogers and Farson, authors of "Active Listening," raise the following issues regarding active listening in relation to organizational goals. Think about these points opposing active listening.

- Write out your reaction to the comments to clarify your own values and assumptions that will affect your active listening.

    "We're in business, and it is a rugged, fast, competitive affair. How are we going to find time to counsel our employee?"

    _____

    _____

    _____

    _____

    "We have to concern ourselves with organizational problems first."

    _____

    _____

    _____

    _____

    "We can't afford to spend all day listening when there is work to do."

    _____

    _____

    _____

    _____

    "What's morale got to do with service to the public?"

    _____

    _____

    _____

    _____

    "Sometimes we have to sacrifice an individual for the good of the rest of the people in the organization."

    _____

    _____

    _____

    _____

**Activity 2:9** continued

- Give this activity to two peers and meet to discuss your responses.
- Review the response by Rogers and Farson below, and briefly state your agreement or disagreement.

One answer is based on an assumption that is central to the listening approach. That assumption is: the kind of behavior which helps the individual will eventually be the best thing that could be done for the work group. Or saying it another way: the things that are best for the individual are best for the organization. This is a conviction of ours, based on our experience in psychology and education. The research evidence from organizations is still coming in. We find that putting the group first, at the expense of the individual, besides being an uncomfortable individual experience, does not unify the group. In fact, it tends to make the group less a group. The members become anxious and suspicious. (Rogers & Farson, 1971, pp. 177–178)

_____
_____
_____
_____

# Activity 2:10

# Public Speaking

According to Dale Carnegie (1977), you should seize every opportunity to practice public speaking. As a new manager you should begin now using good speaking techniques so that this skill grows as your career does. There will be educational and administrative topics you will need to present either to your staff or your peers. Sometimes after committee work on a special project you may be part of a presentation to the entire nursing management group. You may also pursue speaking opportunities in your professional or community organizations. Whatever the occasion, get in the habit of good speaking techniques.

Find an occasion to try out the following checklist:

- ☐ Be sure of your facts.
- ☐ Speak to the interest and level of your audience.
- ☐ Be enthusiastic.
- ☐ Never apologize for being nervous (it makes people watch for it).
- ☐ Speak from an outline—*never* read it.
- ☐ Practice your speech several times before giving it.
- ☐ Use visuals if possible (try them out ahead).
- ☐ Use the tried and true format:

    - Tell the audience what you are about to say.
    - Say it.
    - Tell the audience what you have said (summarize).

- ☐ Humor helps.
- ☐ Seek one-to-one feedback from one or two individuals you respect and add their suggestions to your checklist.

# Activity 2:11

# Presentation "Up the Line"

Whenever you want to "sell" something to your boss (whether to make a change or obtain some item), be prepared with data to back up your position.

Use the following format to organize your data:

State how the present situation is

_____

_____

Explain briefly the problem in terms of

- safe patient care _____

  _____

- quality care _____

  _____

- special needs of patients _____

  _____

- job satisfaction of staff _____

  _____

- compliance with laws, standards, policies, etc. _____

  _____

State options

1. _____
2. _____
3. _____
4. _____

Cost of options _____

_____

Desired change _____

_____

_____

**Activity 2:11** continued

Rationale in terms of cost/quality _____

_____

_____

What you need from your boss:

Item _____

Support _____

Cost _____

## CASE STUDY

Sondra Morris was hired to be the new intensive care unit (ICU) head nurse in a large, sophisticated medical center. Sondra arrived with extensive technical skills and some leadership experience. She was met by a group of highly independent nurses who functioned well despite their lack of "popularity" with nursing administration. Sondra, concerned about this poor relationship, spent time listening to her staff—their needs and their complaints. Sondra also was diligent about "selling" administration to her staff and carrying information "down the line." She told her boss about the good relationship between herself and her staff, the strong team, and the open sharing. Her boss believed that "everything was fine now in the ICU."

Six months later, seven nurses on Sondra's staff went directly to her boss to complain. The nurses said that although they liked Sondra, they were tired of hearing what administration wanted. "It is time for administration to hear what we want," they said firmly.

When Sondra heard of the visit, she was surprised, hurt, and confused. Where did Sondra go wrong?

## SOLUTION TO CASE STUDY

Sondra did one-half of her "linking-pin" function. Her job is to carry information "down the line" to her staff (as she did well) but also to take the issues, needs, and concerns of her staff "up the line." Instead, she told her boss, "All is well." All the trust she built with her team will die if she doesn't represent them to her boss. Without this trust emerging from good representation to administration, all her team building and listening efforts will be in vain. Sondra is a "no-action manager" and must fulfill her responsibility of transmitting staff needs up the line, to administration, to become an effective manager.

**REFERENCES**

Carnegie, D. *Effective speaking*. New York: Carnegie, 1977.

Fayol, H. *General and industrial management*. London: Pitman Publishing, 1949.

Kelly, J. *Organizational behavior* (3rd ed.). Homewood, Ill.: Irwin, 1980.

Kramer, J. H., & Lewis, T. R. Comparison of visual and nonvisual listening. *Journal of Communication*, 1951, *1* (16).

Likert, R. *New patterns of management*. New York: McGraw-Hill, 1961, pp. 103–118.

Morris, J. O. *Make yourself clear*. New York: McGraw-Hill, 1980.

Rogers, C. R., & Farson, R. E. Active listening. In D.A. Kolb, I.M. Rubin, & J.M. McIntyre (Eds.), *Organizational behavior* (3rd ed.). Englewood Cliffs, N.J.: Prentice-Hall, 1971.

Rogers, C. R., & Roethlisberger, F. J. Barriers and gateways to communication. *Harvard Business Review*, 1952, *30* (4), 28–32.

# Chapter 3

# Leadership

**OBJECTIVES**

Upon completion of this chapter, including the activities, the new nurse manager will be able to:

- explain a contingency leadership model, including the behaviors on various levels of the continuum
- state the Theory X and Theory Y assumptions underlying the two extreme management styles
- differentiate between country club managers, task managers, impoverished managers, middle road managers, and team managers
- delineate forces in the manager that affect his or her leadership style
- recognize various stages in group functioning and assess the level of group functioning by observation
- analyze what can be delegated and to whom, considering responsibility, authority, and accountability
- recognize team-building needs and explain interventions to meet those needs

# DEVELOPMENT OF THE NEW NURSE MANAGER™

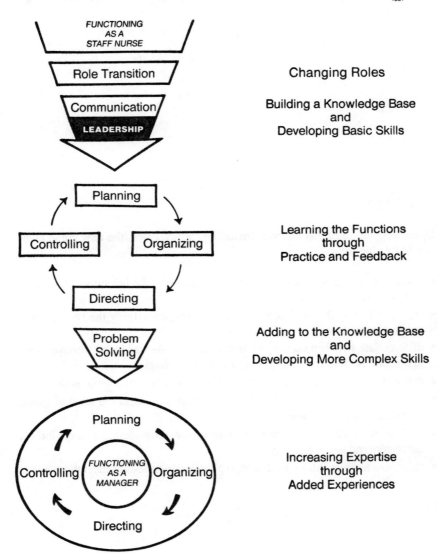

¶ To be an effective manager, you will need a variety of leadership skills. You have subordinates "in line" under you. These people report to you and expect you to "lead" them. "Leadership is the process of influencing the activities of an individual or a group in efforts toward goal achievement in a given situation" (Hersey & Blanchard, 1977).

If you achieved your current position through excellent clinical nursing skills, be assured that the clinical expertise that helped get you promoted to manager is still valuable in this new position. Other skills needed in management and leadership, although totally different than those previously used, are learnable.

Much like the communication model explored in the last chapter, a leadership model can also be used to facilitate learning about leadership styles. This model will help you sort out which leadership style is appropriate in situations you will face as a nurse manager. Through quality feedback and plenty of practice, you can develop the skills you need to be an effective leader.

There was a time when managers simply told people what to do and the employees complied. At that time managers were working under what McGregor (1957) calls Theory X assumptions. These managers believed that:

- people are basically lazy and do not want to work
- people are passive, even resistive, to organizational needs and must be persuaded, rewarded, punished, and controlled
- people are self-centered and not very bright
- people want to be told, shown, and trained
- people lack ambition and responsibility and want to be led.

The style of the manager who believes these Theory X assumptions will be consistent with these negative assumptions. This person will use an authoritarian form of management. You probably remember an authoritarian manager somewhere in your career—the boss who continually looked over your shoulder after telling you what to do, the teacher who habitually addressed the class in a condescending tone. Such authoritarian tactics have limited usefulness today. Although there are situations in which the manager needs to be authoritarian, society in general and professional employees in particular now demand a more sophisticated approach from people in management. The manager's actions today are influenced by many more forces than used to be the case. The increased rate of change and complexity of organizations and decision making require more sophisticated leadership skills in today's managers.

## MANAGEMENT STYLE

Your first concerns as a new manager are probably "How should I act?" or "What kind of manager should I be?" These questions refer to management styles. An extremely rigid, task-oriented manager uses the authoritarian style, which may be based on Theory X assumptions about people. This manager usually favors one-way communication from boss to subordinates. This manager "tells" people what to do. You might see such communication in a nurse manager who is a stickler for following policies and procedures "to the letter," someone who demands an immediate response. For example, a head nurse wants an incident report filled out. She demands that a staff nurse stop what she is doing and complete it "now." The nurse would like to suggest that she write the form after she takes her elderly patient to Physical Therapy (P.T.) and talks with the patient's family about the treatment. The staff nurse does not suggest this alternative because of the authoritarian manner in which she was told to "do it now." She completes the form, the patient is late for P.T., and the family, who had to leave, remains uninformed about their mother's therapy.

The other extreme style of leadership is that of the laissez-faire manager. This manager is good friends with the staff and is more concerned with how the staff feels about things than with what they actually do. Consider the head nurse who places such a high value on interpersonal communications and support to patients that the physical condition of patients' rooms gets little attention. Cluttered overbed tables and countertops prevent easy placement of food trays and obstruct access to patients in an emergency situation.

A trend toward more laissez-faire leadership styles resulted from the humanistic movement in society that began in the 1950s. During this time, leaders began basing their management styles on what McGregor (1957) calls Theory Y assumptions about people. Theory Y assumptions are as follows:

- People like to work and are not naturally passive or resistant to organizational goals.
- All people have potential for development and a capacity for assuming responsibility.
- The work itself is meaningful.
- Most people are capable of controlling their own work and seek responsibility.

Leaders who believe Theory Y assumptions tend to involve their followers more in their decision making. Two-way communication increases.

Which of these two styles is appropriate? The answer is that it depends on or is contingent upon the situation. For example, if a patient's heart stops, a life is dependent upon quick, accurate decisions. A directive or authoritarian approach is appropriate here because of the seriousness of the situation, the time constraint, and because a clear, simple, one-way direction is adequate. Although the appropriate style is directive, the manager does not necessarily "buy into" the Theory X assumptions. The manager chose a directive style because the situation demanded it. In contrast, where to place the coffee pot in the staff lounge is not a decision requiring a directive style, and use of an authoritarian approach in such a situation would be inappropriate.

Thus, the appropriate style for today's manager is contingent upon the situation. A good leader needs to know how to be both authoritarian and laissez-faire. Yet neither of these pure styles will suit all situations. Many in-between styles, reflecting varying amounts and types of two-way communication between manager and employee, are available to the nurse manager.

Research in leadership behavior was initiated in 1945 by the Ohio State University (Stogdill & Coons, 1957). Two distinctive leadership styles were observed. The first, consideration, was characterized by friendly, approachable leaders who found time to listen to their group. The second, initiating structure, was characterized by standard rules and regulations and clear expectations from the leader.

Blake and Mouton (1978) have named the two extreme management styles as task oriented (authoritarian) and country club oriented (laissez-faire). To these two extremes, they added three other management styles: impoverished, middle road, and team. All five are presented in Figure 3–1.

## Figure 3–1 The Managerial Grid

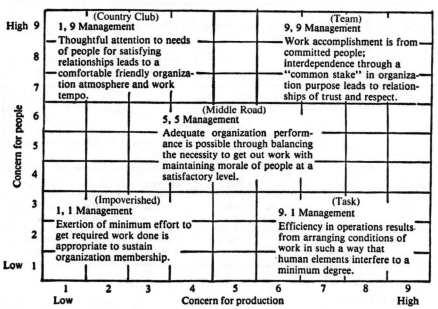

*Source:* The Managerial Grid figure from *The New Managerial Grid*, by Robert R. Blake and Jane Srygley Mouton. Houston: Gulf Publishing Co., Copyright © 1978, page 11. Reproduced by permission.

They defined these five styles based on the amounts of concern for task and concern for people reflected by each. The task manager (authoritarian) has great concern for productivity (task) and low concern for people (two-way communication). The country club manager (laissez-faire) has great concern for people and low concern for task. The impoverished manager shows little concern for either task or people. The middle road manager shows medium concern for both task and people. The team manager shows great concern for both people and task.

To manage well, the nurse manager must be able to use any of these styles and decide which style best suits each situation in light of the variables that are relevant to that situation.

Consider the management styles as being on a continuum from authoritarian to laissez-faire. As you move from authoritarian to laissez-faire, two-way communication increases and the employee has more opportunity to participate in the decisions you make. You are thus increasing your participatory management style—moving from high task concern to high people concern.

Tannenbaum and Schmidt (1958) have presented seven incremental phases, from authoritarian decision making to laissez-faire decision making. Each phase states the manager's role and the group's role in the decision-making process (Figure 3–2). Moving from the left end of the continuum, authoritarian, to the right end, laissez-faire, involves incrementally increasing the group's input.

---

**Figure 3–2** A Continuum of Leadership Behavior

| Boss-centered leadership | | | | | | Subordinate-centered leadership |
| --- | --- | --- | --- | --- | --- | --- |

Use of authority by the manager

Area of freedom for subordinates

| Manager makes decision and announces it. | Manager "sells" decision. | Manager presents ideas and invites questions. | Manager presents tentative decision subject to change. | Manager presents problem, gets suggestions, makes decision. | Manager defines limits; asks group to make decision. | Manager permits subordinates to function within limits defined by superior. |

Range of behavior

There are situations that are appropriate for the use of each style. As a nursing manager, you need to have the ability, communication skills, and self-confidence to use any of the incremental styles. With experience, you will be able to judge which style is best in a given situation. Few situations lend themselves to either extreme of the continuum; most situations fall somewhere in the middle. Exhibit 3–1 gives examples of decision-making situations faced by a head nurse that are appropriate to each style.

Before deciding which leadership style to use in your new role, consider the variables in choosing the appropriate amount of employee participation in a given situation. Tannenbaum and Schmidt call these variables "forces." The term *forces* is appropriate because these entities will push, or force, you into a more authoritarian or more laissez-faire style.

The four types of forces that affect leadership style are found (1) in the manager, (2) in the subordinate, (3) in the situation, and (4) in the environment—both the organizational and the societal environments (see Figure 3–3). These forces are present in various combinations in every situation. Increasing your awareness of the forces is your first step in choosing a management style.

### Forces in the Nurse Manager

The first forces are those in the manager. What are the forces within you that will affect your management style? First, examine your management skills and experiences. What has worked or not worked in the past? How well developed are your communication skills? Can you be assertive when the situation demands it? Then be more mellow and understanding in another situation? What is your natural style? In other words, what are you most comfortable doing? Are you more task oriented? Nurses who work in the intensive care unit, operating room, emergency room, or recovery room often tend to operate more toward the task end of the continuum. This style may frequently be appropriate for safety reasons, since patients in these areas are often in an acute condition. If your background leans more toward psychology, geriatrics, obstetrics, or medical/surgical nursing, your natural tendency may be to choose a more laissez-faire style, as these specialties often demand more people-oriented skills. Thus, you may tend to ask for more input and feedback from your staff and allow more opportunities for employees to share how they feel about a decision.

Values and attitudes play a key role in determining your style. Who were your role models? What were their styles? Review the Theory X and Theory Y assumptions. What are your assumptions? These basic assumptions reflect your values about your employees and will affect your leadership style. How you believe people are motivated will also influence your natural style.

Your own needs also play a role. Perhaps you would like your unit to be able to operate equally smoothly with or without your presence. Therefore, you openly

**Exhibit 3–1  Decision-Making Styles and Examples of Their Appropriate Use**

| Possible styles to use in each situation: | Manager makes decision and announces it. | Manager "sells" decision. | Manager presents ideas and invites questions. | Manager presents tentative decision subject to change. | Manager presents problem, gets suggestions, makes decision. | Manager defines limits; asks group to make decision. | Manager permits subordinates to function within limits defined by superior. |
|---|---|---|---|---|---|---|---|
| When to use: | • Emergency<br>• Down-the-line communication that is clear | • Climate tense<br>• To keep morale up<br>• If you anticipate difficulty with decision | • When group cannot change but may need clarification | • Pretty set but there may be some information you have not considered | • When there is time<br>• When there may be more than one solution<br>• When you want group to "buy into" participation management<br>• People expect it because it is a group norm | • Often used in committees given a specific charge<br>• Report format<br>• Decision has strong implications on group and manager trusts group to make a good decision | • Informal/social |
| Examples: | You are the manager, and you walk into a patient room when a cardiac arrest is in process. You see that CPR is being done by one nurse. You tell another nurse to assist. As two other nurses enter the room, you tell one to call the operator to announce the code and have the other nurse bring the "crash cart." | Due to financial cuts mandated in an economic recession, tuition reimbursement benefits were decreased. You explain that this reduction was preferable to cutting nursing positions. | You receive five vacation requests for Christmas holiday, but safe staffing on your unit only allows three people to be out. You announce your decision, explain rationale, and invite questions. | A recent resignation of a night shift RN needs to be covered. Until a new RN is hired and oriented, you need to schedule staff to fill this slot. You tentatively schedule three nurses to rotate for coverage. This plan is presented to them for their approval or changes subject to your final approval. | Linen usage has escalated on your unit with subsequent large (negative) budget variances. You present this problem to a small group of interested staff members for suggestions to decrease linen use. | For change of shift report—give guidelines, length of time, who must attend, some statement about type of information to be exchanged; let group decide on format. | A $300 check is given to a nursing unit in gratitude for care by a family. Manager reiterates family wishes that the money be used to benefit all unit nurses in some way. |

*Source:* Adapted from "How To Choose a Leadership Pattern," by R. Tannenbaum and W.H. Schmidt, *Harvard Business Review*, March-April, 1958, p. 96.

**Figure 3–3** The Forces That Affect Leadership Style

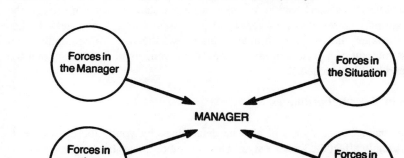

share information and develop your nurses to "fill in" for you. You help them learn management tasks and eventually guide them into management roles. Or perhaps you would like to feel needed; thus, you integrate yourself into every activity and decision of the unit, creating a system dependent upon your presence. Other needs that may affect your style include a need to be surrounded by excitement, change, and creativity or, contrarily, a need for stability and tradition.

Another important force that can affect your management style is the confidence you have in your subordinates. You may delegate work, but as a manager you cannot actually delegate the final responsibility. You are responsible for delegating to people who are competent and who follow through on a given assignment. Your confidence in subordinates must be well founded. This increases with positive experiences. For example, you trust one of your staff to prepare a patient for surgery without giving the nurse specific instructions. If she performs well, you will more readily trust her in a similar situation in the future. If you get a phone call that the patient arrived wearing dentures and nail polish, your trust in that nurse will decrease.

Your propensity to take risks or not is another factor that plays a role in your management style. As a head nurse you may want to try a new rotation pattern with your night staff. This will involve some inconvenience for a few staff members, but the plan will benefit almost all of the staff. Are you willing to give it a try?

The last force that emerges from you, affecting your management style, is your tolerance for ambiguity. If you believe there is one right way to do something and that all other ways are wrong, your tolerance for ambiguity is low. Often, one's tolerance for ambiguity increases with experience. If you believe in the principle of "equifinality" (better known as, "There is more than one way to skin a cat"), your style will be more flexible. Equifinality is defined by Katz and Kahn (1966) as the use of various system configurations to reach the same end or, conversely, the same end may be reached by a variety of processes. A nurse manager who has worked in many hospitals or on many units knows the value of equifinality and often is tolerant of a variety of approaches to a given situation knowing that the same end will be reached.

### Forces in Your Subordinates

Your management style will also be determined by your subordinates. Followers greatly affect the leader's style. Do your subordinates have a great need for independence, or are they very dependent? Often dependency is inversely proportional to the amount of experience a staff nurse has. The new graduate nurse certainly is more dependent than an experienced nurse practitioner—with many levels in between.

Some institutions sort out this variable by having staff nurse levels and criteria for each level. Even if your institution does not have defined staff nurse levels, you know from experience that the notion "a nurse is a nurse" has little validity. The amount of input you, as a manager, seek from your staff in making a decision will often necessarily be related directly to the amount of expertise and experience they have.

Another variable in your subordinates that will affect your management style is whether the staff on your unit are willing to assume more responsibility. It is difficult to delegate to nurses who do not want increased responsibility. If your predecessor "did everything herself," this may be a difficult norm to break. If nurses are willing to assume more responsibility, you must also consider to what degree they identify with the goals of your unit and organization.

Benge (1976) accuses managers of not delegating enough. He claims that most managers have never even analyzed their jobs to decide what should be delegated. Further, managers often fail to analyze their subordinates' abilities to decide who can accept delegation. Benge proposes four reasons why managers do not delegate:

1. doubt that subordinates are capable, smart, or experienced enough
2. concern that subordinates might prove more capable than themselves
3. fear that their own importance will be lessened
4. ignorance of what should be delegated.

Managers should delegate to free themselves from small, time-consuming details to allow time and energy for larger responsibilities. Also, delegation "down-the-line" brings the decisions closer to the front line, where the action is. Chances for better decisions and improved morale increase. Delegation should be used as a major tool through which to develop your staff. Increased responsibility of staff often yields greater "buying into" the unit. Greater creativity comes from diversity in leadership and decision making. Subordinates gain a broader perspective of the organization.

Delegation is not without disadvantages. With delegation may come "less uniformity, duplication of staff functions, conflict, and poor and costly decisions" (Benge, 1976). These problems can be reduced or avoided with proper selection and development of the persons to whom you delegate.

When you delegate a task to someone, assess whether or not this person has the skills necessary for the job. Clearly define the task (responsibility), and give the person the authority (power) to go with that responsibility. For example, if you assign someone the role of charge nurse for a shift, that nurse must have the power to make and alter assignments as needs of the unit change.

After giving responsibility and authority, follow up with an evaluation of your nurse's performance on the delegated task. Ask that person what went well and what did not; then help problem solve or develop skills for any areas that were troublesome.

Although the person to whom you delegate should be held accountable for the task, delegation of your responsibilities does not free you from accountability. Thus, you must be sure to select carefully the persons to whom you delegate; you must clearly define the responsibility, back up their authority to do it, and then hold them accountable and give them feedback. This is the "Circle of Delegation" (see Figure 3–4).

**Figure 3–4** Circle of Delegation

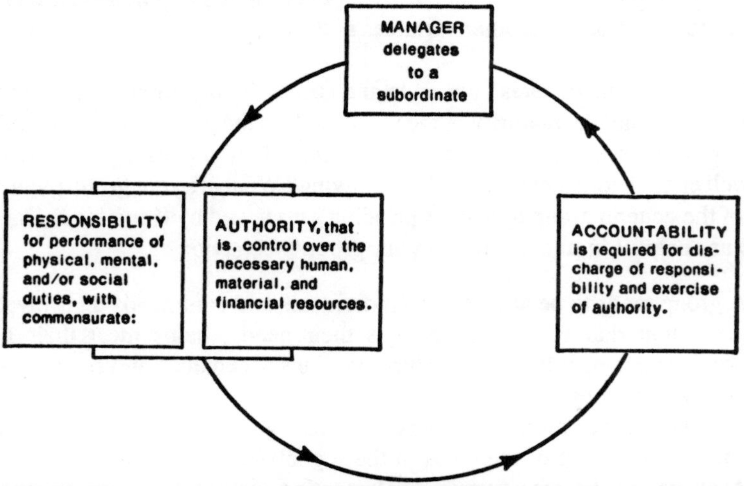
MANAGER delegates to a subordinate
RESPONSIBILITY for performance of physical, mental, and/or social duties, with commensurate:
AUTHORITY, that is, control over the necessary human, material, and financial resources.
ACCOUNTABILITY is required for discharge of responsibility and exercise of authority.

*Source:* Reprinted by permission of the publisher, from ELEMENTS OF MODERN MANAGEMENT by E.J. Benge, p. 130 © 1976 by AMACOM, a division of American Management Associations, New York. All rights reserved.

Besides ability and expertise, the attitude of your staff plays a key part in how independent they will be. This usually varies with the situation. Most nurses are interested in particular problems or issues; no one is interested in all of them. The amount of participation you seek should relate to the amount of vested interest of the subordinates. One reality to be considered here is that some staff members, as in any other profession, will want to "just do the job and go home" while others will have substantial energy to invest in hospital committee work, professional organizations, writing for publication, and/or problem solving and system change. You need to vary your style to accommodate both types of employees.

### Forces in the Situation

Regardless of your preferred style and the expertise of your staff, there are variables that almost dictate the appropriate style. The two most forceful of these variables are the urgency and gravity of the situation. If you walk into a room and a patient is falling out of bed or having difficulty breathing, and if a nurse is not adequately dealing with the patient's urgent need, you will certainly meet that need prior to seeking input from the nurse.

Urgency and gravity can be ranked in terms of Maslow's hierarchy of needs (1959). The most urgent needs, and therefore the first to be met, are the primary physiological needs of safety and security. Second, the social, self-esteem, and self-actualization needs should be addressed. In the foregoing example, the patient's physiological or safety needs took precedence over observing the social graces and talking with the nurse or helping the nurse fulfill her self-esteem needs by working the problem out by herself. After the patient's urgent need is met, you may then take into account other variables and change your style according to the situation.

Another force that dictates your style and comes from your staff is the group's maturity level—not the maturity of the individuals in the group, but the maturity of the group itself (see Chapter 6). How often have they met as a group? Do they work well enough together to do problem solving? What are your group dynamics? Some of the general group dynamics principles reviewed by Knowles & Knowles (1972) are helpful in understanding your group's behavior:

1. A group tends to be attractive to individuals and commands their loyalty to the extent that the group satisfies their needs, helps meet their goals, provides a congenial membership, provides acceptance and security and is highly valued by outsiders.
2. The more input group members have into goals and decisions, the more commitment each of them has to those goals and decisions.
3. A group can be effective in implementing change to the extent that the members of the group share the perception that the change is needed and plan for it.

4. The better individuals understand their own behavior and group behavior, the more constructively they will be able to contribute while preserving their own integrity.
5. Pressure to conform to the group is determined by the group's need for conformity and how attractive the group and the issue are to the individual.
6. The effectiveness of a group is determined by the existence of clear, prioritized, agreed-upon goals that mobilize group energies; agreed-upon plans to reach those goals; and sufficient organization and use of appropriate group processes to reach the goals.

These principles are useful because "every group is able to improve its ability to operate as a group to the extent that it consciously examines its processes and their consequences and experiments with improved processes" (Knowles & Knowles, 1972, pp. 61–64). You can use the Cog's Ladder to assess your group's stage of operation (Pfeiffer & Jones, 1974). Exhibit 3–2 delineates the five stages of group development as:

1. polite stage,
2. why we are here stage,
3. bid for power stage,
4. constructive stage, and
5. esprit de corps stage.

Some groups get stuck in a stage and may need to look at why that is happening. Each time the group meets, they begin at stage 1. A healthy, established task group may move quickly up to stage 4 on most meetings. Even after a group reaches the constructive stage, periodic "backing up" may be necessary to redefine the task (stage 2). Moving from stage 2, defining your task, to stage 3, bid for power, starts with someone taking a risk on sharing an opinion or idea. If criticized, the risk increases for the next group member who tries to share. Some groups have difficulty getting past this stage if there are no risk takers or if every idea is criticized. Brainstorming can help to move a group forward if this happens (see the Brainstorming Activity at the end of this chapter).

To move from stage 3, bid for power, to the constructive stage, someone must move the group from telling to listening. A group member with active listening skills (see Chapter 2) or a facilitator can augment this process. In stage 4, work is done.

Esprit de corps is a natural group feeling of accomplishment as tasks are completed. As a leader, take time to feed back accomplishments and provide recognition to the team to foster the mutual acceptance, high cohesiveness, good will, and camaraderie of stage 5.

To assess how your group is functioning, look at how well it proceeds through these stages. Also consider each of the "group properties" (Knowles & Knowles,

**Exhibit 3–2** Cog's Ladder

| | |
|---|---|
| Esprit Stage | Feel unity and high spirits; have mutual acceptance; high cohesiveness; good will; and camaraderie. |
| Constructive Stage | Begin active listening; accept one another's value systems; in this "team action stage" members are more open-minded. |
| Bid for Power | Attempt to influence one another's opinions, ideas, values; compete for recognition, attention, influence. |
| Why We're Here | Define objectives and goals of group; define task; redefine. |
| Polite Stage | Get acquainted; share values; stay simple; avoid controversy. |

Five Steps of Group Development

1972), including: background of the group, participation patterns, communication, cohesion, atmosphere standards, sociometric pattern, structure and organization, procedures, and goals. (See the group assessment/improvement activities at the end of this chapter.)

If your group is not functioning on a constructive level (stage 4), team building will be helpful. "Probably the most important single group of interventions in organizational development are the team-building activities, the goals of which are the improvement and increased effectiveness of various teams within the organization" (French & Bell, 1978, p. 117). Team-building activities focus on two types of groups. Family groups are permanent work teams composed of boss and subordinates. Special groups include task forces, committees, and new groups resulting from organizational structure changes. A variety of team-building activities are defined by French and Bell (1978) for both types of groups. These activities address five areas: task accomplishment, relationships, group processes, role analysis, and role negotiation (see Figure 3–5). Goal setting for your unit may be a good team-building vehicle with which to begin.

**Figure 3–5** Varieties of Team-Building Interventions

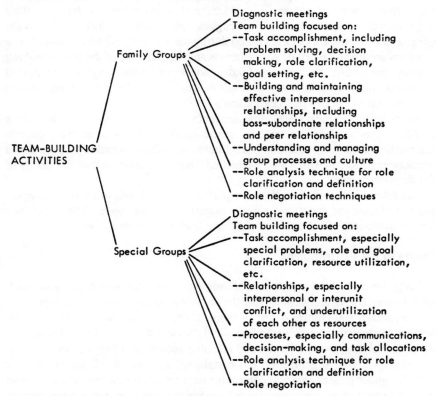

On the other hand, perhaps your group is solidified and works together quite well. You can involve this mature group in more decision making using a more participatory style of management, something toward the laissez-faire end of the Tannenbaum-Schmidt continuum. The currently popular "Theory Z" (Ouchi, 1981) is a participatory form of management used in Japan. Under Theory Z the number of subordinates involved in a decision goes beyond the concerned group or committee. The number of opinions sought is often so large that decision making is a very slow process.

Be careful of a mature group that moves to the top of the Cog's Ladder and "over the edge." An extremely cohesive group could result in groupthink patterns. Groupthink exists in a group when "concurrence-seeking becomes so dominant in a cohesive ingroup that it tends to override realistic appraisal of alternative courses of action. . . . [Members] avoid being too harsh in their judgments of the leaders' or their colleagues' ideas'' (Janis, 1971). This was the alleged cause of the Bay of Pigs fiasco during the Kennedy administration. "The more amiability and esprit de corps there is among members of the policy-making ingroup, the greater the danger that independent critical thinking will be replaced by group think which is likely to result in irrational and dehumanizing actions directed against outgroups'' (Parkinson's Law).

All cohesive groups have some tendency toward groupthink. It is only a problem if new ideas are stifled, critical thinking is not promoted, outside information is not sought, discussion is limited, and decision making is placed on a predictable pattern in which the "we feeling" is more important than the quality of the decision reached.

The subordinate forces are thus complex, including levels of individual expertise and attitude and variations in group maturity and functioning. These variables have a significant effect on the appropriate leadership style for you.

## Forces in the Environment

Many forces beyond you, your subordinates, and your unit affect your leadership style. These forces come from the organization and from society in general. The organizational culture is one of them. Culture is "the way people actually behave, the way they actually think and feel, the way they actually deal with each other. It includes both the formal and informal activities'' (Argyris, 1967, p. 2). For example, your organization has certain values about head nurses; specific attitudes about patient charges; committee expectation norms; perceptions about intensive care nurses; and unwritten rules regarding telephone and memo communications. French and Bell divide the organizational culture variables into two categories—formal (overt) and informal (covert) aspects. They depict these organizational "rules" on the symbolic Freudian iceberg; the formal (overt) aspects are characterized as being above the water. Informal, but equally powerful, "rules" lie below the surface. Information about the formal organization is readily available. Finding out about the informal organization may be difficult (see Exhibit 3–3).

Although the informal aspects of an organization are difficult to assess objectively, they become real should you step beyond them. Perhaps one of the organizational norms in your culture is to promote from within the hospital. If so, when you hire from outside in lieu of promoting a qualified staff nurse from within, your action will probably evoke a strong reaction from your staff. Or your staff will say nothing to you but make it very difficult for the unknowing new employee. Other cultural "rules" include notions that nurses are hardworking people or that hospitals are busy places where physicians have more power than

**Exhibit 3–3** Sources of Information about the Formal and Informal
Organizations

| *The Formal Organization Is Reflected in:* | *The Informal Organization Is Reflected in:* |
|---|---|
| • Policies | • Values |
| • Procedures | • Attitudes |
| • Goals | • Needs |
| • Objectives | • Expectations |
| • Organizational Charts | • History of the Organization |
| • Technology | • Traditions |
| • Job Descriptions | • Group Norms |
| • Human Resources | • Grapevines |
| • Material Resources | • Cliques |

nurses. Get to know your organization's culture. Before you violate the norm, know what the probable consequences will be. Explore the unit culture with your staff, and decide which norms promote increased productivity and smooth working relationships and which norms hinder these processes.

Another covert (or maybe not so covert) force that will affect your style is the style of your boss. If your superior gives you one-way communications, it will become difficult for you to discuss or to "sell" ideas to your staff. If your boss is very open and participatory, you will have more choices about your style.

Some important overt forces in the organization that will affect your management style include:

• budget constraints—these increase in intensity with economic recessions;
• union contracts—once negotiated, these often gravely restrict staffing and scheduling decisions; and
• policies and procedures—these should reflect professional standards of practice and quality care.

The latter go beyond the organization, reflecting societal demands and constraints such as regulations and national trends. Policies and procedures in your organization need to reflect quality health care practice. Implementation of these guidelines is essential to receiving both Joint Commission for Accreditation of Hospitals (JCAH) certification and state licensure for your institution.

Societal demands also encompass results of the 1960s consumer awareness movement. Since the 1960s, patients' questions have not only been answered more openly and honestly but are (and should be) encouraged. Health care teaching is more valued. Patients are told what their temperature is, what medications they are taking and their possible side effects, and alternatives to suggested treatments. In some states patients now have the right to read their own charts. Once the American Cancer Society raised awareness about the dangers of smoking, patients' requests about nonsmoking roommates gained validity, forcing managers to comply.

All these variables have an impact on how much flexibility you have in the leadership style you choose for a given situation and in your approach to decision making. As a good manager, you will need skill in all the styles as well as the ability to weigh significant variables to select the behavioral style appropriate for each situation.

## WHERE DO YOU START?

For a given decision, consider the forces that have the greatest bearing on the situation. Determine, in light of these forces, what the appropriate leadership style would be. Consider the consequences of several alternative styles. Choose and implement the style that you believe best suits the situation—even if it is not your "natural" style. Afterward, evaluate the effectiveness of the decision in terms of the quality of outcome and the satisfaction level of those involved or affected.

Be ready to ask for feedback on others' perceptions of your actions. This process will increase your awareness of how your leadership style affects your followers. You will also become more aware of how it affects your peers and your boss. As awareness increases, you can fine tune your style to be appropriate to any situation. This is how to learn the skills of an experienced leader. Time alone does not teach good leadership skills.

# Activity 3:1

# Contingency Leadership Styles

Tannebaum and Schmidt (1973) suggest that management style is on a continuum. A successful leader is one who can: (1) accurately assess the forces, (2) determine the appropriate behavior, and (3) actually be able to behave accordingly. This exercise is divided into three parts addressing these three criteria.

**Part I.**   To be able to assess the forces accurately, first it is essential to increase awareness.

What are some of the general forces on the Head Nurse in your organization?

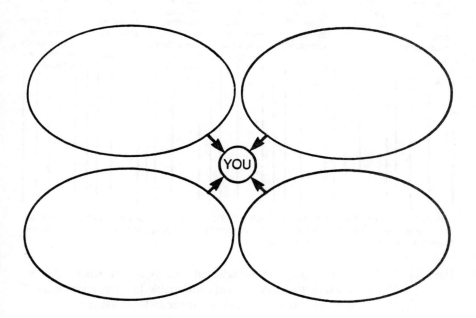

**Activity 3:1** continued

**Part II.**    To be able to determine the appropriate behavior, consider one example of an appropriate situation in your hospital for each of the styles along the continuum. Review these examples with your boss for validity in relation to your organization's authority code and norms about decision making.

**Exhibit I.** Continuum of Leadership Behavior

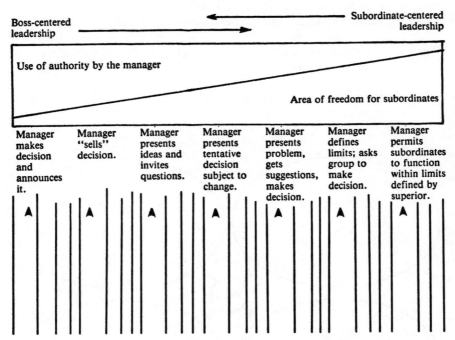

**Part III.**    To behave according to your selected style you must make a choice. You have a style that will be most comfortable for you, your "natural style," and you may want to develop other styles to use in your work. To develop these "less natural" styles will require practice.

• What is your "natural" style (where on the continuum)? _____

• Which styles do you need to practice? _____

**Activity 3:1** continued

- Plan two coming events that will require you to use a style other than your "natural" style. Role play this style with one of your peers, and discuss "how it feels" for you as the manager and "how it feels" to the person playing subordinate.

*Plan I*

Event: _____

Style(s) to try: _____

Peer: _____

How it felt to me: _____

Peer feedback: _____

*Plan II*

Event: _____

Style(s) to try: _____

Peer: _____

How it felt to me: _____

Peer feedback: _____

# Leadership Styles in Your Organization

• In your organization, most styles of leadership can be found. Select three managers with very different management styles, and interview them using the questionnaire below.

*Suggested Leadership Questions for Interviews by New Managers*

1. Would you share some of your background?
   (Clinical, managerial, and professional/educational)
   _____

2. Would you share information about your specialty?
   (Type of clinical expertise, size and location of your unit, etc.)
   _____

3. What do you see as the responsibility of managers in health care?
   _____

4. What are the manager's responsibilities in this organization?
   (Nursing/nonnursing; top management/middle management)
   _____

5. Would you recommend a particular style of leadership?
   _____

6. Can you share some examples of leadership techniques that have worked for you?
   (For example: Once I had a _____situation and I
   did _____because of _____.
   I believe it worked or didn't work because of _____.)

7. What advice can you give to me as a new manager in this organization?
   (What works? What doesn't?) _____
   _____

8. As a leader, what are your goals for this organization? _____
   _____

9. As a leader, what are your goals for yourself? _____
   _____

• What styles were found in your organization by those you interviewed?
   _____
   _____
   _____
   _____

# Activity 3:3

# Predicting Style Results

**Part I.** Employee timecards over the past two to three months have been returned to you with omissions and errors. More than one-third of your staff have to make corrections before cards can be signed off. It takes a large amount of time to track down employees each pay period because of this "carelessness."

Describe how you would approach this problem as each type manager below; what would you say? Also state your predicted response, the pros and cons of each style. Where does this style lie on the Tannenbaum/Schmidt leadership continuum, and what X/Y assumptions underlie this style?

| 1. Autocratic Manager: Based on extreme Theory X assumptions. | | | | | |
|---|---|---|---|---|---|
| You would say: | Predicted Response | Pros of This Style | Cons of This Style | Locate Where on the T/S Continuum You Are | X/Y Assumption Underlying This Style |
| | | | | | |
| | | | | | |
| | | | | | |

| 2. Laissez Faire Manager: Based on extreme Theory Y assumptions. | | | | | |
|---|---|---|---|---|---|
| You would say: | Predicted Response | Pros of This Style | Cons of This Style | Locate Where on the T/S Continuum You Are | X/Y Assumption Underlying This Style |
| | | | | | |
| | | | | | |
| | | | | | |

| 3. Contingency Manager: Based on assumptions of X or Y or both. | | | | | |
|---|---|---|---|---|---|
| You would say: | Predicted Response | Pros of This Style | Cons of This Style | Locate Where on the T/S Continuum You Are | X/Y Assumption Underlying This Style |
| | | | | | |
| | | | | | |
| | | | | | |

**Part II.** You need to deny a vacation request by one of your evening staff nurses.

- Write a script on how you would tell this nurse. Include setting, style, and meeting objectives.

**Activity 3:3** continued

Script

Setting: _____
Planned Leadership Style: _____
Objectives: _____
_____
_____
Script: _____
_____
_____
_____
_____
_____
_____

- Go back and circle those lines that will facilitate your chances of a positive outcome for both you and the staff nurse.
- Underline the lines that may cause either of you to be dissatisfied at the end of the session.
- Try to change as many of your underlined lines to circled lines as possible in the following script rewrites.

Script Rewrite

Setting: _____
Planned Leadership Style: _____
Objectives: _____
_____
_____
Script: _____
_____
_____
_____
_____
_____
_____

# Activity 3:4

# Underlying Leadership Assumptions

Answer the questions below.

**"Assumptions About People: Personal Analysis of Leadership Styles"***

Directions: This instrument is designed to help you better understand the assumptions you make about people and human nature. There are ten pairs of statements. Assign a weight from 0–10 to each statement to show the relative strength of your belief in the statements in each pair. The points assigned for each pair must in each case total ten. Be as honest with yourself as you can and resist the natural tendency to respond as you would "like to think things are." This instrument is not a "test." There are no right or wrong answers. It is designed to be a stimulus for personal reflection and discussion.

1. It's only human nature for people to do as little work as they can get away with. _____ (a)

   When people avoid work, it's usually because their work has been deprived of its meaning. _____ (b)
   10

2. If employees have access to any information they want, they tend to have better attitudes and behave more responsibly. _____ (c)

   If employees have access to more information than they need to do their immediate tasks, they will usually misuse it. _____ (d)
   10

---

*Adapted from M. Scott Myers, *Every Employee a Manager* (New York: McGraw-Hill Book Company, 1970).

David A. Kolb, Irwin M. Rubin, and James M. McIntyre, *Organizational Psychology: An Experimental Approach*, 2nd ed., © 1974. Reprinted by permission of Prentice-Hall, inc., Englewood Cliffs, New Jersey, pp. 241–246.

**Activity 3:4** continued

3. One problem in asking for the ideas of
employees is that their perspective is too limited
for their suggestions to be of much practical
value. _____ (e)

Asking employees for their ideas broadens their
perspective and results in the development of _____ (f)
useful suggestions. 10

4. If people don't use much imagination and
ingenuity on the job, it's probably because
relatively few people have much of either. _____ (g)

Most people are imaginative and creative but
may not show it because of limitations imposed _____ (h)
by supervision and the job. 10

5. People tend to raise their standards if they are
accountable for their own behavior and for
correcting their own mistakes. _____ (i)

People tend to lower their standards if they are _____ (j)
not punished for their misbehavior and mistakes. 10

6. It's better to give people both good and bad
news because most employees want the whole
story, no matter how painful. _____ (k)

It's better to withhold unfavorable news about
business because most employees really want to _____ (l)
hear only the good news. 10

7. Because a supervisor is entitled to more respect
than those below him in the organization, it
weakens his prestige to admit that a subordinate
was right and he was wrong. _____ (m)

Because people at all levels are entitled to equal
respect, a supervisor's prestige is increased when
he supports this principle by admitting that a _____ (n)
subordinate was right and he was wrong. 10

8. If you give people enough money, they are less
likely to be concerned with such intangibles as
responsibility and recognition. _____ (o)

If you give people interesting and challenging
work, they are less likely to complain about such _____ (p)
things as pay and supplemental benefits. 10

**Activity 3:4** continued

9. If people are allowed to set their own goals and
standards of performance, they tend to set them
higher than the boss would. ———— (q)

If people are allowed to set their own goals and
standards of performance, they tend to set them ———— (r)
lower than the boss would.                        10

10. The more knowledge and freedom a person has
regarding his job, the more controls are needed
to keep him in line. ———— (s)

The more knowledge and freedom a person has
regarding his job, the fewer controls are needed ———— (t)
to insure satisfactory job performance.            10

Score the questionnaire as follows:

The theory behind this instrument is discussed in detail in this unit. To get your
scores, add up the points you assigned to the following:

Theory X Score = Sum of (a), (d), (e), (g), (j), (l), (m), (o), (r), and (s).

Theory Y Score = Sum of (b), (c), (f), (h), (i), (k), (n), (p), (q), and (t).

This tool assesses your natural tendency to practice leadership based more on X or
on Y beliefs (McGregor). A balance of both is essential. If you find you have
mostly X or Y points, list the predictable responses from your staff when these
beliefs are activated.

_____
_____
_____
_____
_____

# Activity 3:5

# Assertiveness

**Part I.** Assertiveness Quotient

In order to be a manager, you must be assertive enough to represent your staff. Test your Assertiveness Quotient by completing the following questionnaire. Give each question a 1, 2, or 3 based on how comfortable you feel about each item:

> 1 — I feel very uncomfortable
>
> 2 — I feel moderately comfortable
>
> 3 — I feel very comfortable

## A Q TEST*

### *Assertive Behavior*

- Speaking up and asking questions at a meeting    _____
- Commenting about being interrupted by someone the moment he or she interrupts you    _____
- Stating your views to an authority figure (e.g., minister, boss, therapist, father)    _____
- Attempting to offer solutions and elaborating on them when others are present    _____

### *Your Body*

- Entering and exiting a room where superiors are present    _____
- Speaking in front of a group    _____
- Maintaining eye contact, keeping your head upright, and leaning forward when in a personal conversation    _____

### *Your Mind*

- Going out with a group of friends when you are the only one without a "date"    _____

*From THE ASSERTIVE WOMAN © 1975 by Stanlee Phelps and Nancy Austin. Reproduced for Donna Richards Sheridan by permission of Impact Publishers, Inc., P.O. Box 1094, San Luis Obispo, CA 94306. Further reproduction prohibited.

**Activity 3:5** continued

- Being especially competent, using your authority and/or power without labeling yourself as "bitchy," impolite, bossy, aggressive, castrating, or parental _____
- Requesting expected service when you haven't received it (e.g., in a restaurant or a store) _____

### *Apology*

- Being expected to apologize for something and not apologizing since you feel you are right _____
- Requesting the return of borrowed items without being apologetic _____

### *Compliments, Criticism, and Rejection*

- Receiving a compliment by saying something assertive to acknowledge that you agree with the person complimenting you _____
- Accepting a rejection _____
- Not getting the approval of the most significant person in your life _____
- Discussing another person's criticism of you openly with that person _____
- Telling someone that she or he is doing something that is bothering you _____

### *Saying No*

- Saying "no"—refusing to do a favor when you really don't feel like it _____
- Turning down a request for a meeting or date _____

### *Manipulation and Countermanipulation*

- Telling a person when you think she or he is manipulating you _____
- Commenting assertively to someone who has made a patronizing remark to you _____
- Talking about your feelings of competition with another person with whom you feel competitive _____

**Activity 3:5** continued

### *Sensuality*

- Showing physical enjoyment of an art show or concert in spite of others' reactions _____
- Asking to be caressed and/or telling your lover what feels good to you _____

### *Anger/Humor*

- Expressing anger directly and honestly when you feel angry _____
- Arguing with another person _____
- Telling a joke _____
- Listening to a friend tell a story about something embarrassing, but funny, that you have done _____
- Responding with humor to someone's put-down of you _____

If you have mostly 3's and a few 2's, you are assertive enough to be a head nurse. If you have a few 1's, write each one down and seek out three occasions to try more assertive behaviors in these situations. If you have five or more 1's, you won't make it in the role without an assertiveness course and/or some real work on your part.

| *Assertive Needs* | *Plan* |
|---|---|
| 1. | |
| | |
| 2. | |
| | |
| 3. | |
| | |

If I am not for myself, who will be for me?
If I am not for others, who am I for
And if not now, when?
—*The Talmud*

**Activity 3:5** continued

**Part II.** Assertiveness vs. Aggressiveness

Assertiveness is the use of energy toward another that is:

- declarative
- affirmative
- confident

Aggressiveness is use of energy toward another that is:

- combative
- forceful
- obtrusive

The difference is determined by the situation and the individual. What may be assertive behavior toward one individual or in one situation may be aggressive toward another individual in a different situation.

Assertive behavior is often necessary to make a point clearly or take a firm stand and usually results in respect for you as a person whether or not someone "buys into" what you are "selling."

Aggressive behavior causes your listener to become defensive and angry, thus usually blocking the message you are trying to send.

Some ways to foster assertive behavior and to avoid aggressive behavior when a firm stand is required include:

- Make "I" statements
- Let the other person know you hear what he or she is saying even though you cannot change your position or do not agree
- Clearly, calmly restate your point of view

For each example below, state whether the speaker is understated, assertive, or aggressive. If the statement is aggressive or understated, rewrite it into an assertive statement:

Nurse to Physician: "The patient's blood pressure is down. I think some blood work might help us to understand what is happening."

This statement is:  ☐ Understated

☐ Properly assertive

☐ Overly aggressive

**Activity 3:5** continued

If understated or overly aggressive, restate as assertive:

_____

_____

Nurse to Physician:  "You should have ordered blood work on that patient. Can't you see the blood pressure is down?"

This statement is:    ☐  Understated

                    ☐  Properly assertive

                    ☐  Overly aggressive

If understated or overly aggressive, restate as assertive:

_____

_____

Nurse to Physician:  "Do you think maybe we could possibly consider doing something, like maybe blood work, because it looks like the blood pressure is sort of down some?"

This statement is:    ☐  Understated

                    ☐  Properly assertive

                    ☐  Overly aggressive

If understated or overly aggressive, restate as assertive:

_____

_____

This week watch for opportunities to use assertive behavior. State three examples below of your use of assertive behavior:

1. _____

_____

2. _____

_____

3. _____

_____

# Activity 3:6

# Delegation Analysis

**Activity 3:6** continued

Using the form below, analyze for each of your responsibilities what can be delegated; to whom; specific responsibilities; authority validation; needs of subordinate before delegating; evaluation (accountability); recommendation.

| Head Nurse responsibilities • take from your job description • reduce to tasks | Cannot be delegated | Can be delegated | Specific responsibilities | Authority validation | To whom | Evaluation | Recommendation | Needs of subordinate before delegating |
|---|---|---|---|---|---|---|---|---|
| Example: P.M. Schedule for January | | | Write out Schedule by Dec. 1 using scheduling guidelines | Review with boss before posting | Carole Sparks | Review new union contract and how it affects scheduling | Coaching session to cover contract. Schedule done on time—acceptable, no change | Let Carole do several with my final approval; then she can guide Janis Marhai |

# Activity 3:7

# Level of Group Effectiveness

## Group Effectiveness Questionnaire

This questionnaire examines your personal perception of the effectiveness of your nursing group, whether you are doing your job individually or working with other group members to meet a group goal. The questionnaire deals with seven parts of the group process: planning, problem solving/decision making, use of resources, responsibility, motivation/pride, communications, and climate.

Each part may be scored separately to determine the nursing group's strength or weakness in each of the process areas. The combined scores give a total group effectiveness score. Score each statement as follows: 1 = Strongly disagree. 2 = Disagree. 3 = Don't know or neutral. 4 = Agree. 5 = Strongly agree. The evaluative categories of the combined scores are shown at the end of the questionnaire.

---

| Planning | Disagree | | | Agree | |
|---|---|---|---|---|---|
| (1) Our group goals are clearly defined. | 1 | 2 | 3 | 4 | 5 |
| (2) There is a high degree of commitment toward group goals. | 1 | 2 | 3 | 4 | 5 |
| (3) My group sets high standards of performance. | 1 | 2 | 3 | 4 | 5 |
| (4) The group does advance planning to avoid a crisis-like operating style. | 1 | 2 | 3 | 4 | 5 |
| (5) Our goals are well coordinated with other associated work groups and with higher organizational goals. | 1 | 2 | 3 | 4 | 5 |
| (6) Management asks for my ideas about better planning. | 1 | 2 | 3 | 4 | 5 |

*Source:* Reprinted from *The Nurse's Communication Handbook* by Harry E. Munn, Jr. with permission of Aspen Systems Corporation, © 1980.

**Activity 3:7** continued

(7) When procedural changes are made or new equipment is placed in operation, my group is properly trained and prepared.     1  2  3  4  5

(8) Management provides adequate staffing.     1  2  3  4  5

| Problem Solving/Decision Making | Disagree | | | Agree | |
|---|---|---|---|---|---|
| (9) My group develops several options before proposing a solution to a problem. | 1 | 2 | 3 | 4 | 5 |
| (10) In resolving group problems, each member of our group accepts a responsibility and constructively works toward resolution. | 1 | 2 | 3 | 4 | 5 |
| (11) We quickly resolve operational problems so that personal conflict does not build up. | 1 | 2 | 3 | 4 | 5 |
| (12) There is a general satisfaction concerning the quality of operational decisions that affect our group. | 1 | 2 | 3 | 4 | 5 |
| (13) Management accepts the consequences for a wrong decision and does not pass the blame to subordinates. | 1 | 2 | 3 | 4 | 5 |
| (14) If I have trouble on my job, I can count on my supervisor to be reasonable and to give the necessary assistance. | 1 | 2 | 3 | 4 | 5 |

| Use of Resources | Disagree | | | Agree | |
|---|---|---|---|---|---|
| (15) Group members utilize the skills of other members. | 1 | 2 | 3 | 4 | 5 |
| (16) There is adequate time and money to meet our important goals. | 1 | 2 | 3 | 4 | 5 |
| (17) The group displays a high level of technical or professional skill required for high performance. | 1 | 2 | 3 | 4 | 5 |
| (18) Our group meetings are action-oriented and productive. | 1 | 2 | 3 | 4 | 5 |

**Activity 3:7** continued

(19) Members are efficient in how they spend their time.     1  2  3  4  5

(20) My job makes good use of my skills and abilities.     1  2  3  4  5

(21) People who get ahead in my department deserve to do so because of their high performance.     1  2  3  4  5

(22) When needed, we receive training in a timely manner.     1  2  3  4  5

| Responsibility | Disagree | | | Agree | |
|---|---|---|---|---|---|

(23) Members of my group will go out of their way to help other members achieve their goals.     1  2  3  4  5

(24) Members of my group know each other's assignments and responsibilities.     1  2  3  4  5

(25) Members of our group follow through on assignments.     1  2  3  4  5

(26) My job gives me the chance to learn new skills and techniques.     1  2  3  4  5

(27) My job allows me to identify and solve problems on my own.     1  2  3  4  5

(28) Through discussion with management I can influence the decisions that affect my job.     1  2  3  4  5

(29) My group accepts the consequences when we make the wrong decision.     1  2  3  4  5

(30) My group actively looks for better ways to get the job done.     1  2  3  4  5

(31) I have a personal sense of responsibility to help my hospital be profitable.     1  2  3  4  5

| Motivation/Pride | Disagree | | | Agree | |
|---|---|---|---|---|---|

(32) We have a record of success in our group that provides a sense of pride.     1  2  3  4  5

**Activity 3:7** continued

(33) There is general group satisfaction about our contribution to the survival and future success of our hospital.    1   2   3   4   5

(34) Employee benefits are very good.    1   2   3   4   5

(35) My department recognizes those who consistently show high performance.    1   2   3   4   5

(36) I am making satisfactory progress toward my career goals.    1   2   3   4   5

(37) What happens to my hospital is important to me.    1   2   3   4   5

(38) I take personal pride in doing my job well.    1   2   3   4   5

## Communications     Disagree    Agree

(39) My group enjoys an open, honest, and direct style of communication.    1   2   3   4   5

(40) Disagreements are handled constructively, and we learn from the discussion.    1   2   3   4   5

(41) Members of my group effectively obtain, through a variety of sources, sufficient information to carry out their responsibilities.    1   2   3   4   5

(42) People at the top keep me advised of proposed solutions to problems existing at my level.    1   2   3   4   5

(43) My supervisor is aware of problems existing at my level.    1   2   3   4   5

(44) Management gives credit and recognition to people who do a good job.    1   2   3   4   5

(45) I clearly understand the employee benefits available to me.    1   2   3   4   5

## Climate     Disagree    Agree

(46) Members of my group have a high degree of respect for the competence and ability of the other members.    1   2   3   4   5

**Activity 3:7** continued

(47) My immediate supervisor treats everyone      1    2    3    4    5
fairly.

(48) I can honestly disagree with manage-         1    2    3    4    5
ment without fear of reprisal.

(49) Members of my work group trust each          1    2    3    4    5
other.

(50) I feel that management will fairly           1    2    3    4    5
represent my interests on issues con-
cerned with pay and working conditions.

TOTAL SCORING: 225–250 Superior, 175–224 Excellent, 125–174
Average, 75–124 Fair, 0–74 Poor.

# Activity 3:8

# Understanding the Roles of Unit Staff Members

**Part I.** Roles of Individual Staff Members

The roles (functions) members play in a group were classified as early as 1948 by Benne and Sheats—group building/maintenance roles and group task roles. Knowles and Knowles (1972) have defined these roles and have added the category of nonfunctional roles. Their definitions are included on the chart below. Think about how these roles are played during the average day on your unit. Next to each role and definition, fill in how this role helps the unit and how it hinders unit work. Add any ideas on how you can bring out the positive aspects of this role.

<table>
<tr>
<th rowspan="3">GROUP BUILDING AND MAINTENANCE ROLES</th>
<th rowspan="2">ROLE</th>
<th rowspan="2">DEFINITION</th>
<th colspan="2">How does the person in this role</th>
<th rowspan="2">How can you bring out the positive aspects of this role?</th>
</tr>
<tr>
<th>Help the unit work?</th>
<th>Hinder the unit work?</th>
</tr>
<tr>
<td>Encouraging</td>
<td>Being friendly, warm, responsive to others; praising others and their ideas; agreeing with and accepting the contributions of others.</td>
<td></td>
<td></td>
<td></td>
</tr>
<tr>
<td>Mediating</td>
<td>Harmonizing, conciliating differences in points of view; making compromises.</td>
<td></td>
<td></td>
<td></td>
</tr>
</table>

**Activity 3:8** continued

| ROLE | DEFINITION | How does the person in this role | | How can you bring out the positive aspects of this role? |
|------|------------|----------------------------------|--|----------------------------------------------------------|
| | | Help the unit work? | Hinder the unit work? | |
| Gate Keeping | Trying to make it possible for another member to make a contribution by saying, "We haven't heard from Jim yet," or suggesting limited talking-time for everyone so that all will have a chance to be heard. | | | |
| Standard Setting | Expressing standards for the group to use in choosing its subject matter or procedures, rules of conduct, ethical values. | | | |
| Following | Going along with the group, somewhat passively accepting the ideas of others, serving as an audience during group discussion, being a good listener. | | | |

GROUP BUILDING AND MAINTENANCE ROLES

**Activity 3:8** continued

<table>
<tr><td rowspan="9" style="writing-mode: vertical-lr">GROUP TASK ROLES</td></tr>
<tr><td rowspan="2">ROLE</td><td rowspan="2">DEFINITION</td><td colspan="2">How does the person in this role</td><td rowspan="2">How can you bring out the positive aspects of this role?</td></tr>
<tr><td>Help the unit work?</td><td>Hinder the unit work?</td></tr>
<tr><td>Relieving Tension</td><td>Draining off negative feeling by jesting or throwing oil on troubled water, diverting atten-tion from un-pleasant to pleas-ant matters.</td><td></td><td></td><td></td></tr>
<tr><td>Initiating</td><td>Suggesting new ideas or a changed way of looking at the group problem or goal, proposing new activities.</td><td></td><td></td><td></td></tr>
<tr><td>Information Seeking</td><td>Asking for rele-vant facts or authoritative information.</td><td></td><td></td><td></td></tr>
<tr><td>Information Giving</td><td>Providing rele-vant facts or au-thoritative infor-mation or relat-ing personal experience perti-nent to the group task.</td><td></td><td></td><td></td></tr>
<tr><td>Opinion Giving</td><td>Stating a perti-nent belief or opinion about something the group is consid-ering.</td><td></td><td></td><td></td></tr>
</table>

**Activity 3:8** continued

| | ROLE | DEFINITION | How does the person in this role | | How can you bring out the positive aspects of this role? |
| --- | --- | --- | --- | --- | --- |
| | | | Help the unit work? | Hinder the unit work? | |
| GROUP TASK ROLES | Clarifying | Probing for meaning and understanding, restating something the group is considering. | | | |
| | Elaborating | Building on a previous comment, enlarging on it, giving examples. | | | |
| | Coordinating | Showing or clarifying the relationships among various ideas, trying to pull ideas and suggestions together. | | | |
| | Orienting | Defining the progress of the discussion in terms of the group's goals, raising questions about the direction the discussion is taking. | | | |
| | Testing | Checking with the group to see if it is ready to make a decision or to take some action. | | | |

**Activity 3:8** continued

GROUP NONFUNCTIONAL ROLES

| ROLE | DEFINITION | How does the person in this role | | How can you bring out the positive aspects of this role? |
|------|------------|-----------|-----------|-----------|
| | | Help the unit work? | Hinder the unit work? | |
| Summarizing | Reviewing the content of past discussion. | | | |
| Blocking | Interfering with the progress of the group by going off on a tangent, citing personal experiences unrelated to the group's problem, arguing too much on a point the rest of the group has resolved, rejecting ideas without consideration, preventing a vote. | | | |
| Aggression | Criticizing or blaming others, showing hostility toward the group or some individual without relation to what has happened in the group, attacking the motives of others, deflating the ego or status of others. | | | |

**Activity 3:8** continued

| | ROLE | DEFINITION | How does the person in this role | | How can you bring out the positive aspects of this role? |
|---|---|---|---|---|---|
| | | | Help the unit work? | Hinder the unit work? | |
| GROUP NONFUNCTIONAL ROLES | Seeking Recognition | Attempting to call attention to oneself by excessive talking, extreme ideas, boasting, boisterousness. | | | |
| | Special Pleading | Introducing or supporting ideas related to one's own pet concerns or philosophies beyond reason, attempting to speak for "the grass roots," "the housewife," "the common man," and so on. | | | |
| | Withdrawing | Acting indifferent or passive, resorting to excessive formality, doodling, whispering to others. | | | |
| | Dominating | Trying to assert authority in manipulating the group or certain members of it by "pulling rank," giving directions authoritatively, interrupting contributions of others. | | | |

**Activity 3:8** continued

**Part II.** Individuals within the Group

Using a sociogram, analyze your group's interactions.*

*EXAMPLES*

*YOUR SOCIOGRAM*

**Step One**

Draw table and participants; initial participants.

**Step Two**

Draw arrows for a few minutes show-ing who spoke to whom. Speaking to the group is repre-sented by arrow to center of table.

**Step Three**

Repeat twice during meeting on new table.

**Activity 3:8** continued

**Step Four**

Analyze the
sociograms.
Is there two-way communication? _____
Does everyone participate? _____
Who dominates (or leads)? _____
Are there subgroups? _____
Who supports whom? _____
Are some people "at odds" with others? _____
What issues pick up group interest? _____
_____
_____

# Activity 3:9

# Assessing and Improving the Functioning Level of Your Group

**Part I.** Analyzing the Level of Your Group's Functioning

Using the Cog's Ladder (Pfeiffer & Jones, 1974) observe several group sessions. (You cannot do this if you are leading a group.) Jot down actions and phrases at each stage of the ladder. Watch for task definers, risk takers, and active listeners who move your group forward.

Does your group usually reach the constructive stage?   ☐ Yes   ☐ No

If not, where do you usually get stuck?   Stage _____

*Cog's Ladder*

| Polite Stage | Get acquainted; share values; stay simple; avoid controversy. _____ _____ |
| Why We're Here | Define objectives and goals of group; define task; redefine. _____ _____ |
| Bid for Power | Attempt to influence one another's opinions, ideas, values; compete for recognition, attention, influence. _____ _____ |
| Constructive Stage | Begin active listening; accept other's value systems; in this "team action stage," members are more open-minded. _____ _____ |
| Esprit Stage | Feel unity and high spririts; have mutual acceptance, high cohesiveness, good will, and camaraderie. _____ _____ |

**Activity 3:9** continued

**Part II.**    Improving the Level of Your Group's Functioning, Stage 2 to
Stage 3

Brainstorming is a creative process used to generate a large quantity of unevaluated ideas. This technique can help a group move from Stage 2, where the task is defined, to Stage 3. In this latter stage, the group generates alternatives to deal with the task at hand. The move from Stage 2 to Stage 3 requires risk. Brainstorming minimizes that risk and also increases the quantity of ideas generated.

The rules of brainstorming are:

1. Go for quantity not quality
2. Any ideas are welcome and no criticism of ideas is allowed
3. Build on each other's ideas

- Using the technique and rules of brainstorming, generate a list of cost containment measures for your unit. (Remember—nothing is too absurd for brainstorming and no criticisms are allowed.)
  Write the ideas on a flip chart or blackboard as they are called out by your staff.

**Part III.**    Improving the Level of Your Group's Functioning, Stage 3 to
Stage 4

Active listening (discussed in Chapter 2) can help move your group from Stage 3, "The Bid for Power," to Stage 4, "The Constructive Stage." The Modified Delphi Technique (Kolb, Rubin, & McIntyre, 1971) is useful in bridging the gap between the generation of ideas in Stage 3 to active listening. Originally a forecasting and planning tool, The Delphi Technique is a means of reaching group consensus when putting a list of items into priority order or for any task that requires the group to come to a mutually agreeable rank ordering. The steps are:

1. Number the items to be ranked.
2. Construct a matrix with names plotted against items.

|        | Joan | Mary | John | Jane | Mean | Range |
|--------|------|------|------|------|------|-------|
| Item 1 |      |      |      |      |      |       |
| Item 2 |      |      |      |      |      |       |
| Item 3 |      |      |      |      |      |       |

**Activity 3:9** continued

3. Ask participants to rank order the items, #1 is "most desired," and enter ranks onto matrix.
4. Figure the mean (average) score for each item and the range (high and low scores). Fill these into the chart.

Now the data are available to assist active listening. Discuss reasons for:

- extremes in the range
- first choices
- last choices
- criteria for ranking items
- other thoughts and rationales

The Delphi Technique can be repeated after the discussion to clarify and update group participants' new rankings. More discussion may be necessary prior to a final decision.

- Using the cost containment ideas generated in the Brainstorming Exercise above, move the group through the Delphi Technique to a point of active listening.

# Activity 3:10

# Team Building

Doing a team building is best approached indirectly by having a retreat or workshop or long meeting to deal with the "right" topic. Bell and Rosenzweig (1978) give eight prerequisites to a successful team-building workshop. Their criteria can be used as a checklist for planning your team-building workshop.

☐ Get the right people together; include key people in the group.

☐ Set aside a large block of uninterrupted time on an agreeable date.

☐ Work on high-priority problems or opportunities. See Exhibit 3–3 for ideas and address problems identified by the group.

☐ Seek input in workshop design.

☐ Structure the time in ways that are likely to enhance positive team building and problem solving.

☐ Work toward realistic solutions and action plans.

☐ Facilitate implementation, and seek help from colleagues, boss, or consultant if needed.

☐ Follow up to assess actual versus expected results.

A simple team-building workshop can be planned by using the skeleton agenda below. First, ask at a staff meeting or through a simple survey what issue(s) people would like to address.

### SKELETON AGENDA

- Coffee
- Warm-up: People introduce themselves and answer one question related to the topic of the workshop.
- Why are we here? Brief overview by facilitators or head nurse.

**Activity 3:10** continued

- Define problem or issue to be addressed.
- Brainstorm related solutions or ideas (see Activity 3:9, Part II).
- Put priorities on solutions or ideas, and refine them into goals (see Delphi Technique, Activity 3:9, Part III).
- Break into small groups to reduce goals to action plans with time frames.
- Have one member from each small group report back to large group.
- Seek feedback from the group on what was good about the day and what could be improved.
- Take work back to staff meeting and follow up.

Now plan a retreat for your staff.

_____

_____

_____

_____

_____

_____

_____

_____

_____

_____

_____

_____

## CASE STUDY

Your boss has developed a minisurvey to see if you are prepared for the upcoming JCAH accreditation. She tells you to treat it like a real survey. You know this will mean extra time and energy for everyone because the unit clerks don't always do temperature logs on the refrigerator and the nurses leave the IV poles in the hall because storage is so far away. The blanket warmer gauge also needs checking. It will take a lot of time and effort to "sell" this mock survey to your staff, and you would like to save that energy and effort for the real accreditation.

- Identify the forces impinging on the manager.
- What do you decide to do?
- Select an appropriate leadership style.

## SOLUTION TO CASE STUDY

**Forces**

The force in the manager (you) is: You don't want to do it now or next week either. You wish your unit was "up to par" without much needed work.

The force in the situation is: Your boss developed and is pushing the survey.

YOU

The forces in your subordinates are: They will resist extra work and do not see the need for many of the requirements.

The forces in the environment are: JCAH accreditation is required for receiving federal money; regulations are for the safety of patients.

**Decision**

You decide to get behind the survey wholeheartedly because of the pressures from above and also because a part of you "knows" your unit "should" be up to par anyway.

**Style**

You decide to use a "selling" approach because your staff is not going to decide to do it on their own. You prefer trying to convince them of the need rather than taking the more authoritarian approach of "telling" them to do it.

## REFERENCES

Argyris, C. Some causes of organizational ineffectiveness within the Department of State *(Occasional Papers*, No. 2). Washington D.C.: U.S. Department of State, Center for International Systems Research, 1967.

Bell, C., & Rosenzweig. Highlights of an organizational improvement program in a city government. In W.L. French, C.H. Bell, & R.A. Zawachi (Eds.), *Organizational development: Theory, practice and research*. Dallas: Business Publications, 1978.

Benge, E.J. *Elements of modern management*. New York: American Management Association, 1976.

Benne, K.D., & Sheats, P. Functional roles of group members. *Journal of Social Issues*, 1948, *4*(2), p. 41.

Blake, R.R., & Mouton, J.S. *The managerial grid*. Houston: Gulf Publishing, 1964.

French, W.L., & Bell, C.H. *Organizational development* (2nd ed.). Englewood Cliffs, N.J.: Prentice-Hall, 1978.

Hersey, P., & Blanchard, K.H. *Management of organizational behavior: Utilizing human resources* (3rd ed.). Englewood Cliffs, N.J.: Prentice-Hall, 1977.

Janis, I.L. Groupthink. *Psychology Today*, November 1971

Katz, D., & Kahn, R.L. *The social psychology of organizations*. New York: Wiley & Sons, 1966.

Knowles, M., & Knowles, H. *Introduction to group dynamics*. New York: Association Press, 1959.

Kolb, D., Rubin, I., & McIntyre, J. *Organizational psychology: An experiential approach* (3rd ed.). Englewood Cliffs: Prentice-Hall, 1971.

Maslow, A.H. *Motivation and personality*. New York: Harper & Row, 1959.

McGregor, D.M. The human side of enterprise. In *Adventures in thought and action*, Proceedings of the 5th Anniversary Convocation of the School of Industrial Management. MIT, 1957, pp. 23–30.

Ouchi, W. *Theory Z*. Menlo Park, Calif.: Addison-Wesley, 1981.

Pfeffer, J.W. & Jones, J.E. (Eds.). *The 1974 annual handbook for group facilitators*. La Jolla, Calif.: University Associates Publishers, 1974.

Phelps, S., & Austin, N. *The assertive woman*. U.S.A.: Impact, 1975.

Tannenbaum, R., & Schmidt, W.H. How to choose a leadership pattern. *Harvard Business Review*, March-April 1958, p. 96.

# Chapter 4

# Planning

**OBJECTIVES**

Upon completion of this chapter, including the activities, the new nurse manager will be able to:

- state a variety of reasons why planning is essential and list six steps of planning
- explain why goals are best originated at the top of the organization
- develop a cascading goal plan for goals originated at a higher organizational level
- explain the three sources of goals and the expected outcomes based on the relationships of the goals to one another
- define management by objectives (MBO) and the linking role it plays in an organization
- recognize threats to your own success and happiness as a manager that planning can help you avoid
- analyze the pros and cons of an open-door policy and develop a related policy that works well for you
- describe some major health care trends and project a few plans that will subsequently be needed in your unit

# DEVELOPMENT OF THE NEW NURSE MANAGER™
© 1981

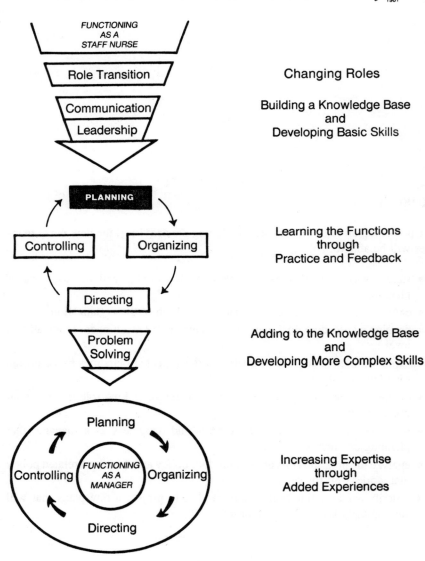

¶ Where do you start? As a new nurse manager, you will need a plan not only to know where to start but also to determine where you are going.

## WHY PLAN?

In Lewis Carroll's *Alice's Adventures in Wonderland*, Alice asked the Cheshire Cat, "Would you tell me please which way I ought to go from here?"

The cat answered, "That depends a good deal on where you want to get to."

"I don't much care where," said Alice.

To which the cat retorted, "Then it doesn't matter which way you go."

If you don't care what your unit, your staff, or your job will be like tomorrow, next month, or next year, as the cat said, it does not much matter which way you go or what you do.

However, "management has no choice but to anticipate the future and to attempt to mold it," says Drucker, a management authority (1973, p. 121).

Planning is beneficial because it provides direction, reduces overlapping and wasteful activities, improves continuity of action, and focuses attention on objectives. It provides clarification because many assumptions may be discussed and questioned during planning. Through planning, change can be anticipated and managed, and both evaluation and control are facilitated.

Several studies have found that organizations that planned significantly outperformed organizations that did not (Ansoff, 1970; Malik & Karger, 1975). Planning also saves time. Greenewalt (1970), former president of du Pont, claims "every moment spent planning saves three or four in execution."

"As work expands and grows more complex, planning becomes imperative to visualize not only what we want to happen but also the various alternatives for accomplishing it " (Mackenzie, 1972, p. 40.)

Mackenzie, another well-known management consultant, says: "In a very real sense, planning is where it all begins in management. It is the rational predetermination of where you want to go and how you intend to get there. Until this has been done, there can be no assurance that effort expended will be in the right direction" (1972, p. 39).

A plan helps you to organize the work to be done. First assess where you are (the current reality or status quo); then decide where you want to go or what you want to happen (a goal). The plan consists of whatever methodology you choose to move toward your goal and the goal itself. In other words, a plan is both a goal and a method to reach that goal.

For example, you realize that a problem with making patient care assignments exists on your unit. You assess the current situation by observing assignment making. You also ask your nurses if they like the system and if it works well for them. You find out the staff is using a modified type of primary care that they call group care—a nurse is responsible for a primary group of patients. Most of your nurses believe the system is not working well for a variety of reasons. Your goal is to implement a system of patient care that meets both patient and staff needs. You bring your staff nurses together to plan a system that will achieve quality patient care and that will also work for them.

The higher you move in an organization, the more time you need to spend planning (Robbins, 1980). As you move from your role of staff nurse to head nurse, your planning time increases substantially. As a staff nurse, you planned care for your patients for a given shift. If you worked as a team leader or in a charge position, you still planned for your patients but also planned who else on the team would care for other patients, and for the staff lunch, relief, patient admissions, and so forth. You did this for the shift in which you assumed the leadership role.

Now, as you move into a head nurse role, you will change from planning for one shift to planning for both patient and staff needs for longer periods of time. You need to plan for ongoing and future staff and unit needs—for such things as more linen for patients or new educational materials for staff. In addition, you have more input into departmental and organizational plans. For example, you become more concerned about the costs of supplies, benefits for staff, and hospital goals.

## WHO SHOULD PLAN?

Who makes the plans? Who sets the goals? Do you? Does your staff? Does your boss? Because the answer is yes to each of these questions, some plans will be in conflict. Your plans may differ from those of the head nurse on pediatrics. In turn, his or her plans may conflict with those of the director of finance, and so on. This is a predictable problem if no organized planning process exists in the organization and plans continuously spring up from a variety of sources.

For example, what if the clinical laboratory decided to run the machine that does a general panel of tests only between the hours of 10 A.M. and 10 P.M. to save manpower costs of running it twenty-four hours? They made this decision in an effort to contain costs in their department. The finance department is happy with this goal, which is in line with their high-priority efforts toward cost containment. However, most head nurses are upset with the limited testing because the doctors have just begun to comply with their requests to order an entire panel on patients who require two or more tests since this is more economical for the patient. With the clinical laboratory's limited hours, doctors cannot order the panel and receive a needed *stat* result, such as a potassium level, during the night hours. Thus, they often order a *stat* potassium in addition to a 10 A.M. general panel. The resulting test duplication costs to patients may outweigh the manpower costs to run the machine twenty-four hours a day. This plan benefited the clinical laboratory but was costly to the overall organization.

Planning must come from the top downward in order to provide a general direction for the organization. Until recently, directional guidelines came down from the top, but usually in the form of a dictate. These one-way communications were packaged in a variety of forms: goals, mission statements, policies, one-way memos, procedures, or laws.

Although this process provides some common direction, it does not meet today's need for multilevel input. The complex planning of patient care requires input from all levels of the organization. Planning requires a participatory approach that must allow "the people being planned" to put their ideas into the body of planning to generate realistic, workable plans and to be committed to them.

## HOW TO PLAN

Planning involves the following six steps:

1. Analyzing the present situation
2. Forecasting the future situation
3. Looking for opportunities
4. Establishing broad goals based on these opportunities
5. Reducing the broad goals to specific, time-bound tasks
6. Evaluating and revising plans

For example, in overall hospital planning, the following may be involved: (1) the chief executive officer (CEO) and hospital administrators gather information from within the organization, such as census levels, levels of disease severity, rising costs, and needs, to analyze the present situation. (2) They also gather information from beyond the organization, including economic forecasts, competition and markets, anticipated community needs, technological trends, and consumer demands. (3) In light of this information, they brainstorm possible directions and look for new opportunities. You may be asked for input by a survey or a meeting or, indirectly, through your capital budget requests, variance reports, or acuteness and staffing reports. (4) The top administrative group then sets priorities on opportunities and establishes broad goals. (5) At this point, all management becomes involved in reducing the broad goals to time-bound tasks specific to departments, units, and individuals. (6) Providing continuous input into the evaluation and revision of plans is an ongoing process throughout the year, based on time frames established in Step 5.

## INVOLVEMENT OF ALL LEVELS IN GOAL SETTING

The broad goals defined by top management offer a general direction for the entire organization. Middle management—you and other nurse managers—need to formulate more specific goals within your units and specialty services. This involves getting staff input because staff members actually accomplish many of the goals.

For example, a hospital goal might be to increase cost containment. If you are the head nurse of the emergency department, you may know that supplies "disappear" frequently. You gather your staff and plan how to maintain the necessary inventory of supplies in a cost-effective manner; together you formulate a plan.

Three levels have participated in formulating this goal. Many other sources of goals and plans, however, are evidenced throughout a hospital. Departments make plans; units make plans; various shifts make plans; individuals make plans.

Hersey and Blanchard (1977) divide the sources of all goals into three general categories: the organization, the boss, and the individual. Whether the goals originate from the top down or not, Hersey and Blanchard propose that the closer these three factors are to each other, the greater the potential for accomplishing the goals of all three (see Figure 4-1). If the goals are further apart, more energy will be required to obtain lesser results.

For example, quality patient care is a goal shared by all levels of an organization. The administrators, the head nurses, the staff—everyone agrees with and supports this goal. Yet in some hospitals quality patient care is not the primary goal. Research or teaching may be a higher concern in a university hospital. Profit may be a higher concern in a corporation hospital. This is not to say that the latter two settings do not support quality patient care, but it does imply a potential source of goal conflict that can be felt throughout the organization. Consider how medical students or interns might want to do histories and physicals on patients late at night to suit their own busy learning schedules. This practice is likely to be debated by nurses as not being in the patients' best interests. Here educational and quality care goals conflict.

---

**Figure 4-1**  An Effective Integration of the Goals of Management, Subordinates, and the Organization Showing Closely Related Goals and a High Degree of Attainment

Source: Paul Hersey, Kenneth H. Blanchard, *Management of Organizational Behavior: Utilizing Human Resources,* 3rd Ed., © 1977, p. 126. Reprinted by permission of Prentice-Hall, Inc., Englewood Cliffs, N.J.

One method of developing interrelated, thus less conflicting, goals is *management by objectives*. Management by objectives (MBO) "operationalizes the planning function through cascading objectives" (Robbins, 1980, p. 171). The organization establishes goals and pushes the goal-setting activity down through all levels of the organization, thus gathering understanding, acceptance, input, and commitment from all levels (see Figure 4–2).

Management by objectives is a management system in which goals are clearly defined and stated in measurable terms with time frames. When this system is used in a hospital, it is usually done within the context of a participatory management system, although it starts from the top, similarly to the planning previously described.

Goals flow downward through the organization. The participation begins when each general goal of the hospital as stated by the administration is reduced to several objectives by each department. These objectives are then further reduced to measurable, time-bound tasks at the unit level. At the unit level, the head nurse and staff make the goals more specific by adding names of persons responsible and time allotments for each task.

What follows is an example of a goal that cascaded down through an organization, gaining detail and commitment as it reached the unit level. The hospital administrators set the goal of improving quality care for patients. One of the nursing department's goals was the establishment of a quality assurance (QA) committee with a representative from each unit to investigate how to improve the quality of patient care administered by the nursing department. Representatives

**Figure 4–2** Cascading of Organizational Plans

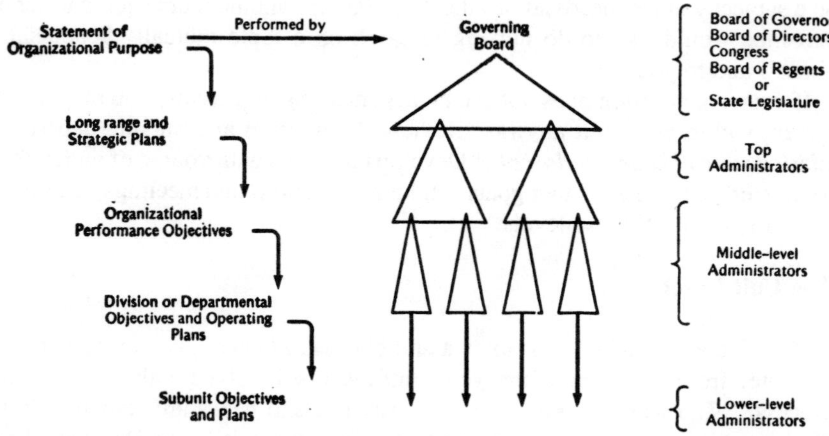

*Source:* From *Managing by Objectives* by Anthony P. Raia. Copyright © 1974 by Scott, Foresman and Co. Reprinted by permission.

shared information with other units. One particular unit, the intensive care unit (ICU), heard about unit-based QA committees from its representative. The ICU then decided to set up a unit QA committee whose first purpose was to audit compliance with medication orders, a suspected problem on the unit. The committee established an action plan and target dates. The plan included a nurse-to-nurse shift report, not about what was ordered, as was previously done, but about what the nurses actually did during that shift. Because the plan came from the nursing staff, it was seen as a professional problem-solving approach to improving quality, not as an imposed monitoring system. The results of the audit were fed back to the unit committee for relevant new goal setting and action plan development. The results were then shared by the unit QA representative up the line, through the departmental QA committee. Subsequently, similar methods were tried by other units.

Management by objectives clearly reinforces the Hersey-Blanchard notion by offering a system in which goals are clearly defined on all three levels (the organization, the boss, and the individual) in a manner that facilitates integration of the entire organization's goals. Management by objectives, used in this manner, also allows the participatory element that is essential to encouraging staff to "buy in" to the goals. This is accomplished by allowing, even encouraging, individual staff members to participate in achieving objectives that are in line with their own personal goals. As a manager, you need to facilitate this process.

In the previous example, nurses who were interested in medication compliance or in quality assurance volunteered to be on the committee. The regional representative had the additional interest of being on a department-wide committee to meet one of her level four staff nurse criteria. A nurse interested in increasing her teaching or speaking skills may help to prepare and give an in-service for the staff on a subject you feel needs some attention. Perhaps another nurse going to school part-time would like to do nursing research on a topic mutually beneficial to himself and to your unit.

If your organization does not use management by objectives, you may use the system within your unit anyway. Review the hospital and nursing department *mission statement and philosophy*. Develop unit goals with your staff within these parameters, adding any other goals you know about through meetings, memos, or key individuals on those levels.

## The Unit Level

Your job as a head nurse is to be a unit planner. Planners, however, cannot be separated from doers; therefore, your staff must be involved in the unit planning process. "The worker's knowledge, experience and needs are resources to the planning process. The worker needs to be a partner in it" says Drucker. If you divorce the planner from the doer, "the planning will cease to be effective and will indeed become a threat to performance . . . the planner needs the doer as a resource and feedback control'' (Drucker, 1973, p. 270).

A plan is essential to getting your job done. Management by objectives addresses many parts of the job you are doing as a head nurse and links the organizational goals with your unit goals. Then it allows you to add your staff's individual goals with time lines.

In this general organizational planning, all levels participate. In addition to this system, you may need to address day-to-day planning needs. This is called operational or tactical planning so that your unit functions smoothly on a day-to-day basis. Existing routines should address this planning need. These routines may be written or unwritten, formal or informal.

An example is your shift report. Perhaps you do something during the shift that you have "always done" and "everyone knows." This is an example of an unwritten but formal system. Another unit might have reviewed and evaluated its shift report process, subsequently writing and implementing a written formal procedure. Both of these are plans. However, the latter may be more efficient and effective if it is consciously chosen, well evaluated, accordingly revised, effectively implemented, and written down for new staff to learn.

Reviewing your routines and systems is necessary to managing a smoothly running unit. Policies and procedures are also plans that guide routines and help the unit to run smoothly. All these plans need to be reviewed periodically to be sure they represent clear, up-to-date, efficient methods for achieving your unit's goals.

Some unit goals are carried out through short-range planning. An example of a short-range plan is staff assignments. This plan states who will be responsible for which patients for a given period of time. Although done routinely, this plan is complex because of the variety of forces impinging on its implementation. The plan cannot be made in a vacuum. When planning staff assignments for patient care, you must consider many factors, including the number of patients, the number of staff, how sick the patients are, and the experience and capabilities of staff. You also need to consider requirements for safe care within legal constraints, physical realities, labor contracts, organizational and unit norms, and numerous other factors. Thus, your assignment plan for a shift reflects much consideration of the constraints of reality in planning to reach your goal. Because of previous experiences, you may already be good at making assignments. How you do it seems to be on a "gut" level. Actually you are considering the many variables already listed, along with organizational norms, various personalities and preferences, and a wide range of skill levels. The many facets of this complex planning task are difficult to define and to teach, but they are essential planning skills for you to teach your charge nurses if you want each shift to run smoothly. The goal of making patient care assignments may not be consciously reviewed each time it is done, but certainly "what you want to happen" is safe patient care with a given amount of staff. This is your minimal expectation and primary goal.

If you examine the preceding goal more closely, perhaps you will be able to identify several subgoals: one is job satisfaction for your staff; another is efficient use of staff; another is quality patient care. These primary and secondary goals may or may not be met. You may not even know whether the goals are met if they are not clearly defined, but you will know if something is wrong. If the goals were met, were they met in a timely fashion? You may not know the answer unless you provided for a projected time line in your plan. But, again, you may know "something" is wrong.

Is your staff working toward the same goals you are? Maybe not, again because of poorly defined goals. The point is that operational goals need to be clearly defined, expressed in measurable terms, and set within time boundaries so that you know whether or not you achieved them. If you expect your staff to contribute to reaching your unit goals, they must clearly understand the goals and they must "buy in." *Buying in,* a term borrowed from the stock market floor, means that the goal falls within an area of acceptability to your staff and that they will own the goal as if it were their own. After "buying in," the staff will put energy into achieving those goals.

## CARRYING OUT PLANS

"Plans must be implemented to be meaningful" (Kelly, 1980, p. 571). It is not sufficient to put goals on paper and then go on doing what you have always done. This can be a pitfall with overdone MBO. Integrate your goals into your unit through staff commitment to individual goals. "A plan agreed to means commitment on the part of those agreeing. Managers involved in the planning process recognize that the ultimate choice of a course of action involves commitment to the achievement of stated objectives" (Mackenzie, 1972, p. 41). Here the term *signing up* represents a stronger commitment than *buying in. Signing up* is borrowed from the military, where once you decide to do something, you "sign up." This shows real commitment because in the military setting, there is no easy out after you sign. The high tech industry has repopularized the term (Kidder, 1981) to mean making a choice to work on something, followed by a serious commitment to see it through to the end. "Signing up" is essential if plans are to become a reality. Your job as a manager is to monitor, evaluate, and revise the plans with your staff's input.

### Planning Your Own Work

Most managers are overworked and underorganized. They suffer from a variety of what Rowan (1978) calls organizing ills. A lack of planning can let organizing ills fester, raising your stress level and decreasing your job satisfaction. These threats to your success and happiness as a manager include:

- high Procrastination Quotients—putting off big projects and major decisions
- Stacked Desk Syndrome—shows how "busy" you are but leaves nowhere to work
- Open-Door Excuse—invites interruptions
- Fat Paper Philosophy—spread by memoitis and copy machines
- Analysis Paralysis—substituting study for courage

Worse than any of the preceding is Planning Paradox—failure to plan because it takes time. In his classic article "The Manager's Job," Mintzberg (1975) refutes the folklore that the manager is a reflective, systematic planner. How much time did you spend planning last week?

Managers not only need to be good planners, but also need to begin by planning well for themselves. "If your aim is management, it must be self-management first. Besides the task of acquiring the ability to organize a day's work, all else you will ever learn about management is but child's play" (Osborn, 1959, p. 26). Too often, says Hummel (1967), we are "slaves to the tyranny of the urgent" (p. 11). In "The Case of the Fragmented Manager," Berkwitt (1969) claims it is the interruptions that gives the manager's job a nightmarish quality. Baruch (1967) attributes all his failures and errors to action without thought.

Clinical nursing is an action-oriented job. As you become a manager, you need consciously to balance action with time to think and plan. If you were very good at organizing patient care and planning your day before you became a manager, those skills are transferable. If you have always had problems with planning a patient care day, the added scope of planning in your new job could be a constant threat to success. Take a time management course. Set aside several days to implement what you learn, and stick with those systems. Many books and workshops offer gimmicks for planning time. If these work for you, use them.

The following planning tools are essential for managers:

- *Know Your Priorities.* Always do your first priority (or some part of it) first. Decide what to do in what order and, most important, what *not* to do. Recognize that you will probably not get everything done, so set priorities continually.
- *Control Your Own Time.* Go through your in-basket, and dispose of items quickly—they are others' priorities. Say no if some task falls outside your priorities and your time available to do it well, or negotiate to do some part of it by a date reasonable for you.
- *Always Carry a Calendar.* Write down every appointment, meeting, and block of time needed for assigned work. Allow time on your calendar for routine but essential tasks and for something that "recharges" you like a half-

hour walk or lunch with a friend and colleague. Add a daily "To Do Today" card to your calendar each morning or the night before for the following day.

- *Be Careful of Reverse Delegation.* When a staff member sees you in the hall and dumps a problem on you, that is reverse delegation. Ask that person to gather data or suggest alternatives for follow-up.
- *Complete Tasks.* Get things done and "out the door." "Compulsion to closure" (Mee, 1969) is a positive motivating force in managers because achieving an objective yields a sense of accomplishment.
- *Delegate. Delegate. Delegate.* Teach your staff, and let them do parts of unit and staff management. One of your primary goals is staff development. Find out who wants to learn what. Teach them. Although it is faster to do it yourself at first, both you and your staff member will benefit from delegation in the long run.

As a head nurse, your priorities include staff development and quality care on your unit. Many of the tasks within these two responsibilities can be delegated. Be sure that whatever responsibilities you take on outside your unit, such as committee work, are in line with your own growth goals or unit needs.

Your boss's priorities must become your priorities. Most bosses are open to negotiation, however, about timing and amounts. Instead of saying no, explain your perspective and offer suggestions. For example, your boss may want you to revise the blood transfusion policy by next week. You look at your calendar and see that it is full. Find out whether a two-week wait is acceptable or if another project, already assigned, could be delayed to allow time for this one. Also, consider taking the project on if you can delegate it to one of your staff nurses.

Always keep in mind your overall organizational goals, unit goals, and personal goals and how they interrelate. Plan your overall and daily priorities in accord with these goals. "Good results without good planning come from good luck, not good management" (Jaquith, 1972, p. 39).

With planning, you will know where you are going, and you will have plans for how to get there. In the next chapter we look at whether you are properly organized to achieve your goals.

## Activity 4:1

# Unit Plans

☐ Find the set of plans (goals) for your unit, if they exist.

☐ Update the plans by adding your own plans (goals) for your unit and deleting those that are inappropriate; get staff input. If no unit plans exist, begin to develop some with staff input.

☐ Share the newly developed or revised plans with your staff at a staff meeting. Plan implementation and follow-up evaluation.

# Activity 4:2

# Integrating Unit Plans

- How do your unit plans relate to your organizational plans? Rate each unit goal developed in Activity 4:1 on whether or not it aligns with your organizational goals.
- Discuss any unit plans not in conflict with organizational plans with your boss to ascertain the appropriateness of the unit plan.

_____

_____

_____

_____

_____

# Activity 4:3

# Organize Your Time

1. Buy a calendar, and carry it with you (write in pencil).

   - Inside back cover, write regularly scheduled meetings. Transfer this information to calendar regularly.
   - Tape a small note pad in back of calendar; use for:
     —Anecdotes about employees. Write them on the spot with date and time; then drop these notes into their files back in your office—useful for performance evaluations. For example: A peer passes you in the hall and mentions Mary Brown, your R.N., did a great job when floated to her unit. Jot it down. Drop it in Mary Brown's file back in your office.
     —Messages to forward or information to drop in a file back in your office. For example: Someone mentions at lunch the need for an in-service on Total Parenteral Nutrition (T.P.N.). Jot this down and file under staff nurse meeting (to recruit a volunteer for the presentation) or in the file labeled with your unit's in-service educator's name for discussion during your next meeting with her. Keep a file for all persons you meet with regularly, and take the file out before meeting with them to review.
   - Write in frequently used phone numbers.
   - Put rubber band around front to today's page. Slide a list of priorities written on an index card onto the front of the book (see below).

2. Write a list each day of what you must and should do; set priorities. Carry it on the front of your calendar. Cross off each completed task. Write a new list each morning, referring to leftover items.
3. When you schedule meetings, allow time to get from one meeting to another; plan for meetings.
4. Cross off time on your calendar for your office work (in-basket, writing performance evaluations, etc.). Treat it as scheduled time, and hold telephone calls during that period.
5. Keep a running list of questions to ask your boss to review at your regularly scheduled meeting.

# Open-Door Policy

Open-door policy is disputed by the time management authorities, who claim it is inefficient, and the behaviorists, who say you should be available to your staff. *Open-door policy* can mean literally that your door is always open—anyone can stop in anytime.

- State the pros and cons of open-door policy.

| Pros | Cons |
|------|------|
| _____ | _____ |
| _____ | _____ |
| _____ | _____ |
| _____ | _____ |
| _____ | _____ |

- Describe a modified open-door policy that would work for you. *(Example: Anytime between 8 A.M. and 10 A.M. or 3 P.M. and 4 P.M. anyone may stop in for anything; or an appointment sign-up posted on your door; or stop in anytime for . . . (state limitations).*

_____

_____

_____

_____

☐ Plan to convey your open-door policy to your staff by putting it on the next staff meeting agenda.

# Activity 4:5

# Plan

List the multiple roles you play and the activities of each role.

Plan ways to integrate the many facets of your personal and professional roles. For example:

- early AM staff meetings as head nurse
- drive PM carpool that day as mother
- work on a disaster committee as head nurse
- write a paper on disaster nursing as master's student

| ROLE | ACTIVITIES | INTEGRATION IDEAS |
|------|-----------|-------------------|
|      |           |                   |
|      |           |                   |
|      |           |                   |
|      |           |                   |

# Clarifying Your Plans

"It seems intuitively right that specific plans would always be preferable to directional or loosely guided plans" (Robbins, 1980, p. 136).

Suppose that in your staff meeting someone says, "We really should write better patient care plans on our Cardex." Everyone agrees. The plan "to write better care plans" is too loosely defined. Use the format below to make this a more specific plan.

- State goal _____
  _____

- State plan _____
  _____

- Define steps (tasks) of plan with a time line (deadlines).

Step 1 _____     Due date _____

Step 2 _____     Due date _____

Step 3 _____     Due date _____

- Evaluation date _____
- Did you meet goal above? _____
  _____

# Activity 4:7

# Analyze One Goal through the Organization

Select one goal, long-range plan, or the mission statement of your hospital. Fill it in on chart below in the top triangle. Reduce it to two objectives: one by nursing and one by some other department, such as dietary. State two related objectives for the two units, and fill in the small triangles. Reduce these objectives to the unit tasks and state them under arrows at bottom. These unit tasks are related to your mission statement.

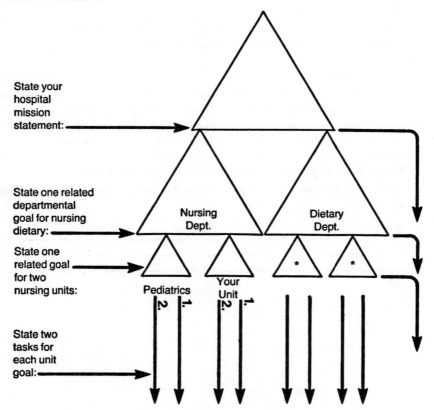

*Source:* Based on Anthony P. Raia, *Managing by Objectives* (Glenview, Ill.: Scott, Foresman, 1974), p. 30.

# Activity 4:8

# Teaching Planning

Select a staff nurse who needs help planning and organizing patient care. Using the format below, help the nurse to plan his or her patients' care for the shift.

- *Assess the status quo*

  _____
  _____
  _____

- *Set goals*

  _____
  _____
  _____

- *Make a plan*

  _____
  _____
  _____
  _____
  _____
  _____

- Set priorities as part of the plan (number the preceding items).
- *Have a coaching session with the nurse to discuss what worked and what did not.*

  Notes from coaching session: _____
  _____
  _____

# Activity 4:9

# "Megatrend" I.Q. Test

Naisbitt (1982) looked at trends and projects them into the future in his best-seller *Megatrends: Ten New Directions Transforming Our Lives*. The quiz below is based on "The New Health Care Paradigm" in Naisbitt's book.

Read each statement and circle T if you agree with the statement; F if you disagree.

1. During the 1970s interest in diet and nutrition soared.     T    F

2. The general public consider acupuncture, acupressure, vitamin therapy, charismatic faith healing, or preventive health care through diet and exercise as alternatives to annual physical exams, drugs, and surgery.     T    F

3. The next big trend in health care is likely to focus on the environmental influence on health.     T    F

4. Since 1960 there has been a 100 percent increase in regular exercises.     T    F

5. The $2.5 billion home health care business of 1981 is expected to reach $10 billion in sales by 1990.     T    F

6. Through the hospices movement many people are reasserting personal, nonmedical control over the beginning and end of life (birth and death care).     T    F

7. More than 500 U.S. companies have fitness programs managed by full-time directors.     T    F

8. In one state Blue Cross/Blue Shield approved insurance coverage for a holistic cancer treatment program aimed primarily at overcoming negative feelings.     T    F

9. There are currently more than 2,100 certified nurse-midwives in the United States, and about 200 graduate annually from accredited schools.     T    F

10. More than 500,000 self-help medical groups have been formed to support home self-care.     T    F

**Activity 4:9** continued

Answers:  1. T          6. T
          2. T          7. T
          3. T          8. T
          4. T          9. T
          5. T         10. T

*If you have:*

- 8 to 10 correct, excellent. You are very aware of health care trends.
- 6 to 7 correct, good. You are generally aware of health care trends.
- 1 to 5 correct, not very good. You need to look beyond your unit into what is happening in health care today. Try reading more health care journals and articles in publications that cover health care issues, such as *Business Week, Fortune,* or *Harvard Business Review.*

# Activity 4:10

# Projecting Trends

Drucker (1980) says unique unforeseen events cannot be "planned." However, you can prepare to take advantage of them by understanding trends in your business; learning your strengths; meeting your needs; and planning to try to optimize tomorrow the trends of today.

Define your unit's business.

_____

_____

What are your strengths?

_____

_____

Do your strengths and your business match? If not, are you in the wrong business?

_____

_____

What are the trends in patient care on your unit (e.g., shorter stays and need for greater patient education)?

_____

_____

If you project these trends ahead for three years, what plans do you need to make now to be ready?

_____

_____

## CASE STUDY

A major hospital goal related to facilities is to allocate funds for the new wing now under construction. Your unit will be moving to that wing in four years. Your unit is not currently in compliance with state requirements regarding the number of electrical outlets. The shortage is also a major inconvenience to your staff. How might you bring your unit goal and the hospital goal closer together?

## SOLUTION TO CASE STUDY

Often when hospitals are concentrating on building new facilities, the day-to-day operating condition of the current facility grossly deteriorates. This is compounded by increasing regulations for higher standards. In order to get some attention for this urgent operating need, you will need to plan a well-grounded petition to your boss. Find out about safety issues and code violations. Add related job satisfaction deterrents. Look for cost-effective alternative solutions, perhaps temporary ones that will be less in conflict with the facilities goal. With facts gathered and organized, make an appointment to discuss the problem with your boss. Be ready to gather more information if it is needed, but be careful not to let Analysis Paralysis deter you from moving forward.

## REFERENCES

Ansoff, H.I. Does planning pay? The effects of planning on success of acquisitions in American firms. *Long Range Planning*, December 1970, pp. 2–7.

Baruch, B. Quoted in Engstrom, T.W., & Mackenzie, R.A. *Managing Your Time*. Grand Rapids, Mich.: Zondervany, 1967.

Berkwitt, G.J. The case of the fragmented manager. *Dun's Review*, April 1969.

Carroll, L. *Alice's adventures in Wonderland*. Avon, Ct.: Heritage Press, 1941.

Drucker, P. *Management: Tasks, responsibilities, practices*. New York: Harper & Row, 1973.

Drucker, P.F. *Managing in turbulent times*. New York: Harper & Row, 1980.

Greenewalt, C. Quoted in Mackenzie, R.A. *Managing Time at the Top*. New York: The President's Association, 1970, p. 41.

Hersey, P., & Blanchard, K.H. *Management of organizational behavior: Utilizing human resources* (3rd ed.). Englewood Cliffs, N.J.: Prentice-Hall, 1977.

Hummel, C.E. *The tyranny of the urgent*. Chicago: Inter-Varsity, 1967.

Jaquith, D. Quoted in Mackenzie, R.A. *The Time Trap*. New York: McGraw-Hill, 1972, p. 39.

Kelly, J. *Organizational behavior: Its data, first principles and applications* (3rd ed.). Homewood, Ill.: Irwin, 1980.

Kidder, T. *The soul of a new machine*. Boston: Little, Brown, 1981.

Mackenzie, R.A. *The time trap*. New York: McGraw-Hill, 1972.

Malik, Z.A., & Karger, D.W. Does long-range planning improve company performance? *Management Review*, September 1975, pp. 27–31.

Mee, J. The zeigarmik effect. *Business Horizons*, June 1969, pp. 53–55.

Mintzberg, H. The manager's job: Folklore and fact. *Harvard Business Review*, July–August 1975, pp. 49–61.

Naisbitt, J. *Megatrends: Ten new directions transforming our lives*. New York: Warner, 1982.

Osborn, E.B. *Executive development manual*. New York: Economics Laboratory, September 1959.

Raia, A.P. *Managing by objectives*. Glenview, Ill.: Scott, Foresman, 1974.

Robbins, S.P. *The administrative process* (2nd ed.). Englewood Cliffs, N.J.: Prentice-Hall, 1980.

Rowan, R. Keeping the clock from running out. *Fortune*, November 6, 1978, pp. 76–83.

# Chapter 5

# Organizing

## OBJECTIVES

Upon completion of this chapter, including the activities, the new nurse manager will be able to:

- explain the organization of your hospital
- state the lines of responsibility from board of directors to head nurse
- identify types of input into your unit system and give examples of each
- analyze incongruencies on your unit between any two of the four transformation factors—task, individual, formal system, informal system
- describe and give an example of the link between outputs of one system and inputs of other systems
- explain a nine-step process for diagnosing and decreasing unit inefficiencies
- explain how your staff is organized to meet patient care needs, including your patient classification system (or alternative), staffing, and scheduling

# DEVELOPMENT OF THE NEW NURSE MANAGER™
© 1981

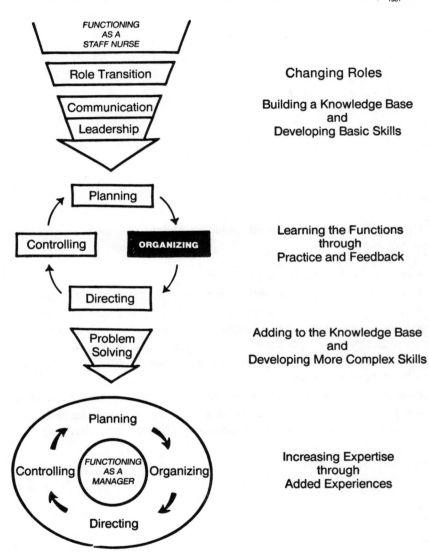

¶ If someone asked you what your job is as a manager, you might answer that you organize and process work efficiently. Drucker, a writer on twentieth-century management, says the manager's organizing function is to analyze activities, decisions, and relations. Based on these analyses, the manager must classify the work and divide it into manageable activities. These activities need to be subdivided further into manageable jobs and matched with competent staff who will perform those tasks (Drucker, 1974).

Because your job is to oversee all patient care on your unit and to provide that care through your staff, you are responsible for dividing up the tasks in a manageable way. This is division of labor on the unit level. To organize work, you may use one of the following nursing care styles: functional, team, or primary nursing. You must also have scheduling patterns providing for sufficient numbers of qualified staff to carry out the chosen nursing care system on a twenty-four-hour basis.

## THREE CATEGORIES OF WORK

Drucker (1974) divides work into three categories: top management work, innovative work, and operating work. In the last chapter, we emphasized the need for plans and discussed how management by objectives (MBO) addresses this need. MBO is a system to plan the process. You can use it for the first two work categories: top management work (setting organizational goals) and innovative work (participating in the goals of the unit and at individual levels).

Near the end of the last chapter, we addressed the less visionary, but essential, goals of performing everyday tasks. Let us consider this everyday work, what Drucker calls "operating work," the third of his three categories. Operating work includes routines and systems for getting daily work done. As a manager, you need to review everyday methods of providing patient care to assess whether or not the current way work is organized is the most efficient and effective method.

## FITTING TOGETHER TASK, PERSON, AND ORGANIZATION

"Structure and job design have to be task-focused, but assignments have to fit both the person and the needs of the situation" (Drucker, 1974, p. 524). The task must match the ability of the person performing the task. In a given situation the task cannot be separated from the person.

For example, a complex dressing change may require special skills that one of your new graduate nurses has not yet acquired. Therefore, this person and this task do not "fit." This would not be a good assignment. You could alter the situation slightly to improve the fit by assigning an experienced staff nurse to teach the new nurse how to do the dressing. This alteration provides a better fit.

Tasks must also be structured to meet the organization's needs. The persons performing the tasks must comply with established standards, policies, and task procedures. Although the staff may have and should have input into the standards and systems of task performance, the task definition precedes the direction of the staff. These definitions are the existing standards of care in an organization. Every health care organization has many established standards of care reflected in procedures at the task level. More general statements of these standards are called policies. A staff nurse must follow existing procedures to provide continuity and predictability for at least a safe level of care. Deviations from procedures need to be evaluated by more than one person. Policy and procedure updates should reflect changes in clinical practice. These changes are not made lightly. Policy and procedure changes come only after careful scrutiny by a variety of practitioners—usually a committee. For a given standard, such as the frequency of changing the urinary drainage system between catheter and bag, each nurse must follow the existing procedure. If newer research or current literature reflects a need for change, it is not the role of the individual nurse to implement this change clinically. The nurse should take the change suggestion with supporting data to be evaluated by the procedure review or quality assurance committee. If the change is made, it should become the organization's standard procedure. Otherwise, conflicting professional standards will diminish predictable levels of quality.

The unit's tasks should clearly reflect the specific purpose for which the organization exists. The next chapter, "Directing," discusses how the staff fits into this system. This is not to say that the task is more important than the person; both are essential. The organization's tasks delineate what skills and knowledge its people need. These tasks should be structured to provide systems fostering quality staff performance and contributions.

Because organizations are dynamic and changing entities, the systems need to be reviewed periodically and changed based on current patient needs, staff abilities, and economic, social, and environmental pressures. For example, perhaps you want the PM dietary trays delivered to your patients later, so the PM shift has more time to get organized, give medications, and check IVs before the food "gets in the way." You decide to hold the food on the heated carts. Evening shift nurses become better organized, and the medications on that shift are given closer to schedule. You also notice a decrease in the number of IV restarts needed because of their running dry. All these positive results came about in less than a week.

However, your desk is flooded with patient complaints about cold food, soggy vegetables, and late dinners. You also have received a telephone message from the dietary supervisor complaining that her staff is increasing overtime waiting for trays from your unit. You have solved a subsystem problem with a solution that affects other subsystems—dietary and patients.

Consider changes in light of "ripple effects" on other subsystems to prevent conflicts between parts of the system. What is the ripple effect? If you toss a pebble into a pond, a splash occurs where the pebble hits the water. However, a greater effect is also seen. Concentric circles ripple out beyond the point of the splash. Static in the water's surface reaches beyond your focal point. So it is with change. One directed change causes ripples altering the status quo beyond the target site. The bigger the change (or pebble), the bigger the ripples. Although it is usually not possible to make changes without affecting others, you can enhance your chances of creating positive effects on others or minimizing negative effects.

For example, if you are having problems with syringes, you take the problem to the Hospital Products Committee. If you do not have such a committee, you can pull together the equivalent by calling someone from the laboratory, someone from materials management (or purchasing), and perhaps other nurses who are having the same problem. Together you review the problem and generate alternative solutions. In this case you may review various companies' syringes. Together you make a decision about which syringe would best meet everyone's needs. This approach will probably produce a high-quality decision about a product everyone agrees to use. Moreover, the organization as a whole benefits from the cost break of the large purchase.

Not every change can be approached in this manner, but changes you make can be shared with those who will be affected. They can make suggestions on minimizing problems for themselves while they help you solve your problem. Before changing any existing system on your unit, first evaluate the task efficiency of current systems.

## Where To Start

You can use the Congruence Model for Diagnosing Organizational Behavior (Nadler & Tushman, 1979) to review your unit's organization of work activities (see Figure 5–1). The model is based on open system theory. Systems can be a way of thinking about the organization of a hospital or hospital unit. "Systems thinking means viewing the organization in terms of its larger environment and treating the organization both as a whole and as a set of intricately related parts" (Burach & Torda, 1979, p. 42).

Each system is actually a subsystem, or a part of a larger system. For example, consider your unit as a subsystem of the larger system, the hospital. Organizing work for efficiency involves facilitating a positive fit between various parts within your subsystem, the unit, and the fit of your subsystem into the larger system, the hospital. If the parts of the system "fit," the system runs smoothly; if conflicts exist between those parts, the system will function poorly.

**Figure 5–1** A Congruence Model for Diagnosing Organizational Behavior

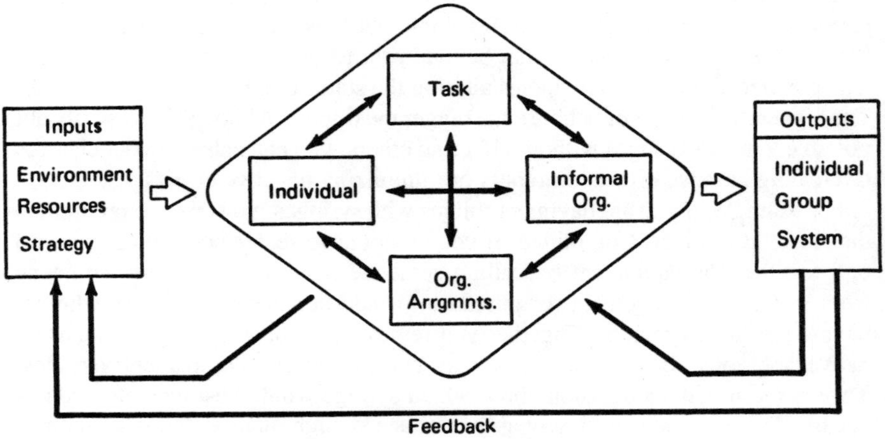

*Source:* Reprinted with permission of M.L. Tushman, "A Congruence Model for Diagnosing Organizational Behavior." In D.A. Kolb, I.M. Rubin, & J.M. McIntyre, *Organizational Psychology: A Book of Readings* (3rd Ed.). Englewood Cliffs, N.J.: Prentice-Hall, 1979.

## Overview of Systems

An open system has four basic components: input, throughout, output, and a feedback loop (see Figure 5–2).

The input, according to the Nadler–Tushman model, includes the environment, the resources, and the organizational strategies. *Environment* is a broad term used here to mean the "givens" in: your hospital, the economy, your unit, the nursing profession, the law, patient needs, and conditions in society as a whole. Resource inputs include both material resources, such as your unit's supplies and square footage, and human resources—your staff. Organizational strategy inputs include rules and norms in the formal and informal organization—for example, policies, procedures, tradition, and habits.

Although you need to be aware of these inputs, a manager actually needs to focus more on the second component, the throughput. Throughput, also called transformation processes, addresses what a manager does to organize work. During the throughput, there is interaction between four major components: task, organizational arrangement, informal organization, and individuals. We explore this component in the greatest depth because managers are intimately involved in this stage of the system.

**Figure 5–2** Model of an Open System

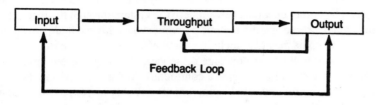

The output of your work includes the productivity, staff attitudes, and patient changes. This output can become part of new input through the feedback loop.

First we consider the four parts of a system individually. Then we relate the general model to your unit, a subsystem of your hospital. Using the Nadler–Tushman diagnostic model, we explore two perspectives of "fit." The first concerns your understanding of how the parts of your unit fit together so that you have a method to diagnose your unit efficiency. The second perspective concerns your understanding of how your unit fits with the rest of the organization so that you have some information to diagnose your unit's fit with the overall organization (the hospital) and other subsystems (various units and departments in the hospital).

After you understand what is working and what is not through this "fit" diagnosis, you can better organize unit activities for the benefit of patients, staff, and overall organizational efficiency.

Given the inputs, the manager organizes the throughputs to produce some outputs. To understand this better, consider economic changes that are input to your unit in the form of a mandate to decrease overtime. You still have the same tasks to do; the same staffing patterns still exist; you have the same staff members; yet you need to reorganize the throughput to produce the output of reduced overtime.

How you deal with this input of mandated overtime reduction and produce the output of actual overtime reduction requires energy and creativity. The "how" could be accomplished through your people, perhaps by changing a unit norm— pride in leaving on time, instead of pride in being the last to leave. Or the "how" could be accomplished through changing a task—begin having a walking report as opposed to a conference-type one to decrease report time. The "how" might combine task and people approaches by meeting with your staff and having them help you redefine a unit task to comply with the mandate. Whatever approach you decide to use, the decision of how to handle your unit's input to produce desired output is one of your greatest management challenges.

The output of a system affects individual behavior, group behavior, and the way a system functions in terms of goal achievement, resource utilization, and adaptation. In other words, various outputs are possible based on how the manager organizes and processes the input. Those outputs can then be measured against predetermined goals, such as the amount of overtime you reduced in the previous example. The output becomes new input to the system through the feedback loop. The reduced overtime and the method by which you achieved it are now input into the system. Outputs may also include greater efficiency or decreased job satisfaction. Again you will have to manage these variables in the throughput stage. As you can see, the model represents a continuous flow and a dynamic process.

Outputs of your unit system become inputs not only to your system but also to other systems. As an input, you receive a memo on Friday afternoon stating that the parking lot where your staff usually park is going to be resurfaced during the next week. You post the notice (your throughput) before you leave for the weekend. On Monday morning you have several overtime slips on your desk (output). The reason stated for each is essentially the same: "had to work overtime because the next shift reported for work late." After asking your staff several questions, you find out there was difficulty parking, so incoming nurses sat in the parking lot or drove around looking for a space for an average of 30 minutes. Consequently, they arrived late to hear the report, and their predecessors had to stay late. You now have the added input of overtime requests and the continued input of decreased parking. Your transformation process the first time (notifying your staff by posting the message) did not prevent the undesired and unanticipated output of overtime.

This time, you manage the throughput differently. You call security and explain the problem. The security department, which handles parking at the hospital, informs you that yours is the fourth call about this problem today, and they have arranged parking one-half block away, with a shuttle bus for PM and night shifts. Security also says that a memo is being sent out immediately, but you decide to inform your staff verbally first and then post the new memo. Security guards will also inform the next shift. Your output this time is decreased overtime related to this parking problem.

## YOUR UNIT SUBSYSTEM

Let us consider how each element of the model can help you to assess the efficiency of your unit's systems.

### Effect of Input on Your Unit

Your unit does not operate in a vacuum. Outside influences play a large role in your unit's activities. These outside influences are inputs to your unit. The three classes of input identified by Nadler & Tushman (1979) are: (1) the environment of the system, (2) the resources available to the system, and (3) the organizational strategies that are developed over time.

Let us consider each source of input and how that input affects your unit's systems. We will also consider how each of these influences might be changed to improve unit efficiency. Keep in mind that changing outside influences (input) may be difficult or even impossible. First try to change something in the throughput to achieve the desired outcome.

Begin by examining the environment of the system. What factors in the environment influence your unit? How do these outside environmental influences affect your unit's activities?

Recently, the Joint Commission for Accreditation of Hospitals (JCAH) imposed a standard requiring written patient care plans on all patients. JCAH accreditation is essential if your hospital wants to receive government funds. If you were head nurse when this change happened, you would be responsible for compliance on your unit. When the hospital is visited by JCAH, your unit may be checked to see whether care plans are present. Since noncompliance carries severe consequences, this environmental input obviously demands certain throughput on your part as a manager. You cannot decide that each patient on your unit should have a unique, creative care plan for each shift that would be planned on a blackboard in the patient's room and erased after each shift. A decision not to have care plans is equally unacceptable. You also do not have the choice of doing nothing about this so that some nurses write care plans and some do not. You must regard this input as a priority, requiring you to take some throughput action that produces the desired output—a care plan for every patient.

Policies and procedures are input to your unit, and your staff's compliance is the required output. Economic constraints are input challenging your creativity in the throughput stage. Other departments also have given your unit input that necessitates some action on your part.

For example, a memo from materials management or finance or hospital administration lists lost charges for the previous month and asks nurse managers to help decrease this revenue loss. You cannot ignore this input, because revenue generation is essential to the survival of health care institutions. Having seen many charge stickers in the utility room and occasionally in patient rooms, you realize your unit is an offender. This input demands action by you and your staff. (This particular problem is explored in Chapter 8, "Problem Solving.")

Your hospital may have planned some long-range strategies that will eventually come to your unit as input with great impact. Suppose you are head nurse of the emergency department and hear that your hospital is planning to open an outpatient surgery (OPS) unit. You currently do some outpatient surgery in your unit, so this planning deserves your attention now. Find out what impact this will have on your unit. Will you need less staff when the new OPS opens? What will happen to your staff? Can some transfer to the new department if they wish? How will this change affect your budget? Your staff's morale? Although you may not be able to change the plan and perhaps would not even want to, you need to be aware of the plan so that you can work out your throughput based on the expected input.

Have some of these inputs decreased the efficiency or quality of your unit's activities? What can you do to change these influences? Based on current literature, perhaps an existing procedure could be updated, and this change would increase quality and efficiency. For example, you may have read about a new method of dressing the IV insertion site that resulted in less skin abrasion. You or some member of your staff could propose a change in policy or a pilot study based on the data you have gathered.

Are there some inputs that decrease your staff's job satisfaction? How might you change that input? Outmoded, annoying dress codes, crowded cafeteria, or poor ventilation on your unit may be inputs worth trying to change.

## Transformation Processes

The need to change the input to your unit is based on a lack of "fit" between your unit and some other subsystems of the hospital or beyond. Sometimes a better fit can be achieved by changing the organization of various tasks within the unit. Using the throughput component of the model, the transformation processes, you (as a manager) have the ability to make many changes to improve the fit of activities within your unit and between your unit and other hospital subsystems. This is the area where most of your power lies to increase the efficiency of unit activities and to improve your functioning with the rest of the organization.

Let us explore each of the four transformation process components and how they interact. If an interaction works well with other components, you will have unit efficiency. If not, you may need to plan how to change that unit activity to achieve a better fit and increased efficiency.

The four components of the transformation process represent the four basic characteristics of behavioral systems. They are tasks, individuals, organizational arrangements, and informal organization. We review each component and give some unit examples. Then we look at several components and see how they fit together by looking at examples of fit or misfit between the components. Finally, we look at some alternatives that might increase your unit's efficiency by lessening the number of misfits or the severity of a misfit. These alternatives will not be ranked or selected, because selection of alternative solutions to problem solving is covered in Chapter 8. This chapter focuses on identifying the problems or misfits.

### The Task Component

The task component concerns the nature of the tasks or jobs that must be performed by the organization, groups, and individuals. The most important aspects of tasks include the extent and nature of interdependence between tasks, the level of skill required, the degree of autonomy, the extent of feedback, the variability of the task, the potential meaningfulness of the task, and the types of information needed to perform the task adequately.

For example, think about the task of starting an IV on your unit. What is the required level of skill for this task? On some units this may be considered a basic skill possessed by most nurses. However, if you are the head nurse of an intensive care or geriatrics or pediatrics unit, the required skill level may be greater or at least more specific. If your unit employs many new graduates who do not learn this skill in school, the amount of information needed will increase, affecting the nature of the task. Thus, you may have an incongruency or conflict between two dimensions within the task component—a large number of new graduates without IV skills and a large number of IVs that are difficult to start. This incongruency, or misfit, is a problem. The problem may be solved or the incongruency may be lessened by: not assigning new graduates to these units, hiring an IV therapist to start all IVs, teaching an IV class, or instituting peer teaching. Some of these solutions may not work in your organization. Some are not good solutions in any hospital because of their cost. Alternative solutions need to be considered in light of the specific criteria. The problem-solving model reviewed in Chapter 8 will help you use criteria to examine alternative solutions. You can then implement the solutions in an attempt to lessen your incongruencies and evaluate them to determine whether you did lessen them and increase fit and unit efficiency. Discovering misfits might thus be equated with problem identification.

Many new nurses on the night shift might be another misfit related to incongruencies between the dimensions of a task. That is, you may find a poor fit between the skills of new nurses and the demands of night shift tasks. With a large number of nurses on night shift, this problem increases. This misfit demands some problem solving on your part.

## The Individuals Component

The individuals component "refers to the individuals who are members of the organization. The major dimensions of this component relate to the systematic differences in individuals which have relevance for organizational behavior. Such dimensions include background or demographic variables such as skill levels, levels of education, and so on, and individual differences in need, strength, personality, or perceptual biases" (Nadler & Tushman, 1979).

You are sure to find "misfits" within the individuals component because people come to your unit from various backgrounds and with various experiences and personal values. These differences usually enrich their contributions to a unit. Moreover, various points of view are essential to healthy decision making. Open sharing of perspectives will increase tolerance for differences—especially if all perspectives are valued. For example, you may have several diploma-school graduates who are very highly skilled nurses and several baccalaureate graduates with strong theoretical backgrounds but without much clinical experience. There is a possible misfit here between two groups of nurses with differing backgrounds. The problem can be worsened if you place greater value on one or the other of these groups. However, you can take advantage of the differences and set up a norm on your unit for sharing skills and knowledge. Perhaps your degree nurse can hold an in-service on understanding blood gases, and your diploma nurse can assist someone who has never actually drawn blood.

Some other misfits related to individual staff members may stem from personality clashes or patient care preference differences. These situations are often handled well in coaching sessions. Sometimes they are temporary and can be ignored; sometimes they require your intervention by a clear statement of your expectations.

### Organization Arrangement

"This includes all the formal mechanisms used by the organization to direct structure or control behavior. Major dimensions include leadership practices, microstructure (how specific jobs, systems, or subcomponents are structured), and macrostructure (how whole units, departments, and organizations are structured)" (Nadler & Tushman, 1979). An example of a leadership practice misfit is to promote a task-oriented nurse to the position of head nurse on a psychiatric unit. An example of a microstructure misfit is to have one nurse give all medications when using a primary care system. An example of a macrostructure misfit is to have various units start at different hours when you have a centralized staffing float system.

Organizational arrangement is demonstrated in a hospital by organizational charts, job descriptions, and committee structures. Misfits here might take the form of committee structures that undermine the line of authority. For example, an interdepartmental quality assurance committee needs to report back to the line administrators at some point so that this information goes down the line to the limit level. Otherwise, power, authority, and responsibility become "muddy." Who really reports to whom becomes less clear. Job descriptions also need to reinforce the organizational structure by clearly stating to whom the person in each job reports.

### Informal Organization

The fourth component of the transformation process is the informal organization. "In addition to the formal prescribed structure that exists in the system, there is an informal social structure that tends to emerge over time. Relevant dimensions of the informal organization include the functioning of informal group structures, the quality of intergroup relations, and the operation of various political processes throughout the organization" (Nadler & Tushman, 1979). This component of the organization is more difficult to define and assess. The informal organization exists to deal with individual needs that are unmet by the formal system. Some examples of attempts to meet needs through informal systems include the p.r.n. family (potluck dinners, wedding and baby showers), T.G.I.F. parties, and newcomer events. Other more academic, informal mechanisms meet unit intellectual needs, such as journal clubs, writers' support groups, and back-to-school support groups. In addition, colleagues can forward and earmark articles, leave them in the lounge for others, and sign up for continuing education classes together. Not all informal systems are positive and reinforce the formal systems. The informal system may also perpetuate resistance to change and adherence to tradition or may foster animosity between staff and management. As a manager you need to be especially aware of the informal system.

### The Concept of Fit

Understanding these four components is only the beginning. In order to manage efficiently, you must understand and be able to change (when necessary) the dynamics between these variables. The concept of "fit" can be used to explore the congruence or harmony *between* components as we have just explored the concept of fit *within* components. Nadler and Tushman define fit as "the degree to which the needs, demands, goals, objectives and/or structures of one component are consistent with the needs, demands, goals, objectives and/or structures of another component. . . . Other things being equal, the greater the total degree of congruence or fit between the various components, the more effective will be organizational behavior at multiple levels. Effective organizational behavior is defined as behavior which leads to higher levels of goal attainment, utilization of resources, and adaptation" (Nadler & Tushman, 1979).

A high level of congruence from unit to unit and from department to department ensures a high degree of goal attainment for all levels of the organization and for individuals.

### Diagnosing Unit Activity Inefficiencies

Let us look at the congruence, or lack of congruence, between a few simple components that might affect your unit's organization. For example, with regard to fit between task and individual on an intensive care unit, the individual needs to be task oriented and to have high-level technical skills to match the nature of the intensive care job. When examining the fit between individuals and organizational arrangement, consider the fit between an organizational policy of every other weekend off and only full-time employees—a definite misfit and an impossibility in most hospitals. The formal and informal organizational systems usually balance each other. What is missing in one is usually found in the other. The head nurse who is incompetent will maintain the title, but the staff will find another person to seek out for help. If the head nurse does not pass information down the line, the staff will look elsewhere for their information. The informal system will also be the way of handling a misfit between task and a formal system. If a task procedure is out of date and attempts to change it through the appropriate lines or committees fail, staff will support each other in ignoring the procedure. Thus, the informal system picks up the slack between the task at hand and an outmoded aspect of the formal system. Identifying and decreasing incongruencies will definitely increase your unit's efficiency.

The number of possible incongruencies or misfits between variables is great. Although we could not possibly explore them all, this model provides a framework through which you can understand and solve an organizational or unit problem. The transformation or throughput part of the model is the section over which you have the most control. Here, you can try to change components of your unit that do not fit with other components. Your efforts here have the greatest impact on your unit.

**Output from Your Unit**

For every action you take on your unit, an output results. Therefore, whenever you make a change, a *new* output results. Possible outputs include *individual affect and behavior, group behavior,* system functioning in terms of *goal achievement, resource utilization,* and *adaptation.* Let us explore each of these output components with unit examples. Individual affect and behavior are seen in the nurse who continues to work overtime after asking staff to cut back. *Group behavior output* is the term used to describe a group action, such as no one complying after you change the time of report. Goal achievement outcome could be demonstrated by a departmental in-service offered and presented by your staff to meet a current "hot" clinical issue. Evaluations from the participants help make this goal (output) more measurable. Resource utilization output could be measured in something as concrete as pounds of linen. Perhaps your unit decided to cut back on wasted linen and measured their goals in pounds per week. Adaptation to a situation is another outcome that could be expected after some type of intervention during the transformation process. For example, if you installed a new monitoring system and offered one-to-one training and a feedback test for people slated to use this equipment, after a period of time, adaptation could be noticed in terms of the number of staff qualified to use the new equipment.

**Feedback**

Remember, you do not operate in a vacuum, and neither do other hospital units and departments. Your output will affect other units, departments (subsystems), and the hospital as a whole. This is the ripple effect described earlier. Also, changes made in other departments and units will send out ripples that affect you.

The ripple effect can be seen, for example, if your unit decides to change shift hours. Perhaps you decide that if your nurses arrived at 6:30 A.M. instead of 7:00 A.M., this would facilitate getting your patients to surgery on time. The ripple effect of this change may cause many problems. A staff nurse may have difficulty finding a sitter for her child at this hour. Your unit clerk's car pooling with someone from another unit may be disrupted because that unit, like the rest of the hospital, changes shifts at 7:00 A.M. Because the float pool cannot meet your needs any earlier (float assignments are made based on the entire staffing picture), float nurses will miss report and not be in synchronization with your unit hours. The evening shift may not find parking at their subsequent earlier starting time. Your patient classification system readings will change because they do not reflect many late afternoon admissions when done one-half hour earlier. This means evening staffing will often be low.

Many ripples extend from your initial change, causing new input into other subsystems. Often these ripples are predictable and some can be prevented by slightly altering the initial change. If ripples cannot be prevented and may cause undesirable input to other subsystems, meet with the managers of those systems to inform them and to problem solve together.

## USING THIS MODEL TO DIAGNOSE INEFFICIENCIES IN ACTIVITIES

We have examined each part of the system: input, throughput, output, and feedback. We have also looked at incongruencies between the components of each part of the system. To facilitate the process of diagnosing and rectifying these incongruencies, including an evaluation of whether or not our action worked, we will use a nine-step model by Nadler and Tushman (1979). The model mimics a problem-solving model, and the information in Chapter 8 on problem solving will help you to use the model even more effectively. The material in Chapter 8 complements this material; the steps of problem solving explored in depth there are treated more generally in this chapter. This model does, however, provide a place for the notion of "fit" and is especially useful in diagnosing your unit's inefficiencies.

Step 1. *Identify the system*. Are you looking at a specific unit or a vertical part of the organizational structure, such as the nursing department, or a horizontal grouping, such as all head nurses? You may even be considering a group within and beyond your organization—for example, all nurses who belong to your state nursing organization.

Step 2. *Determine the nature of the key variables*. In the situation or problem you are examining, what are the key inputs, and which of the four throughput components are relevant? Perhaps someone else instituted a change that caused an undesirable input into your system, affecting your staff in a negative way. Your staff is the "individual component," and their behavior is the output.

Step 3. *Evaluate the fit and identify misfits*. Focus on misfits that are causing negative outputs.

Step 4. *Identify critical system problems*. Based on undesired outputs, decide which key components need some change to improve output.

Step 5. *Generate alternative solutions*. These solutions should be directed at inconsistent fits to improve the output. This step of problem solving and steps 6, 7, and 8 are discussed in depth in Chapter 8.

Step 6. *Evaluate alternative solutions*. To what extent does each alternative improve the fit between components? To what extent does each alternative create a misfit with another component? There are no perfect answers and infinite possibilities, so what you are seeking is the fit that works best while solving the critical system problem you've identified in step 4.

Step 7. *Choose a strategy to implement*. Theory, research, experience, and input from a variety of sources aid in this selection process. Weigh the various advantages and disadvantages, and choose an action plan.

Step 8. *Implement strategy*. Consider the likelihood of acceptance or rejection, and use change strategies (see Chapter 8) to increase your chances of success.

Step 9. *Evaluate and feed the results back to the unit*. Did the fit improve? Did output improve? What was the cost in terms of human/material resources and component change?

The preceding model appears long at first, but you can use it easily with practice. Many experienced managers automatically go through these steps before answering questions asked in the hallway or a meeting. They think quickly through the steps, calling a halt where more information is needed to move to the next step, perhaps needing some time to think of additional alternatives or to make a phone call to assess the impact on another subsystem.

## A UNIT INEFFICIENCY EXPLORED THROUGH THE DIAGNOSTIC MODEL

To understand better how to use the model, let us use it to sort out an example of a misfit on a unit level.

Step 1. The system is your unit, all three shifts.

Step 2. The key variables are the three shifts of staff. They are also the "individuals component." There is friction between shifts about leaving a messy utility room, incomplete shift reports, IVs running out at change of shift, and other change-of-shift issues in which each shift blames the prior shift and denies responsibility to the following one. You notice that the output, or behavior, is a growing animosity between shifts. It is not uncommon for you to hear, "The day shift left all the water pitchers empty"; "The evening shift did not check to be sure we had new medication orders filled and on the unit"; and "The night shift isn't getting the early OR patients ready on time."

Step 3. The lack of fit is between day and evening shifts, evening and night shifts, and night and day shifts. These are all parts of the individual component and the task component.

Step 4. The critical problem, as described in step 2, is conflict between shifts. It is necessary to make some changes in the individual and/or task components in order to clarify responsibilities and pull together with a team spirit.

Step 5. You can consider various methods to reach your goal of creating smoother working relations between shifts and getting the work done. Perhaps a task force from all three shifts can propose a clearer delineation of responsibilities (tasks) of each shift (people) to be considered by all staff. Some team-building efforts would also be useful. (Team building is addressed in Chapter 3.)

Step 6. Which of the preceding alternatives will produce better team spirit and get the job done? What are the benefits and consequences of each? Setting dates and criteria for evaluation are essential.

Step 7. Choose your strategy, and consider the best action plan for its implementation in light of human and material resource costs and possible ripple effects. Try to find a solution that satisfies staff and that is cost-effective.

Step 8. Implement your action plan using unfreezing strategies, discussed in Chapter 8. In this situation, the more people involved, the better your chances of a successful resolution.

Step 9. At the prescribed time, make an evaluation based on preset criteria and current fit. Feed new problems back to step 1. Reinforce what is working, and work on new solutions as needed.

Through this process you can explore congruence between various elements related to your unit's efficiency and plan how to increase fit between parts within and beyond your unit.

As a manager, your job is to organize and process work efficiently. In this chapter, we have looked at a framework for analyzing activities, decisions, and relations with an emphasis on task efficiency and fit between variables. We mentioned that the task is integrated with those persons performing the tasks. The next chapter focuses on the performers of the activities and your job as a manager to *direct* them.

## Activity 5:1

# How Your Hospital Is Organized

- Collect the following:

  ☐ Your hospital organizational chart
  ☐ Your nursing department organizational chart
  ☐ Your unit organizational chart (if it exists)

- Answer the questions below:

  What is the function of your hospital board?
  _____
  _____

  Who are your board members, and who appoints them?
  _____
  _____

  What issues are resolved by your hospital board?
  _____
  _____

  ☐ Ask if you can attend a hospital board meeting.
  ☐ Review the organizational charts with your boss to clarify who reports to whom.
  Comments _____
  _____
  _____

- Ask your boss for an example of a decision made on each level.

  Board _____
  Hospital administration _____
  Nursing administration _____
  Unit _____

**Activity 5:1** continued

- Ask the name of the president (chief executive officer or hospital administrator) and vice presidents (associate administrators) of your hospital.

_____President
_____Vice-president
_____Vice-president

Which areas of responsibility report to which administrators?

_____

_____

_____

- Try to find out about informal decision making in your organization. Circle in red the administrators who are perceived as the most powerful.

_____

_____

- Who is your director of nursing? _____

What is the job description of that person? (Obtain job description and summarize below.)

_____

_____

_____

_____

_____

_____

Who reports to your director of nursing?
(Names and positions)

_____

_____

_____

What are the responsibilities of these managers (associate directors of nursing or assistant directors of nursing)?

_____

_____

_____

_____

**Activity 5:1** continued

- Where do you (head nurse) fit into the organizational chart? _____
  What are your support systems, and how do each of them fit into the organization (e.g., staffing, office, unit managers, in-service)?

  _____
  _____
  _____
  _____

  How do you use them? _____

  _____
  _____
  _____

- Where do policies and procedures originate in your organization?

  _____
  _____

  How do you change a policy or procedure?

  _____
  _____
  _____
  _____

- How do the evening and night supervisors fit into your organization? Do they have primary authority over any particular persons or units (e.g., hire, fire, performance appraisal)?

  _____
  _____
  _____
  _____
  _____

# Activity 5:2

# Unit Organization

- If your unit has an organizational chart, obtain a copy. Discuss with your boss how this structure reinforces and/or undermines (fits with) the people and tasks on your unit.

  Reinforces: _____
  _____
  _____

  Undermines: _____
  _____
  _____

  Together, discuss any needed changes: _____
  _____
  _____

- If your unit does not have an organizational chart, begin one with the head nurse at the top; include R.N.s, L.V.N.s, N.A.s, and unit clerks. Share it at a staff meeting.

```
                    ┌─────────────┐
                    │ Head Nurse  │
                    └──────┬──────┘
                           │
    ───────────────────────┴───────────────────────
```

# Activity 5:3

# Unit Committee Assessment

- Fill in the names of your unit committees (or task forces) on left.
  Fill in information about the committees in next columns.
  Add any needed committees at bottom.
  *If you have no unit committees or task forces, use this form to begin planning needed committees or to analyze departmental committees to which your staff belong.*

| Committee Names | Purpose of Committee | Current Tasks of Committee | Is this committee active and productive? | Committee Chair & Member-ship | Would this be a good committee for me to be on? Why? | How does a staff member get on or off this committee? |
|---|---|---|---|---|---|---|
|  |  |  |  |  |  |  |
|  |  |  |  |  |  |  |
|  |  |  |  |  |  |  |
|  |  |  |  |  |  |  |
|  |  |  |  |  |  |  |

- Should any of these committees be deleted? _____
  What is your plan for terminating them? _____
  _____
  _____

- Should any committees (or task forces) be added (e.g., unit-based quality assurance, cost containment, social, patient education)? If so, draft the purpose and tasks, and add to your unit meeting agenda.

# Activity 5:4

# Unit Level Throughput Congruence Analysis

**Activity 5:4** continued

Analysis of fit among tasks, individuals, formal organizations, and informal organizations.

**Part I.** Develop a Data Base—Fill in Chart Below.

| Tasks<br>List the tasks of your unit. | Individuals<br>List the needed skills, education, and experience for each task listed at left and who has those skills. | Formal Organizations<br>List the formal organizational structure that relates to each task. | Informal Organizations<br>List the informal norms that relate to each task. (You may want to ignore lines and make a general list of norms that affect many tasks.) |
|---|---|---|---|
| Examples<br>Patient teaching on diabetes; prepping a patient for surgery. | Examples<br>Must be R.N.; must understand diabetes; must know how to chart temperatures. | Examples<br>Job description; policy, procedure, or organizational chart that specifies rules about this task. | Examples<br>Mary Smith is excellent at diabetic teaching and usually does most of it for the unit's diabetic patients. |
| 1. | | | |
| 2. | | | |
| 3. | | | |
| 4. | | | |

| | | | |
|---|---|---|---|
| 5. | | | |
| 6. | | | |
| 7. | | | |
| 8. | | | |
| 9. | | | |
| 10. | | | |
| 11. | | | |
| 12. | | | |
| 13. | | | |
| 14. | | | |
| 15. | | | |

**Activity 5:4** continued

**Part II.** Identify Incongruencies on Your Unit.

- Look at task 1. Does it fit with the information in the individuals column? In other words, do your staff have the skills, education, and experience necessary for the task? If yes, your fit between task and individual for task 1 is good.
- Check the fit between the tasks and individuals columns for each task. Circle any incongruencies on the data base chart above using red.
- Compare tasks and individuals with the formal organization. Circle any incongruencies in blue.
- Compare tasks, individuals, and formal organization with the informal organization. Circle any incongruencies in green.

Circles indicate incongruencies between two or more columns. These incongruencies are called misfits.
List your identified misfits:

_____

_____

_____

_____

_____

_____


**Part III.** Analyze Incongruencies on Your Unit.

Copy incongruencies (misfits) on *left side of chart below* (one per square). Explain the misfit. Suggest solutions on right side of chart.*

| (Circle two or more) Misfit 1 is between task— individual—formal org.—informal org. | What could you change to improve fit? |
|---|---|
|  |  |

*If you identify problems without identifying obvious changes to improve fit, use the problem-solving format in Chapter 8. This tool is useful for identifying and defining problems but not for involved problem solving. Column 1 (above) can be used for problem statement in the problem-solving format, and column 2 (above) can be used as a beginning list of alternative solutions in the problem-solving format.

**Activity 5:4** continued

| | |
|---|---|
| Explain misfit: | |
| (Circle two or more)<br>Misfit 2 is between task—individual—formal org.—informal org. | What could you change to improve fit? |
| Explain misfit: | |
| (Circle two or more)<br>Misfit 3 is between task—individual—formal org.—informal org. | What could you change to improve fit? |
| Explain misfit: | |

**Activity 5:4** continued

| (Circle two or more)<br>Misfit 4 is between task—individual—formal org.—informal org. | What could you change to improve fit? |
|---|---|
| Explain misfit: | |
| (Circle two or more)<br>Misfit 5 is between task—individual—formal org.—informal org. | What could you change to improve fit? |
| Explain misfit: | |
| (Circle two or more)<br>Misfit 6 is between task—individual—formal org.—informal org. | What could you change to improve fit? |
| Explain misfit: | |

# Activity 5:5

# Understanding the Larger Organization

Fill in the answers below to understand better the overall organization.

• How and when did your hospital start?

_____

_____

• How old is your current facility? _____
What are your current facility's modernization plans?

_____

_____

_____

• Who owns your hospital (e.g., government, university, church, community, corporation)? Do you have profit or nonprofit status?

_____

_____

_____

• What services are offered in your hospital (e.g., general medical, surgical, ear, nose, throat)?

_____      _____

_____      _____

_____      _____

• Do you provide long-term care (over 30 days)? If so, what percent is long-term?

_____

• Do you provide ambulatory care? Hospice care? Any other community services?

_____

_____

_____

• What are the closest hospitals to yours? How do they differ and how are they similar?

_____

_____

_____

**Activity 5:5** continued

• What is the average length of patient stay in your hospital? What are the ten most frequently treated diagnoses of patients in your hospital?

_____

_____

_____

• Do you have nursing students, medical students, interns, or residents in your hospital? From what teaching facilities do they come? Where can you find policies and procedures regarding what they may do in your hospital?

_____

_____

_____

• Which physicians in your hospital are paid directly by the hospital, which are self-employed, and which are under contract?

_____

_____

_____

_____

# Activity 5:6

# Organization of Patient Care

• *Assessment of your Method of Delivering Patient Care:* Below is a comparison of three methods of delivering patient care. (Kron, 1981, pp. 228–232)

Circle for each factor the method you are currently using on your unit. Ignore labels at the top for now, because most units do not use a "pure" method. If it differs for each shift, use three colors (Blue = day; Green = PM; Red = night).

## COMPARISON OF THREE METHODS OF DELIVERING NURSING CARE

| FACTOR | METHOD OF NURSING CARE: | | |
| | FUNCTIONAL | TEAM | PRIMARY |
| --- | --- | --- | --- |
| Assignments | Head nurse or nursing co-ordinator assigns to staff members tasks that fall within their job descriptions. | Team leader assigns to team members tasks that fall within their job descriptions. | Head nurse or nursing co-ordinator assigns individual patients to professional nurses, matching the patient's needs to the nurse's skills. |
| Assessment, planning, and evaluation | Related to a specific need of each patient; done by any member of the nursing staff; no continuity. | Related to specific needs of each patient; done by the team leader; a limited continuity depending on how long a person remains team leader. | Related to specific needs of each patient; done by the primary nurse; maximum continuity, since primary nurse remains throughout patient's stay on hospital unit. |
| Implementation | Different members of the nursing staff do tasks for a given patient. | Each team member does tasks for all patients, according to job description; the team leader often does medications and charting for the team. | Each primary nurse delivers total care to all assigned patients ("For the first time I feel that somebody knows who I am"). |
| Documentation | Staff members make notations on only those actions or aspects of care done by them. or A staff member is assigned to "chart" for a given number of patients; usually no nursing care plan is in evidence. | Team leader usually documents care for patients cared for by most, or all, team members; sometimes a team member makes certain entries on patient charts; the team leader documents the nursing care plan. | Each primary or associate nurse documents care given to each assigned patient during shift; the primary nurse documents the nursing care plan. |

*Source:* Reprinted from *The Management of Patient Care,* edited by T. Kron, with permission of W.B. Saunders, © 1981.

## Activity 5:6 continued

### COMPARISON OF THREE METHODS OF DELIVERING NURSING CARE (Continued)

| FACTOR | FUNCTIONAL | METHOD OF NURSING CARE: TEAM | PRIMARY |
|---|---|---|---|
| Reporting at end of shift | A "charge" nurse gives report on patients to another charge nurse; most of the information shared is based on reports of other workers. | The team leader gives report on the group of patients to the oncoming team; most of the information shared is based on reports of other workers. | The primary nurse gives report on each assigned patient to oncoming nurse who will care for the patient; the nurse who reports has interacted directly with all the patients about whom reports are given. |
| Responsibility for planning care | No one person is responsible for planning unless this is assigned as a functional task to a specific R.N. for a given period. | The team leader is responsible for planning the nursing care for the assigned group of patients. | The primary nurse is responsible for planning the nursing care of all primary patients, from the time they are admitted to a nursing unit until they are discharged from that unit. |
| Responsibility for providing care | Nursing care is delivered in a fragmented manner, with many staff members interacting with the patient as the various tasks are done. | As in functional nursing, delivery of nursing care is a "mixed bag." | The primary nurse directly delivers all nursing care to the primary patients when on duty. |
| Decentralization of authority, for continuous decision-making and follow-up of nursing care | Total decentralization—decisions are made on basis of separate tasks done by individual staff members for each patient on the unit. | The team leader makes final decisions about nursing care for the patients in the group on basis of feedback (some of which is lost) from team members. | Each primary nurse makes final decisions about nursing care for the assigned patients. |
| Accountability to patients, families, peers, physicians, interdepartmental staff, administration, and community | | | |
| *For professional actions* | Professional nurses are each answerable for their own professional actions. | Professional nurses are each answerable for their own professional actions. | Professional nurses are each answerable for their own professional actions. |
| *For coordination and outcomes of nursing care* | No one nursing staff member is answerable for the coordination and outcomes of nursing care; the head nurse often answers to everyone for the entire staff. | The team leader, who plans care but often does not give it, is answerable for the care of each patient in the assigned group and for the coordination and outcomes of nursing care. | The primary nurse who plans and delivers the care to each assigned patient is answerable for the coordination and outcomes of nursing care. |
| *For follow-up on patient problems* | Physicians, administrators, and other interdepartmental personnel can rarely pinpoint responsibility for follow-up on problems. | The team leader is responsible for follow-up on patient problems, which are often generated by other staff. | The primary nurse is responsible for follow-up on problems of assigned patients. |

## Activity 5:6 continued

COMPARISON OF THREE METHODS OF DELIVERING NURSING CARE *(Continued)*

| FACTOR | METHOD OF NURSING CARE: | | |
|---|---|---|---|
| | FUNCTIONAL | TEAM | PRIMARY |
| — "Passing the buck" | "Passing the buck" prevalent. | Moderate amount of "buck passing" due to change in staff assignments from day to day. | Minimal, if any, "passing the buck" because of constancy of staff assignments to same patients. |
| Comprehensiveness of care, in terms of: Patients' needs | Not possible; focus of care is on tasks, not on the patient as a unique individual with a broad spectrum of needs and resources. | Theoretically, and sometimes actually, possible, since team members are expected to communicate ideas related to patient needs and nursing action to meet those needs; a united approach is the goal; however, plans are often designed with minimal patient/family input, and focus is on nursing action rather than on patient goals. | Inherent in the system, because continuity in same nurse/same patient relationships is maximized; focus of nursing care is on patient goals rather than on nursing action. |
| Documentation | Nursing care regimens are rarely documented, so individual approaches are inconsistent. | Documented nursing care plans are encouraged but can rarely be demanded, because nursing case load is too large. | Documented nursing care plans are mandated and are facilitated by smaller case load of each nurse and by constancy of assignment. |
| Communication Between nurses and patients or clients | Patient, family, and significant others find it difficult to identify a nursing staff member with whom to relate on a continuing basis. | Patient, family, and significant others may be confused as to identity of the nursing staff member to whom questions and problems may be directed. | Patient, family, and significant others can clearly identify the nurse and can share ideas, feelings, and problems freely with this person. |
| Between nurses and staff of other departments | Physicians, administrators, and interdepartmental staff address questions and problems to nurses or to head nurse on unit, but often satisfactory answers are delayed or are not available. | Same as in functional nursing, except team leader rather than head nurse may be consulted. | All communications are directed to the primary nurse for each patient. Satisfactory answers are more likely to be forthcoming. Persons may find difficulty in locating specific nurses. |
| Between nurses and supervisors | Instructions often have to be repeated because of changes in staff assignments and lack of consistent documentation of nursing care plans | Same as in functional nursing | Dramatic decrease in repetition of instructions for particular patients due to constancy of assignments and mandatory care plans. |

**Activity 5:6** continued

**COMPARISON OF THREE METHODS OF DELIVERING NURSING CARE** (*Continued*)

| FACTOR | FUNCTIONAL | METHOD OF NURSING CARE: TEAM | PRIMARY |
|---|---|---|---|
| Cost-effectiveness | Not cost-effective, * because:<br><br>a. Product (nursing care) is of poor quality owing to fragmentation; this results in many complaints from consumers. | Not cost-effective, * because:<br><br>a. Product is of only moderate quality, since expertise in judgment and communication cannot be delegated from the care-planners (team leaders) to the care-givers (team members). | Most likely to be cost-* effective, because:<br><br>a. Product is of high quality since the person most prepared and best equipped to perform does so on a continuing basis for the same patients. |
| | b. Nursing staff easily becomes frustrated and turnover rate is usually high, thus increasing cost of orientation and of staff development. | b. Turnover of nursing staff is moderate but variable. | b. Turnover of nursing staff is minimal because of higher level of satisfaction experienced by nurses. |
| | c. Output from professional nurses is low, since they are not required to perform the full job—the total nursing process—for which they are being paid. | c. Same as for functional nursing. | c. Professional nurses do the job for which they are being paid; "unproductive" time decreases dramatically. |

*The opinion of T. Kron

- What is the predominant method of care delivery on your unit?

  _____

- Can you change any factors in your methods of care delivery to improve the quality and/or cost of patient care delivery on your unit?

  _____
  _____
  _____

# Activity 5:7

# Organization of Staff To Meet Patient Needs

**Part I.** Assessing Staffing Patient Care Needs

"A patient classification system permits categorization of patients by levels of nursing care required. The resultant tools for each classification provide the basis for defining the nursing workload, the number of nursing hours required on each shift" (Ganong & Ganong, 1980, p. 233).

- Is your staff centralized or scheduled by units/regions? _____
- Do you have a float pool, and how are these staff assigned and budgeted?

  _____
  _____

- Do you use agency nurses? How are they assigned and budgeted?

  _____
  _____

- Find out if your hospital uses a patient classification system to staff each shift.

  Yes ☐     No ☐

---

*If yes:* Find a mentor to teach you the system. Discuss the questions below: What are the critical indicators of care?

_____
_____
_____
_____

Who gathers the data? _____

How often are the data collected? _____

---

**Activity 5:7** continued

Trace the process from data generation to unit staffing for the shift.

_____
_____
_____
_____

What is the origin of your patient classification system?

_____
_____

What are its strengths?

_____
_____

What are its weaknesses (inaccuracies)?

_____
_____

In what way are the weaknesses compensated?

_____
_____

Do you have a float pool available? _____

---

*If no:* Find a mentor to teach you how staffing is determined for each unit for
     each shift.
How is staffing determined for each unit? For each shift?

_____
_____
_____

What are the primary factors (critical indicators) considered?

_____
_____
_____
_____

Who makes the decision? How do you give input?

_____
_____

What are the strengths of this system?

_____
_____

**Activity 5:7** continued

What are the weaknesses (inaccuracies)?

_____

_____

Does your system represent changes in census and changes in acuteness of illness? How?

_____

_____

_____

_____

_____

**Part II.** Understanding Scheduling

Some organizations use computerized cyclic staffing and hire people for a specific "slot." The schedule is usually for six weeks and repeats itself over and over. This person agrees to work this specific schedule when hired.

Some organizations do manual scheduling every month on a unit basis; each month is different.

Many varieties of scheduling exist between these two extremes.

Answer the following questions about scheduling for your hospital:

- Is scheduling done by a central office, for each region specifically, or by the units? _____
- What is your responsibility for staffing?

  _____

  _____

  _____

- How do you give input? Who are your support people?

  _____

  _____

  _____

- What effect does the union contract (if one exists) have on scheduling?

  _____

  _____

  _____

**Activity 5:7** continued

   • How are individual requests handled?

   _____

   _____

   _____

   • What are the observed holidays, and how are they handled?

   _____

   _____

   _____

   _____

   • How do you assure the needed level of staff nurses' skills for each shift
     in the schedule?

   _____

   _____

   _____

_____

☐ If you will be responsible for making out a monthly unit schedule, find a
   mentor and do three practice schedules for critique.

## Activity 5:8

# Simplifying Unit Work Methods

- At a staff meeting, ask your staff to think about this question (before the next meeting): "What tasks are difficult to do on this unit?" Share what will be done at the next staff meeting. (See sample flip chart.)

- At the following staff meeting, allow some time for staff to share their answers to the above question. Write their answers (tasks) on the left side of the flip chart for all to see. Then ask: "For each task identified, what can we do to simplify this task without sacrificing quality or increasing the cost?" Write ideas on the right side of the chart.

Sample Flip Chart

| Difficult Tasks | Simplification |
|---|---|
|  |  |

## CASE STUDY

A directive from the chief executive officer mandates each department to cut its operating budget by 5 percent. The housekeeping department has subsequently decided to cut 30 minutes off the end of each shift. You receive this information via memo as a *fait accompli* (already decided and implemented).

This output from housekeeping ripples to your unit as unwanted input. Multiple interunit transfers occur between 2:30 and 3:00 P.M. The unavailability of housekeeping to clean beds at this time delays your moving patients out of your "stepdown" unit to medical units. Thus you cannot take transfers from intensive care, and that unit is not able to take patients from the emergency department, the operating room, or the recovery room.

What do you do?

## SOLUTION TO CASE STUDY

It is unacceptable to leave the situation "as is." It is also unacceptable to have nurses routinely clean the beds. You need to meet with your colleagues and housekeeping to work out an acceptable solution.

Since housekeeping services are so vital to you at the time they have been cut, perhaps the half hour could be cut from the other end of the day for this particular shift. Another possibility would be to have all the cut time in the early morning, a "down time" for housekeeping, by setting up shifts from 7 A.M. to 2:30 P.M., 2:30 P.M. to 10 P.M., and 10 P.M. to 4:30 A.M., with no coverage from 5:30 A.M. to 7 A.M.

This problem probably cannot be solved acceptably without going beyond your unit.

**REFERENCES**

Burach, E.H., & Torda, F. *The manager's guide to change*. Belmont, Calif.: Wadsworth, 1979.

Drucker, P. *Management: Tasks, responsibilities, practices*. New York: Harper & Row, 1973.

Ganong, J.M., & Ganong, W.L. *Nursing management* (2nd ed.). Rockville, Md.: Aspen Systems, 1980.

Kron, T. *The management of patient care*. Philadelphia: Saunders, 1981.

Nadler, D.A., & Tushman, M. A congruence model for diagnosing organizational behavior. In D.A. Kolb, I.M. Rubin, & J.M. McIntyre (Eds.), *Organizational Psychology* (3rd ed.). Englewood Cliffs, N.J.: Prentice-Hall, 1979.

# Chapter 6

# Directing

## OBJECTIVES

Upon completion of this chapter, including the activities, the new nurse manager will be able to:

- adapt his or her leadership style to the task-relevant maturity level of staff
- differentiate between attitude, training, and system misfit problems as sources of performance discrepancies
- use Maslow's hierarchy to describe unmet needs as motivators of new graduate nurses
- describe satisfiers and dissatisfiers according to Herzberg and how these factors are related to staff motivation
- list job enrichment characteristics
- use Pasmore's six-step Data Feedback Change Strategy to identify and correct job dissatisfaction
- use Fournies' system of coaching for one-to-one problem solving and one-to-one goal setting
- develop a standard hiring interview guide
- explain disciplinary action and grievance procedures in your hospital

# DEVELOPMENT OF THE NEW NURSE MANAGER™ © 1981

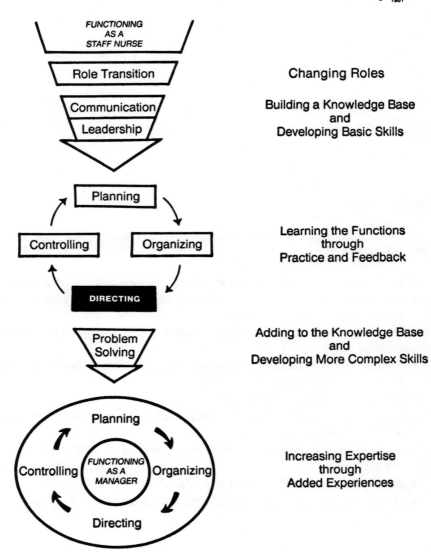

¶ Your job as a manager involves the constant challenge of getting work done through other people. The last chapter explored the work and the unit activities. Chapter 3 explored the various leadership styles available to you. This chapter discusses selecting a management style that helps the people under you get the work done. Included in this chapter is the need for staff training and motivation.

## SITUATIONAL LEADERSHIP

You begin with an individual or group and something you want them to accomplish. Based on who they are and how much they know about the task, you can determine what leadership style you should use to attain the desired results.

For example, suppose a decision is made that your orthopedic unit will begin accepting neurology patients. Start by assessing your staff's neurological nursing skills and determining how much skill development these nurses need for basic care of this patient population. In this situation, your leadership style needs to be directive (authoritarian) to bring your nurses' skill levels up to a safe standard in neurology.

### Task-Relevant Maturity Levels

Consequently, you formulate a list of performance standards that all staff must be able to meet within two months. The standards are based on the skills needed to give safe nursing care to neurology patients. You are being directive in that all staff *must* learn these new skills. In this situation, you have chosen a directive style of leadership because your assessment has shown that most of your staff have little ability to care for neurology patients. Hersey and Blanchard (1977) call this assessment a diagnosis of task-relevant maturity in their Situation Leadership Model (see Figure 6–1). Task-relevant maturity refers to an individual's or group's ability and willingness to take responsibility for a particular task. It also involves their education and related experience and their ability to set high but attainable goals. In the neurology situation, you may have a willing staff, but their ability, education, and experience may be limited and may therefore require your direction.

The task-relevant maturity of your subordinates is the basis for determining which leadership style is appropriate for each particular task. In other words, task-relevant maturity will diagnose the situation and dictate which style will work best in that circumstance.

Hersey and Blanchard (1977) divide task-relevant maturity into four levels. These levels range from a maturity level of 1 (a low level of experience and education) to level 4 (a high level of experience and education). Leadership styles are also divided into four groups, decreasing in directiveness. These four styles are

**Figure 6–1** Situational Leadership Model

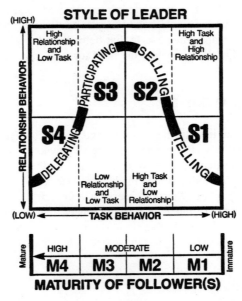

called "telling," "selling," "participating," and "delegating." The leader needs to assess the maturity level of the followers (levels 1, 2, 3, or 4), then apply the appropriate leadership style.

Matching your leadership style with the task-relevant maturity of your subordinates for a given task is based on two variables—your concern for the task and your concern for the people. Concern for the task is characterized by one-way communication and specific directions (authoritarian).

What follows is an example of a situation that would require you to use a very directive style and to show great concern for the task at hand. You develop a written guideline sheet for float nurses coming to your unit. The guidelines are clear, one-way directives about how to work on the unit. This "telling" style is used for a low task-relevant maturity. The low level of maturity does not mean the float nurses are not mature; rather, it indicates that, given this situation (a new unit on which to work), their experience is low and requires directive leadership.

Some situations may require high concern not only for the task but also for the person or group. The appropriate leadership style for this situation is "selling." For example, you receive a memo saying that one section of the time card will be changed. The change requires your staff to make an increased effort to fill out the new form. The maturity level of your staff is not zero; they know how to fill out a time card. However, the task-relevant maturity level is still low (a maturity level of 2 on a scale of 1 to 4), requiring some specific directions from you related to the changes. Besides this high task requirement, you also need to show a strong concern for your staff. This change requires increased time by your staff. After giving directions about the task, you allow time for the staff to ask questions and share their concerns about the new format and additional time requirements. You encourage them to try the new system with an open mind, informing them of the additional benefits the system will provide, such as more accurate overtime pay.

When one of your more experienced staff nurses comes to you with a report about a change in a patient's condition, your concern is mostly for supporting the person rather than the task. In other words, this nurse has a fairly high task-relevant maturity (a maturity level of 3 on a scale of 4), so you focus on supporting the nurse's decision rather than questioning her ability to perform the task of good patient assessment. The leadership style you use is "participating." Together you discuss the clinical assessment; you support the decision to call the physician immediately.

Any member of your staff can demonstrate the highest maturity level. For example, your unit routine specifies that nursing assistants take vital signs after the morning report. In this situation, you use a "delegating" leadership style with your experienced aides. They have a high level of task-relevant maturity, having taken vital signs for many years. They also require little support from you for this particular task. To be directive in this situation can be condescending or demoralizing to your staff.

For each situation, you must look at the task-relevant maturity level of the subordinates. Based on their experience and education, you choose your leadership style. This method will provide you with a useful way of determining which style is most likely to achieve the desired results.

In a broader sense, this model will provide you with guidelines for dealing with your staff as they grow. New graduates have a task-relevant maturity level of 1 on most tasks, requiring more direction and support. Experienced nurses usually perform on a high task level, requiring less support and direction. Fluctuations of maturity level can be expected on new procedures. A nurse experiencing significant personal stress may perform on a level lower than usual. For example, a nurse who is going through a divorce may require increased support, even on clinical decisions.

## ATTITUDES AND NEEDS

Hersey and Blanchard's (1977) model provides a clear guide for determining the appropriate leadership style to use, given the education and experience level of a particular staff nurse. The model also guides your style choice for leading a group, as in the ortho/neuro unit example. Through this model, the knowledge and skill and experience levels of your staff determine what degree of directiveness is appropriate in a specific situation.

Your staff's willingness (in addition to their ability) is another factor to consider in the task-relevant maturity diagnosis. If you assess someone's skill level as high, but the work is not getting done or the quality of work is poor, perhaps attitude is the problem. Attitudinal problems, or lack of motivation, demand more directive leadership styles.

For example, a particular nurse frequently requests specific days off. Usually these are weekends and holidays that many nurses desire to have free. You have worked out a rotation system with your staff, and most of them comply. This particular nurse, however, calls in sick whenever she does not get her requested day off. Regardless of the nurse's general task maturity level on clinical issues, this problem requires a directive style on your part because the nurse is not accepting the responsibility for coming to work as scheduled.

Mager and Pipe (1970) have developed a useful flowchart model for exploring "performance discrepancies"—differences between someone's actual perform-ance and the performance you desire from them. Mager and Pipe suggest identify-ing whether the nature of the discrepancy is a training problem (an educational/experiential need) or an attitude problem (a lack of motivation to perform the activity). To these we add system misfits as a third cause of performance discrep-ancies.

When staff members are not performing assigned or expected activities, discuss with them whether or not they understood what was expected. Remember that perceptions, values, and other "noise" (Chapter 2) may have interfered with communication of the assignment from the sender (you or your delegate) to the receivers.

If staff members understood what was expected of them, why did they not do it? Let us consider three alternatives. First, they did not know how—a training problem. Some examples of this might be improperly charted vital signs or improper disposal of syringes and needles. Perhaps new staff members do not follow isolation techniques correctly. The discrepancy between what is done and what is desired should be discussed with the employees to ascertain knowledge and skill levels for these tasks. If the employees do not know how to perform the functions, you have a training problem. As a manager you can deal with this problem through one-to-one teaching, adding the information to your unit orienta-tion program, sending a memo to the employees concerned, or having one of your staff help these people.

A second possible reason why your staff did not perform an expected activity could be a misfit in your unit's systems. You may hear this as "insufficient time" or "too much to do" or some other problem of an organizational nature. This reason, if not masking an attitude problem, should be reviewed in light of possible misfits between components (see Chapter 5). Be sure to assess whether it is a unit problem or an individual's training problem.

For example, if most nurses finish charting on time but one nurse consistently complains that he has insufficient time to chart, continually using overtime, you may have an individual training problem, not a unit problem. What this nurse may need is some help in organizing assigned work, setting priorities, and developing time management skills.

The third possible reason for a performance discrepancy is attitude. As mentioned earlier, this problem is usually masked under "I didn't have enough time" or "I was too busy." An attitude problem can also be masked as a training problem when a person with education and experience appropriate to a specific activity replies, "I don't know how," when asked to perform that activity.

Management literature addresses attitude problems under the topic of motivation. Maslow (1943) describes motivation as an unmet need. Maslow arranged such needs into a five-level hierarchy, explaining that lower-level needs must be met before a person is motivated by higher-level needs.

The theory is exemplified by the "Challenge: New Graduates . . . Descending and Climbing Back Up the Hierarchy." (Walker, 1982).

> Moments of great change in our lives produce the vague underlying anxiety from fear of the unknown. During this unrest each of us welcomes the support offered to us by understanding others. The support may not provide total comfort, but even a lesser discomfort is welcomed during this time of unrest as we struggle to meet our needs.
>
> New graduates are certainly plunged into this state of unrest during their transition from student nurse to professional Registered Nurse. Many new stimuli bombard the new graduate—new faces, new places, new paces. Although the challenge may be welcome, the plunge into so much newness at once may temporarily drop one to a basic level on the needs hierarchy (Maslow, 1943). In order to smooth the transition from student to professional, we offer help to the new graduate in meeting some needs on each level.
>
> On the basic physiological level—food, shelter, and clothing needs— we have arranged for temporary housing for the relocated, new graduate coming to Stanford. On level two, safety and security, we assist the nurse in maintaining safe practice through orientation and an extensive preceptorship program. In terms of financial security, Stanford nurses are not only some of the best paid in the country but also receive excellent health, dental, and retirement programs.
>
> To help the new graduate meet the first of the upper-level needs, the social need, a Newcomers Club now meets regularly. Newcomers offers

an opportunity to get acquainted with other recent graduates, meet new Stanford colleagues, and learn about the community.

Our recent graduates satisfy self-esteem needs (level four) as they move through a clearly defined clinical ladder with regular feedback and help. Opportunities to meet self-actualization needs (level five) are readily available in this environment, which is laden with opportunities for self-fulfillment and growth.

Although we traverse up and down the hierarchy throughout life—indeed throughout the day—the understanding and support of others help in the great unrest of major change. We continue to strive to ease the new graduate's climb from the unrest of career beginnings toward excellence and fulfillment in nursing practice. (pp. 1–6)*

This example illustrates the programs and resources offered by Stanford nursing management to meet the new graduate's predictable needs. The hierarchical order addresses basic needs first. The order is essential to success in management's motivation of the new graduate because, in fact, no one can motivate someone else. You can only become aware of a need and offer ways to meet that need; that is motivation.

Herzberg (1966) carries Maslow's theory one step further by combining the five levels into two basic categories—primary and secondary. Primary needs, also called hygiene factors, include physiological and safety/security needs. Secondary needs, also called satisfiers, include social, self-esteem, and self-actualization needs. According to Herzberg, meeting your employees' primary needs will not motivate them; however, these needs must be met before you can address higher-level needs that will motivate employees. A poor benefits program leaving employees without the security of health insurance or life insurance is an example. This primary need is not a potential motivator, but it is a strong dissatisfier. If you meet this need, the dissatisfier is removed, but that only brings the employee up to neutral. Neutral is the best you can do with primary needs. You cannot satisfy an employee by increasing the amount of a hygiene factor; you can only remove the dissatisfier by meeting the need. For example, if employees have sufficient health insurance to meet their security needs, they will not be motivated by more health insurance.

## JOB SATISFACTION

After removing dissatisfiers or meeting primary needs, the manager must offer opportunities to employees to meet secondary needs. These are the needs that

---

*Source: Reprinted with permission from "Challenge: New graduates . . . descending and climbing back up the hierarchy." *Stanford Nurse,* formerly *Nursing at Stanford,* 1982, *4*(4), pp. 1, 6.

determine the employees' level of job satisfaction. Herzberg's studies (1966) revealed five factors that stand out as strong indicators of job satisfaction: achievement, recognition for achievement, the work itself, responsibility, and advancement.

Some of your staff will be easier to motivate than others. They make their motivating needs known and help find opportunities to meet those needs—for example, a new graduate nurse who needs practice catheterizing. When she hears of a patient needing this, she offers to do it, finding an experienced nurse to help her. She thrives on learning and growing.

Another nurse might be quite adept at patient care for your unit's patients, but is learning and growing by giving in-services to newer nurses and by serving on nursing/dietary committees to contribute to the larger organization. Perhaps you have a nurse who does an average job but contributes to the nursing profession through writing for professional journals. These nurses are all finding job satisfaction and are also a source of job satisfaction for you.

Some staff members, however, are more difficult to motivate. You may have a nurse who complains frequently and totally resists change, saying, "We've always done it this way, and it's worked just fine." Motivation of such nurses will require much more effort on your part. You need to find out what will "turn these people on." How can you get them involved? Hackman and colleagues (1979) identified three things that matter to workers: meaningful work, responsibility for outcomes of their efforts, and knowledge of results. They reviewed recent research related to job enrichment and summarized core characteristics of jobs that fulfill the three criteria of "what matters." These fulfilling jobs included skill variety, task identity, task significance, autonomy, and feedback. Primary nursing enhances all these characteristics in nursing. Other ways to increase your staff's opportunity to experience these job enrichers include:

- teaching and managing tasks for enhancing skill variety
- peer input into performance appraisal and unit system evaluations for enhancing feedback
- project and committee work to enhance autonomous task-related enrichers

You probably have some less autonomous staff who are very needy and require much positive feedback, or "stroking," from you. You may be fortunate enough to have some staff who are self-motivated and who seem to exude motivation. Such staff members spread positive feedback, peer support, and a friendly collegial spirit around the unit, raising nearly everyone's level of job satisfaction, including your own.

You probably have a "gut" reading on the job satisfaction level on your unit. You need to test that reading. Many tools are available to assess your staff's level of job satisfaction—from very simple, informal methods to more complex organizational climate models. You can get a good idea of your staff's satisfaction by asking two questions four times a year at staff meetings. "What makes you happy at work?" will elicit their satisfiers. "What annoys you at work?" or "What makes your job difficult?" will elicit dissatisfiers. Together you can explore ways to increase satisfiers and decrease dissatisfiers.

Other tools used to gather job satisfaction information include quality circles, formal surveys, organizational climate questionnaires, and organizational development (OD) techniques. Often these types of assessments are done through an entire organization simultaneously to identify trends and issues. However, the basic principle is the same on any scale. To understand better the satisfaction level of employees, simply ask them. The main difference between the various tools already mentioned is the method of asking. Quality circles consist of people gathering from various organizational levels to identify and solve problems. Proponents of this method believe people share more information verbally. Formal surveys and organizational climate questionnaires offer anonymity, which some believe increases open, honest sharing. Organizational development (OD) techniques are the latest fad in exploring job satisfaction. These various techniques include the survey and the interview. OD is a system through which many aspects of an organization's functioning, not only job satisfaction, may be explored.

Whether using a complex, organization-wide system or a simple suggestion box, you need to act on the information gathered. Pasmore (1979) uses a method called Data Feedback Change Strategy, an OD technique, to identify and correct job dissatisfaction. He arranges six steps in a vertical flowchart, moving slightly from left to right in a waterfall pattern. The process is as follows:

1. *Surveys and interviews are conducted.* You can use any of the methods already described to collect these data.
2. *Data are fed back to employees.* This is best accomplished at a meeting. You may want to get the raw data out ahead of time to allow time for thought. An all-day retreat away from the hospital is ideal. If you do an all-day retreat, step 1 can also be done in a verbal brainstorming format, and steps 1, 2, and 3 can be combined.
3. *Problems are discussed.* The format used in Chapter 8 for problem solving provides a useful format here. You will not be able to solve all problems but may be able to lessen many dissatisfiers. For a long list of problems, set priorities on the ones to solve first. You can use the Delphi Technique (see Activity 3:9, Chapter 3) to set priorities on items by groups. A facilitator is a welcome addition so that you can be free to participate.
4. *Changes are initiated.* The change process is discussed in Chapter 8. Change requires planning, time, and unfreezing to avoid reverting to a

former state. Planning change with your staff increases their "buying in" and decreases the need for "policing" to maintain change.

5. *Attitudes improve.* Morale, the enigma that defies measuring, is defined by Webster as "the moral or verbal condition with respect to cheerfulness, confidence and zeal." Simple asking (step 1) often raises morale through your overt concern. Participatory problem solving and collaborative change initiation also improve morale.

6. *Performance improves.* Although it is difficult to show a direct relationship between increased morale and improved performance, a study by Pasmore and King (1978) indicates that turning people on to work requires their involvement, changes in the work itself, and the creation of supportive immediate work contexts.

This flowchart offers you a method not only to reduce performance discrepancies but also to improve morale and render attitude problems more manageable so that you, as the manager, can identify and implement needed changes in the unit work and create a supportive environment for your staff.

Consider the following example of the waterfall process at work after a need was identified in an emergency department nursing staff survey. When employees were asked to identify several dissatisfiers in their jobs, one need predominated: a nice place to go for breaks to get relief from the department's chaos and stress. This information was fed back to employees. The availability of some space but no budget allotment emerged from the subsequent problem-solving session. The need was significant enough to the staff that they decided to do the work if the hospital supplied the cost of materials. Together, the staff painted and decorated a dull room into a cheery escape. The team spirit was contagious for other unit work, and the stress breaks seemed to improve the energy level for performance.

Any survey should question whether both primary and secondary employee needs are being met. Some of the needs not being met can then be reviewed with the staff in a meeting (as described above). Together the staff can problem solve and plan change to improve attitudes and performance. Some problems, however, may be beyond the control of your unit and not appropriate for unit-based problem solving. These problems need to go up the line to your supervisor. If they are ignored, problems can arise; unions are often fueled by unresolved issues.

Some dissatisfiers to work on with your staff include getting out of work on time, implementing a method of performance appraisal that is perceived as fair and useful, providing unit-based in-services on new products, opening lines of communication with other departments when ongoing problems exist, some environmental changes, and encouraging positive feedback. Some needs must be handled on a higher level. They include a poor benefits package (health insurance, vacation, and sick days), staffing shortages, safety infringements, overtime pay, and capital budget item needs.

## YOUR ROLE AS A COACH

Your job as a manager is to get work done through others. We have examined the following functions: delegating based on task-relevant maturity; determining the most effective leadership style for a task; dealing with discrepancies between delegated activities and performance based on attitude, organization, and training problems; and assessing job satisfaction from feedback. One further element of your management function in relation to your staff is to direct. Although implicit in all of the above, it deserves specific attention here. This is your role as a coach.

In *Games Mother Never Taught You*, Harrigan (1977) defines the coach as the ultimate authority and motivator. The coach has the power to evaluate skills, assign positions, and decide who plays in the first line up, who gets benched, and who is substituted. She says the coach's job traditionally is to "build fearless, aggressive, unflinching, courageous, unstoppable, unemotional, single-minded robots programmed to synchronize their efforts to win the game." Although Harrigan considered use of the word "coach" to be a fad in management, the term has endured. Currently, coaching carries a less harsh connotation in management development. (1977, pp. 75, 108).

Fournies (1978) reduces coaching to a formula through a performance analysis that elicits desired performance from an employee. The formula,

$A = \dfrac{(P + T) M}{E} = R$ looks formidable at first, but it is easily related to the

factors covered earlier regarding performance and performance discrepancies. The abilities, $A$, go into the formula. The results, $R$, come out of the formula. A person's abilities, $A$, are the raw materials used to produce some product or result. Similar to the systems framework in the previous chapter, the abilities represent input, and the results of that person's performance represent output. Again, the

place for you to focus is on throughput. Throughput is $\dfrac{(P + T) M}{E}$. This means

performance, $P$, plus telling, $T$, times motivation, $M$, divided by external influences, $E$, will produce some result given some ability. In other words, motivation greatly enhances a person's job effectiveness and his or her use of training. Results can be greatly decreased by external influences, $E$, such as obstacles to performance and lack of support.

Although Fournies (1978) approaches coaching primarily as a one-to-one process for solving a problem, the process is useful in directing a staff member to grow and achieve more. The framework can be used to guide a subordinate to greater job fulfillment and personal development. The steps below have been adapted from Fournies for both one-to-one problem solving and one-to-one goal setting.

1. Get agreement that a problem exists or that developmental goals need to be set. The latter is easier in an organization that uses MBO (see Chapter 4).

You should begin coaching on a problem as soon after you become aware of its existence as you can set an appointment with the staff member involved. You should begin goal setting in your employee's performance appraisal. The content of the goal often comes out of a problem or weakness or need identified in a performance appraisal.

2. Discuss alternative solutions or goals. These should be acceptable to both of you and should achieve the desired result. Both alternative solutions or goal statements must be behaviorally measurable.

3. Mutually agree on the action to be taken to solve the problem or reach the goal. Set a reasonable time frame with incremental, measurable progress checks.

4. Follow up to ensure that the agreed-upon action has been taken. Offer support when needed. Renegotiate what turns out to be unrealistic goals or solutions or time frames.

5. Recognize any achievement. The positive feedback you offer for achieved interim goals will reinforce and help maintain behavior, morale, and self-esteem.

6. Evaluate. Do not forget to assess the situation at the end of the time frame and evaluate with your employee what worked and what did not work. Set new goals as needed.

As your primary resource, the staff are essential to your unit's productivity. Although all of these mechanisms (surveys, coaching, and training) require much time and effort on your part, staff care will yield great returns. Together with your staff, you can create a unit that works in harmony to provide excellence in patient care.

Reviewing the main topics of the book, we have addressed your role transition, communication and leadership skills, goals, plans, and unit activities, along with persons performing those activities. Chapter 7, "Controlling," looks at how you are doing in all those areas. Through evaluative processes, you can determine how well you are achieving your goals. You can also determine how to maintain quality or how to change your systems and/or management style for better management in a dynamic environment.

# Activity 6:1

# Interviewing To Hire Staff

- Decide which type of interview you would like to use when hiring staff:

  ☐ panel of several staff nurses

  ☐ head nurse interview

  ☐ other _____

- Develop standard interviewing guide of information and questions to ask during the hiring interview of registered nurses.

  *Give information about:*

  _____ the job that is open
  _____ brief background on the organization
  _____ the salary range
  _____ the expectations (include shift work, overtime, etc.)
  _____ the orientation

  *Ask questions about:*

  _____ educational preparation
  _____ work experience (where, specialty, length of time, description)
  _____ philosophy of nursing
  _____ strengths
  _____ growth areas
  _____ why he/she choose this unit
  _____ expected salary
  _____ other interests and activities

- Answer any of interviewee's questions
- End on a positive note
- Be polite and friendly throughout
- Follow up with a letter

# Understanding Disciplinary Actions and Grievance Procedures

**Part I.** Disciplinary Action

For managers having problems with employees, the sequence of disciplinary actions, from verbal warnings to suspension, is clearly defined in a Disciplinary Action Procedure.

- Obtain and read a copy of your hospital's Disciplinary Action Procedure from Personnel. (If you have more than one union, or part union and part non-union, you may have more than one procedure.)
- Write the steps you would take for an employee who failed to show up for work. Write down any assumptions you make about the employee or the situation.

_____

_____

_____

_____

_____

**Part II.** Grievance Procedure

For employees who feel they have been unfairly treated, a Grievance Procedure defines the steps they must follow.

- Obtain and read a copy of your hospital's Grievance Procedure.
- Write the steps an employee would take who was upset about his or her performance appraisal. Write down the actions you would take as the person against whom the grievance was directed.

_____

_____

_____

_____

_____

**Activity 6:2** continued

**Part III.** Follow-up

- Meet with your boss and review the above actions.
- Make a contact in the personnel department who you can call with questions about disciplinary actions and grievance procedures.

Name _____ Telephone Extension _____

# Nursing Unit Climate Survey

- Have your staff complete the form below anonymously.
- Analyze the survey results with your boss.
- Feed back the results at a team-building meeting.
- Choose two variables where the left and right columns differ greatly, and develop a plan with your staff to improve each.

| On a scale of 1 to 10, rate your unit on each variable: | Unit Variables | On a scale of 1 to 10, rate the way you would like your unit to be: |
|---|---|---|
| | working together | |
| | problem solving | |
| | patient teaching | |
| | sharing responsibility | |
| | clinical skills | |
| | professional attitudes | |
| | sharing ideas | |
| | fairness | |
| | organizational clarity | |
| | support for each other | |
| | leadership | |
| | recognition for a good job | |
| | support for new graduates | |
| | team spirit | |
| | consistency | |

## Activity 6:4

# Coaching To Meet Individual Developmental Needs

You have a unit clerk who is abrupt on the telephone. You schedule a coaching session with her.

- Role play the coaching session with a peer using Fournies's (1978) six-step coaching model. (Plan your strategies first using format below.) Seek feedback from your peer on how he or she felt and on what would have helped make the session more productive.

1. Get agreement that a problem exists.

   _____

   _____

2. Discuss alternative solutions or goals.

   _____

   _____

3. Agree on problem-solving action.

   _____

   _____

4. Follow up to be sure action was taken.

   _____

   _____

5. Recognize any achievement toward the goal.

   _____

   _____

6. Evaluate and set new goals if needed.

   _____

   _____

## Activity 6:5

# Knowing Your Personnel Limits

Federal laws (E.E.O.C., for example) and state laws are reflected in your personnel policies and union contract.

- Obtain a copy of your personnel policy manual. Read the table of contents, and skim the manual, developing a list of 20 questions to ask personnel experts. Include federal, state, and state board regulations.

1. Question _____
   Answer _____
2. Question _____
   Answer _____
3. Question _____
   Answer _____
4. Question _____
   Answer _____
5. Question _____
   Answer _____
6. Question _____
   Answer _____
7. Question _____
   Answer _____
8. Question _____
   Answer _____
9. Question _____
   Answer _____
10. Question _____
    Answer _____
11. Question _____
    Answer _____
12. Question _____
    Answer _____
13. Question _____
    Answer _____
14. Question _____
    Answer _____

**Activity 6:5** continued

15. Question _____
    Answer _____
16. Question _____
    Answer _____
17. Question _____
    Answer _____
18. Question _____
    Answer _____
19. Question _____
    Answer _____
20. Question _____
    Answer _____

- Meet with your personnel contact, and find out the answers to above questions. Also, ask that person what the most common mistakes made by new managers are; list them below:

_____
_____
_____
_____
_____
_____

## Activity 6:6

# Assessing Your Staff's Level of Job Satisfaction

- Many sophisticated tools exist to measure job satisfaction. One simple but very effective method is to ask your staff at a meeting the two questions below. Put answers on a flipchart for all to see.

FLIPCHART SAMPLE

* What satisfies you?

* What dissatisfies (frustrates) you?

This process replaces steps 1 and 2 of Pasmore's Data Feedback Change Strategy.

- Using the information on the flipcharts, do steps 3 and 4:
  discuss problems, initiate changes. _____
  _____

- Check back with staff at a later meeting to measure their perception of improved attitudes and improved performance—steps 5 and 6.
  _____
  _____
  _____
  _____

# Activity 6:7

# Assessing Education and Training Opportunities for Staff Members

Ganong and Ganong (1980) divide the educational functions into two responsibility categories, the patient unit and the staff development department. The latter is also known as in-service, educational services, human resources, or education and training.

## Part I

Using their chart below as a guide, interview the head of your hospital-wide or of nursing department's staff development. Circle all the functions done by his or her department (mostly in left column). Cross out any functions not done in your hospital. Write the names of other departments who perform any of these functions. Star any functions expected of you (mostly in right column).

Also ask about the reporting system of the staff development department and any educational benefits offered (e.g., tuition reimbursement, in-house courses, speakers, consultants).

| *Staff Development Department* | *Patient Unit* |
| --- | --- |
| 1   For Orientation | |
| • To the agency and nursing department and the overall organizational structure, philosophy, goals, objectives, policies, and rules. | • To the unit and its specific organizational philosophy, goals, objectives, policies, and rules. |
| • To the layout of physical facility. | • To patients, records, reports. |
| • To the nursing department's patient care program. | • To unit personnel, staffing, patient assignments, unit meetings and conferences, performance responsibilities, and performance evaluation plan. |
| • To agency and nursing department systems and techniques. | • To the unit's physical layout details. |
| | • To the unit's patient care program. |
| | • To the unit's application of systems and techniques. |

*Source:* Reprinted from *Nursing Management.* 2nd ed., by J.M. Ganong and W.L. Ganong, with permission of Aspen Systems Corporation, © 1980.

**Activity 6:7** continued

2. For In-service
   - Plan, organize, coordinate, implement, and evaluate.
   - Agency and department-wide in-service programs—such as CPR, fire and safety, disaster, new procedures, systems, and techniques.
   - Clinical conferences of broad interest to the department.
   - Assist unit nurse managers as needed and requested in unit-level in-service programs.
   - Collaborate with other agency departments in programs as appropriate.
   - On-the-job training for agency and department-wide procedures and tasks.
   - Knowledge and skill sessions specific to a unit.
   - Problem-solving clinics.
   - Clinical conference specific to a unit.
   - On-the-job training for new procedures and tasks specific to unit.

3. For Continuing Education
   - Plan, organize, coordinate, implement, and evaluate residency program for newly graduated nurses.
   - Clinical specialty development programs.
   - Nurse manager development program.
   - Nurse educator programs.
   - Assist with clinical experience aspects of residency program for the newly graduated nurse.
   - Support and reinforce on the unit new learnings of self and staff for each of the programs conducted by others for unit personnel.

4. For Patient Education
   - Help update staff on current patient teaching principles and techniques.
   - Provide resources for nursing staff and unit personnel.
   - Offer direct bedside teaching.
   - Support patient learning sessions as part of nursing care plan.

**Activity 6:7** continued

**Part II**

At a staff meeting, ask for inservice topics of interest or need. (Repeat every six months.)

date _____

topics _____

_____

_____

plans _____

_____

_____

Information from Interview:

_____

_____

_____

_____

_____

_____

**Part III**

Post a calendar with planned inservices. Include speakers, topics, dates, times, and places. Also include nonunit educational programs. Update as programs are added.

☐ Calendar discussed at staff meeting

☐ Calendar posted

## CASE STUDY

A staff nurse who has been at your hospital for two years takes great pride in being a unit role model and in teaching others. She writes comprehensive nursing notes stating patient care in a clear format that includes subjective data, objective data, assessment, and a plan (S.O.A.P.). Her clinical assessments of patients' situations are very accurate. Patients comment about her concern and interest in them.

Although skilled at patient care and charting, she is often one to two hours overtime doing her charting. Other care givers report that her patients' rooms are often untidy. She has difficulty setting priorities and often starts two things at the same time.

You would like her to be a preceptor for a new graduate because of her excellent clinical skills, but she would be a poor role model for organizational skills and time management.

What do you do?

## SOLUTION TO CASE STUDY

Meet with your staff nurse and use Fournies's (1978) six-step coaching guide. Before step 1 give positive feedback about clinical skills and excellent patient care.

1. Get agreement that a problem exists. This is usually simple, but in case of denial, be prepared with anecdotes and overtime documentation.
2. Discuss alternative solutions or goals. Have some ideas ready, but hold off. The nurse's own ideas will receive more commitment than yours. Two alternatives include a time management course or mentoring to learn organizing skills by critique with a written plan preshift and feedback/discussion postshift.
3. Mutually agree on an action and time frame. Be realistic about the time frame. Be sure goals are behaviorally measurable.
4. Follow up to ensure action is taken. Schedule a follow-up meeting during this coaching session. Offer assistance in the interim.
5. Recognize achievement. If the goals are complex or long range, break them into smaller subgoals (tasks). Give positive feedback for each subgoal accomplished.
6. Evaluate and set new goals as needed. When the goals are reached, set new goals if needed to help this nurse move into a competent preceptor role.

## REFERENCES

Fournies, F.F. *Coaching for improved work performance*. New York: Van Nostrand Reinhold, 1978.

Ganong, J.M., & Ganong, W.L. *Nursing management* (2nd ed.). Rockville, Md.: Aspen Systems, 1980.

Hackman, J.R., Oldham, G., Janson, R., & Purdy, K. A new strategy for job enrichment. *California Management Review*, 1979, *27*(4), 57–71.

Harrigan, B.L. *Games Mother never taught you: Corporate gamesmanship for women*. New York: Warner, 1977.

Hersey, P., & Blanchard, K.H. *Management of organizational behavior: Utilizing human resources*. Englewood Cliffs, N.J.: Prentice-Hall, 1977.

Herzberg, F. *Work and the nature of man*. New York: World Publishing, 1966.

Mager, R.F., & Pipe, P. *Analyzing performance problems or "You Really Oughta Wanta."* Belmont, Calif.: Fearon Publishers, 1970.

Maslow, A.H. A theory of human motivation. *Psychological Review*, 1943, *50*, 370–396.

Pasmore, W.A. Turning people on to work. In D.A. Kolb, I.M. Rubin, and J.M. McIntyre (Eds.), *Organizational psychology* (3rd ed.). Englewood Cliffs, N.J.: Prentice-Hall, 1979.

Pasmore, W., & King, D. Understanding organizational change: A comparative study of multi-faceted interventions. *Journal of Applied Behavioral Sciences*, 1978, *14*, 455–468.

Stevens, B.J. *The nurse as executive*. Wakefield, Mass.: Nursing Resources, 1980.

Walker, D.D. Challenge: New graduates . . . descending and climbing back up the hierarchy. *Nursing at Stanford*, 1982, *4*(4), 1, 6.

# Chapter 7

# Controlling

## OBJECTIVES

Upon completion of this chapter, including the activities, the new nurse manager will be able to:

- maintain and improve performance on the unit using a three-step process
- identify unit standards, including job descriptions, individual goals, union contract clauses, personnel policies, federal and state laws, clinical policies and procedures, and American Nurses' Association standards
- monitor personnel performance in relation to identified standards
- develop plans for change where unit norms and unit standards differ
- explain and monitor unit compliance with the Joint Commission for Accreditation of Hospitals (JCAH)
- assess unit environmental control
- develop a tool to assess patient satisfaction
- assess the climate on your nursing unit
- explain revenue and expenses of your unit budget, including materials and manpower aspects
- explain the capital budget process of your hospital
- set up a system to monitor unit-based, quality assurance problem solving
- identify and explain sources of power in the head nurse role

# DEVELOPMENT OF THE NEW NURSE MANAGER™
1981

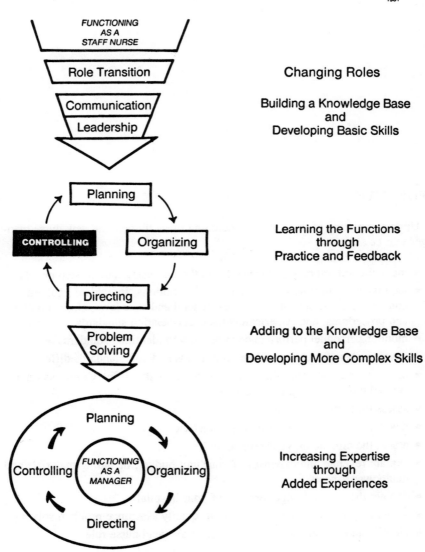

FUNCTIONING
AS A
STAFF NURSE

Role Transition

Communication

Leadership

Changing Roles

Building a Knowledge Base
and
Developing Basic Skills

Planning

CONTROLLING

Organizing

Directing

Learning the Functions
through
Practice and Feedback

Problem
Solving

Adding to the Knowledge Base
and
Developing More Complex Skills

Planning

Controlling

FUNCTIONING
AS A
MANAGER

Organizing

Directing

Increasing Expertise
through
Added Experiences

¶ *Control* is a word that has lost popularity since the advent of the human relations movement. Because old-fashioned, authoritarian management systems often abused the notion of control, the pendulum has gone to the other extreme— negating the notion of control and often equating the concept with the currently humanistic taboo—manipulation.

Yet your job as a head nurse demands that you have control of your unit. This is not manipulation, but control in the sense that Webster defines as "power or authority to guide or manage." This authority is essential to all your other responsibilities as a head nurse. The authority to control your unit comes from the legitimate power of your position as a head nurse. This power is known as *positional power*.

Levenstein (1978) says, "At the heart of management lies this concept of control." He goes on to say that routine is desirable and rules are essential. Head nurses are expected to see that their units conform to the rules and routines of the organization. "A hospital that does not have general rules governing a thousand and one detailed tasks would collapse into a state of incoherence and disorganization. People would not know what is expected of them and how they can coordinate their functions with those of others" (Levenstein, 1978, p. 25).

You are responsible for two basic types of control on your unit—quality control and cost control. Quality control refers mainly to compliance with standards. Cost control refers to economic use of resources—both human and material resources. In other words, how do your staff's performance and productivity measure up when compared to the standards of the organization? What is the cost of your unit's performance? You can measure, maintain, and improve performance and productivity on your unit using these three steps:

1. Identify what the organization's standards are for quality and for cost.
2. Compare the quality of performance and the total costs for your unit to the standards to determine any discrepancies.
3. Plan for change, if needed.

This chapter will help you identify the standards in your organization and offers useful methods to assess the status quo on your unit. Then you can compare that reality to your organizational standards. If you find any discrepancies between what is happening on your unit and the organizational standards, you need to decide whether the discrepancy is a problem. We look at examples of when a discrepancy is a problem and when it is not. Then we examine ideas for lessening undesired discrepancies so that your unit will meet the organizational standards for which you are responsible.

## QUALITY CONTROL

"Quality assurance is one of the major issues facing the health-care industry . . . its central goal is making certain that care practices will produce good patient outcomes" (Mayers, Norby, & Watson, 1977, p. 3). As front-line manager, you are the primary person responsible for making certain this happens. It will not happen by chance. "It is the result of deliberate decision making and action . . . based upon information obtained through evaluation" (Mayers et al., 1977, p. 3). Weiss (1972) calls *evaluation* "an elastic word that stretches to cover judgments of many kinds" (p. 1). Weiss's main point is that evaluation is "the notion of judging merit. Someone is examining and weighing a phenomenon (a person, a thing, an idea) against some explicit or implicit yardstick" (Weiss, 1972, p. 1). The "someone" who needs to examine the quality of nursing care on the unit is you. The "phenomena" you will weigh are staff performance, unit activities, and patient care costs. The "yardsticks" you will use are called standards; they are many and varied. Using the three steps described above will help you to weed through a very complex system to make certain that care practices on your unit produce quality care at standard costs.

### Step One: Identify the Standards

*Job Description*

Max Weber, "the father of modern bureaucracy," recognized the need for rules or administrative regulations to guide "modern officialdom" as early as 1946 in his essay "Bureaucracy." In this essay, Weber (1978) identified the three characteristics of a bureaucracy. These characteristics provide the framework for today's organizational standards, especially job descriptions.

The essense of what Weber said was this: First, the purposes of an organization are carried out through regular activities, and these need to be divided into official duties. In your organization, you will find the purposes translated into tasks. These tasks then become the responsibilities of various persons in your organization and are delineated in various job descriptions.

Second, the "authority to give the commands required for the discharge of these duties" exists in today's job descriptions as "reports to" or "is responsible for," or under such euphemisms as "relationships with superordinates and subordinates." It is important for every job description to state clearly to whom the persons in that job will report and who will report to them.

Third, Weber (1978) states, "Methodical provision is made for the regular and continuous fulfillment of these duties." This means you need to hire, fire, and recruit as necessary. He also advocates "execution of corresponding rights," usually stated today as benefits, personnel policies, and negotiated rights as stated in a union contract. Weber continues, "Only persons who have the generally regulated qualifications to serve are employed.'' Today's job descriptions usually state qualifications in terms of education, experience, and licensure requirements.

Therefore, a job description, essential for each type of position classification, must contain the functions, responsibilities, and specific qualifications for the job. The job description is the standard providing the criteria against which your staff will be measured for their performance appraisals. Having job descriptions with the above elements and using them to measure your staff's performance are requirements of the Joint Commission for Accreditation of Hospitals (1980).

In some organizations, detailed job descriptions have been developed. The clinical ladder is an example of a detailed task delineation in a staff nurse job description. The clinical ladder includes all three characteristics of a job description but provides particular details for the task. The tasks, stated in behavioral terms, are presented in three or four levels of increasing complexity. All of the level 1 tasks (easiest) become the standards for a staff nurse one. Level 2 tasks (in addition to level 1 tasks) form the standards for a level two nurse, and so on. Although tedious in developing and monitoring, this system provides clearer standards for the evaluation and growth of a staff nurse.

An example of a staff nurse's standard in a typical job description is ''to plan, coordinate, and supervise patient care.'' However, a similar standard in a clinical ladder format might expand the plan section to much greater depth (see Exhibit 7–1).

The clinical ladder certainly provides a clearer delineation of the task, and both the staff nurse and the head nurse have clearer expectations of what the nurse is expected to do. Neither task definition addresses quality, but the clinical ladder delineates more objectively the details of the task.

The delineation of responsibility is another job description section that is sometimes detailed. This became popular in the early 1980s as ''matrixing.'' The word *matrix* is used in this context to mean that someone reports to two bosses. This occurred in high technology industries because specific product line managers and traditional departmental managers both supervised one technical/professional.

For example, a manager of the calculator product line might have an engineer and a finance person report to her. However, the engineer would also report to the engineering department manager and the finance person, to the finance department head. This format requires detailed functions and responsibilities and detailed authority codes for each function where there may be a dual responsibility.

The process of clarifying who reports to whom on each behavioral function involves much time and work if all concerned are involved in deciding. If only a few develop these reporting lines, decision time is less, but the compliance and/or satisfaction will probably diminish. As quickly as matrixing came in, just that quickly it is disappearing. Reporting to two bosses is costly, inefficient, and often frustrating for the employee.

**Exhibit 7–1** Staff Nurse's Job Description in Clinical Ladder

| Level I<br>*Develops a Written Plan of Care Using Assessment Data Base* | Level II<br>*Develops a Written Plan of Care Using Assessment Data Base* | Level III<br>*Develops a Written Plan of Care Using Assessment Data Base* | Level IV<br>*Develops a Written Plan of Care Using Assessment Data Base* |
|---|---|---|---|
| 1. Documents overt patient problems requiring intervention, including teaching needs and discharge planning. | 1. Documents overt and covert patient problems requiring intervention, including teaching needs and discharge planning. | 1. Documents overt, covert, and potential patient problems requiring intervention, including teaching needs and discharge planning. | 1. Documents overt, covert, and potential patient problems requiring intervention, including teaching needs and discharge planning. |
| 2. Contributes to a plan of nursing action based on existing problems, expected patient response, and the medical plan of care. | 2. Develops and contributes to a plan of nursing action based on existing patient problems and obtainable responses. Incorporates the medical plan of care. | 2. Develops and contributes to a plan of nursing action based on existing and potential patient problems and obtainable patient responses. Incorporates the medical plan of care. Utilizes past experiences to provide a range of options for nursing actions. | 2. Develops and contributes to a plan of nursing action based on existing and potential patient problems and obtainable patient responses. Incorporates the medical plan of care. Utilizes past experiences to provide a range of options for nursing actions. |
| 3. Utilizes resources (patient, family, nurses, and written material) to contribute to the written plan of care. | 3. Utilizes resources (patient, family, nurses, physicians, and written materials) to formulate a written plan of care. | 3. Utilizes resources (patient, family, nurses, physicians, other health team members, and written material) to formulate a written plan of care. | 3. Utilizes resources (patient, family, nurses, physicians, other health team members, and written material) to formulate a written plan of care. Seeks out new resources when needed. |

4. Communicates the plan of care by using methods that include action plans, goals, and time frames. Gives shift report according to unit guidelines.

4. Communicates the plan of care by using methods that include action plans, goals, and time frames. Gives shift report according to unit guidelines.

4. Communicates the plan of care by using methods that include action plans, goals, and time frames. Gives shift report according to unit guidelines.

*Source:* Reprinted with permission of Duane D. Walker, R.N., M.S., F.A.A.N., Associate Administrator/Director of Nursing, Stanford University Hospital, Department of Nursing, Stanford, California.

Two positive outcomes of this management fad include: team building—when people get together to discuss and clarify reporting systems—and increased recognition of the need for flexibility in today's increasingly complex society.

The third characteristic of a job description, qualifications, may also take on written and unwritten extras in some organizations. Besides requirements, such as having a current nursing license in your state, some job descriptions list what is desirable. This may include such items as one year of prior intensive care experience, a baccalaureate degree, or primary care knowledge. These preferences may be clearly stated in a job description but often exist only in the head of the hiring head nurse.

Two new (actually recycled) qualification processes that are currently popular are "experiential interviewing" and "panel interviews," also called "search and selection." Experiential interviewing actually tests the applicant before or during the interview for the characteristics desired. This has been used in Ivy League school admissions and Fortune 500 companies. Once carried to an extreme, it is now back in a modified form. You might adapt this notion during your hiring interviewing by explaining a particular situation to a nurse and asking what he or she would do. A more elementary form of experiential interviewing some hospitals use is a written test on certain areas of pharmacology in which questions are asked about specific drugs, dosages, methods of administration, and side effects. A passing grade is a prerequisite for employment.

Panel interviews are conducted by several employees who will work with the newly hired person. Sometimes the group develops criteria ahead of time. These written criteria replace hiring preferences in the head nurse's mind. The group may combine some techniques from experiential interviewing. One major benefit of group hiring is the built-in support system for the new hiree. Those who selected that person will want to see the new employee succeed. (Remember this if you were hired this way—it is a good place to start your own support system.) The obvious drawback to this detailed development of qualifications is the time and energy a large number of people invest.

You should, however, spend some time thinking about the qualifications needed on your unit when you hire staff. Be sure to use the same type of interview and questions when interviewing each potential employee in fairness to the candidate and to provide you with better information in making an informed decision when hiring. Be aware of equal employment opportunity laws and avoid asking discriminatory questions related to sex, race, religion, or age. (More about this under federal law standards later in this chapter.)

### Individual Goals

In some organizations, individual sets of standards may exist in the form of employees' goals. These goals may have been written as part of an MBO program (see Chapter 4), at the employee's former performance appraisal, or during a coaching session (see Chapter 6). These negotiated goals, although not relevant for all employees, become standards by which to measure the performance of the individual who agreed to achieve this goal by a specific date.

## Unions

Another source of standards comes from union contracts. Both parties must adhere to the negotiated contract—your staff and you, as part of management. An example of a negotiated clause could be related to weekends off for staff. One specific issue related to this topic is the definition of a weekend by night shift nurses. Some nurses consider Friday/Saturday a weekend; other nurses define the weekend as Saturday/Sunday. To resolve this issue, one union negotiated the following terms: "A weekend is defined as Saturday and Sunday for the day and evening tours of duty. Shifts beginning Friday and Saturday, or Saturday and Sunday as designated in writing by the individual nurse will be considered a weekend for the night tour of duty to the extent extensive scheduling permits. All such designations will remain in effect for a period of six (6) months" (Committee for Recognition of Nursing Achievement [CRONA], 1982, p. 35).

This clause is in a section of the contract called "Weekend Staffing" in which the definition of a weekend needs to be very clear if such issues as every other weekend off are to be negotiated. You need to be very clear about what is in your nurses' contract; you should read it several times a year and be very familiar with its contents.

## Personnel Policies

Policies also provide standards. As a head nurse, you will need to be familiar with the whole body of knowledge unique to your organization—personnel policies. These policies guide such actions as how often you must evaluate your staff; these standards are usually quite specific in an attempt to maintain fairness across departments.

For example, after you hire a new employee, that person is on probation for a set period, perhaps three months. This time is provided to allow you and the new employee to "try each other out." You are responsible for observing this person during probation and for documenting your observations. At the end of the probation time, your personnel policy may state a performance appraisal is due. Another may be due in six months, then annually on the six-month anniversary of hiring. You must be aware of and comply with this standard. You must also be aware of whether and to what extent salary is related to performance appraisals. Personnel policies warrant a good slice of your time as a manager. Be familiar enough with the personnel policy in your hospital that you know what topics are included: Find a knowledgeable contact in the personnel office you can call with questions. Personnel policies are usually based on history of the organization, state or federal laws, accreditation requirements, or union contracts. Your infringement of these policies can have grave consequences.

For example, if you do not follow your disciplinary action procedure to the letter, when an employee takes you to grievance, you may lose the grievance. You may end up having to reinstate an employee you terminated, even though you had "just cause" for firing the person, if you did not follow the procedures.

### Federal Laws

Although you may feel far away from federal laws, they will provide many standards for you in your new management role. Often federal laws are reflected in your personnel policies. You are responsible for staying within these laws.

For example, the Equal Employment Opportunity Commission (E.E.O.C.) prohibits discrimination by employers on the basis of age, nationality, religion, or sex. You are responsible to know this law's implications. To ask a possible night nurse during a hiring interview how she would provide care for her children while she works is sex discrimination. If she brings up the issue, however, you can ask if she sees it as a problem.

### State Laws

State laws come in 50 versions. The laws may be statutory (congressionally made) or case law (judicially made or tested). You are responsible for complying with state laws affecting your organization. Someone from personnel can brief you on these laws.

An example of a state law, taken from California Title 22 #70445, is in relation to Chronic Dialysis Service Staff: "There shall be a registered nurse for the nursing service who has had at least twelve months general nursing experience or six months experience in the care of patients with end stage renal disease." Each specialty unit has specific nursing background requirements. State laws also govern such items as how cold the refrigerator in which you store blood must be.

Within the body of state law, the Board of Registered Nurses offers many guidelines demanding your attention. These laws govern such actions as: Can a newly graduated nurse who has not yet heard the results of state board exams practice as a nurse in the interim? Is a Licensed Vocational Nurse (L.V.N.) allowed to give all types of injections? Are continuing education units (CEUs) mandatory for relicensure? Can foreign nurses practice as registered nurses on a temporary permit? For how long? And what should you do if one of your nurses is suspected of taking narcotics?

Besides state and federal laws, another source of outside control is the Joint Commission for Accreditation of Hospitals (JCAH). Although accreditation by this organization is voluntary, the government will not reimburse Medicare patients in your hospital if it is not JCAH accredited. Because of this tie to reimbursement, JCAH control is real.

An example of a JCAH standard affecting your functioning as a head nurse is Standard VII under *Nursing Services*. Standard VII states: "Written policies and procedures that reflect optional standards of nursing practice shall guide the provision of nursing care" (JCAH, 1980, p. 120). Ten areas are defined by JCAH in which you must have annually updated policies and procedures. For example, it is mandatory to have policies and procedures related to "assignment of nursing care consistent with patient needs as determined by the nursing process" (p. 120). During a site visit by JCAH representatives, you will be evaluated on this point. You, or perhaps a charge nurse you have delegated, may be asked, "How do you make patient assignments?"

JCAH has a variety of standards of which you need to be aware. Besides the section on *Nursing Services*, the *Quality Assurance* section has one standard with definite implications for nursing. "There shall be evidence of a well-defined, organized program designed to enhance patient care through the ongoing objective assessment of important aspects of patient care and the correction of identified problems" (p. 152).

This standard includes: identifying problems related to patient care; prioritizing both the investigation and resolution of patient care problems in relation to adverse impact on patient care; implementing solutions to eliminate problems; monitoring and documenting results. Many hospitals have a hospital-wide committee for quality assurance. However, the retrospective audits (looking at charts after patients are discharged) alone do not meet recently revised JCAH standards. Quality assurance interventions by only doctors or only risk management do not meet standards either. "Each clinical discipline is responsible for identifying and resolving problems related to patient care" (p. 153).

One currently popular method of quality assurance in hospital nursing departments is the concurrent unit-based model. In this model, problems are identified and solved on a unit basis. They are reported upward, to be reviewed by a committee looking for specialty or hospital-wide trends. For example, a unit may do a concurrent (patient still in the hospital) audit to check one specific standard—whether the patient's response to a given pain medication is recorded on the chart. Problem assessment and data collection are done on the unit by staff members who decide to keep a bar graph on the lounge wall. In this case, increased awareness may itself spur the problem's resolution. However, the problem assessment, resolution, monitoring system, and results are documented and reviewed by the department-wide committee for any necessary problem solving on that level.

Unit-based quality assurance programs can also incorporate nursing research. Zalar (1982) lists the major components of hospital quality assurance program goals as:

1. The promotion of ongoing monitoring of patient care.
2. The investigation of barriers to quality patient care.
3. The improvement of patient care through use of the nursing research process and implementation of nursing research findings.

The intimate involvement of nurse clinicians in the study of nursing practice will help to focus research on urgent concerns and will produce findings which have practical application. These nurses are in the best position to identify the problems that most urgently need study, to collect data with the least disruption of patient care, and to implement the worthwhile solutions. (Welches, 1982, pp. 1, 3)

### Clinical Policies

Policies, usually general in nature, state a philosophical perspective and the reason behind that perspective including assumptions. For example, an intensive care policy may read: "Registered nurses may perform defibrillation in an emergency situation" (Stanford Statement of Policy, IC & IIC, 1983, p. 3–01.520). Another hospital might have a policy in direct opposition to this.

### Clinical Procedures

Procedures are more specific and usually give a step-by-step approach to a task. Procedures explain the "how to" of a policy. An example of the procedure for the above policy might be called: "The Procedure for Emergency External Defibrillation, Intensive Care and Intermediate Intensive Care." This procedure could include a diagram of the equipment used, a description of the equipment, a statement of purpose, step-by-step nursing actions and rationales, specifics about charting, and even directions for cleaning and storing equipment (Stanford ICU and IIC, 1982).

### ANA Standards

American Nurses' Association (ANA) Standards for Professional Practice also guide your unit's professional practice. Consider, for example, Standard V from ANA's Standards of Nursing Practice: "Nursing actions provide for client/patient participation in health promotion, maintenance, and restoration" (1974, pp. 11–12). Nurses address this standard by developing useful patient teaching tools to help patients better understand their illness and how to care for themselves in light of their illness to promote a higher level of health. Two such tools include *After Your Heart Surgery* and *Ophthalmology,* published by Stanford nurses who teach the patient using the booklet, then give the publication to the patient for reinforcement after discharge (Stanford Nursing, 1982, 1983).

### Step Two: Compare the Reality or Status Quo on Your Unit with the Standards

How do you look at all these standards related to providing at least minimum required quality on your unit and check your unit for compliance? Many tools are already in place that can provide regular readings of how things are. The most useful monitoring device, however, is informal and relatively simple; it has a high degree of accuracy for identifying at an early stage any problems with standard compliance. This monitoring device is head nurse daily rounds. As your unit's chief monitor, you are responsible to get out there and see what is happening first-hand.

Observe nurses' station activities, stocking of supplies, answering of telephones, and attitudes toward visitors. Observe your staff giving patient care. Talk with patients, visitors, staff, doctors, and other visiting departments such as dietary, housekeeping, and clinical laboratory. Ask them how it is for them to be on this unit, what they like, what they would change, and how they would change it.

After observing—document, document, document. Formal documentation is not usually necessary, but keep notes with names, dates, times, and other specifics. Write both positives and negatives. Get to know what is happening on your unit and how people feel about your unit. What is the climate? Does it change with different staff and on different shifts? What works and what does not work? Be open. Listen without criticism. Use active listening skills (see Chapter 2) to let people know you really do want to know their thoughts, feelings, perceptions, and suggestions about your unit.

If you do this every day you work, in the morning and at other sporadic times around the clock, any other monitoring device mentioned here will be a weak second in terms of the amount of information you receive for the amount of time invested. However, other monitoring devices are essential considering the number and diversity of standards for which you must account. Looking back through the standards above, how might you monitor each on your unit?

*Personnel Monitoring*

You need to know if your staff are performing up to standards. Knowing each staff member in this depth is tedious but necessary work. If you have a large number of staff and have an assistant head nurse, or one for each shift, some of the individuals can be delegated to report primarily to a particular assistant. You must periodically audit the charting and care plans for those persons reporting to you and must keep attendance sheets including sick, tardy, late, and overtime hours. Give your nurses feedback. Use coaching (see Chapter 6), and goal setting (see Chapter 4) techniques. Talk with the patients they care for; again, give feedback.

Keep anecdotal notes on your staff as you observe and coach. Keep a folder on each staff member or a page in your daily calendar for each staff member where you can easily jot down notes documenting behaviors. Rather than keeping notes until an annual performance appraisal, give feedback as needed. Do not forget positive feedback that says "I value you, and I do notice you are doing a great job." Feedback should be specific—"Thank you, Jane, for helping our new graduate nurse change Mrs. Kellog's dressing. Your excellent technique is good modeling for her." As you give this feedback, watch for or listen for the response. Often job satisfaction surveys reveal nurses do not hear positive feedback.

Incident reports also monitor deviations from the norms. These forms state, from a participant's or observer's perspective, something unusual that happened. Your attitude toward incident reports will become clear to staff very quickly. Although you would not like to foster the incidents, you should foster the reporting of incidents. The form should be viewed as documentation of an unusual occurrence from the writer's perspective—a chance to "tell your side." Complete documents are especially important if legal action follows an incident. Two years later details will have been forgotten. Let your staff know that you value timely and complete incident forms. Do not use incident forms for punishment, or you will see few of them and they will have sketchy information. Incident reports need to be evaluated as one-time strange occurrences or as dangerous patterns. They should be used as problem-solving initiators. Selected ones (perhaps patterns, such as an increased number of falls on day shift) could be investigated by a unit-based quality assurance committee for resolution.

How about monitoring all those federal, state, and JCAH requirements? Either you or a unit task force can audit both environmental and clinical requirements related to your unit. Together, identify what is reviewed by JCAH during an accreditation site visit. Also, identify federal and state laws having a direct impact on your unit. Bring in experts from nursing administration, personnel, and your legal department to help. From the gathered information, make up a unit audit in checklist form. Have staff members sign up for turns to audit compliance monthly using the checklist. This will have the added benefit of educating your staff on the standards imposed by external sources. Their participation will increase compliance with the standards.

Another monitoring device that can be structured and formal or informal and random is patient satisfaction surveys. On your rounds you will be interviewing patients about their hospitalization and their care. Although this is a useful method to assess patient satisfaction, you may want to supplement it with an occasional written questionnaire, survey, or interview done by a neutral person (from outside your unit).

In "Patients' Evaluation of Their Care: Why Don't They Complain?" Nehring and Geach (1973) suggested that patients will not give negative feedback if they believe it will be held against them and they might therefore receive lesser care or if they believe they were not sick enough to warrant care by a professional R.N. Be sure to provide an atmosphere conducive to honest feedback, both positive and negative, regardless of your data collection method.

Quality circles is an entire system for problem identification and resolution. Essentially, quality circles bring together employees from all organizational levels who volunteer to be part of this regular meeting circle. The group discusses problems and plans solutions. Although the concept is essentially a fad, its principles, based on participatory management, are sound. You might implement some aspects of the quality circles by having 10 or 20 minutes of your staff meeting to bring up problems. Solutions could be worked on there; or the problems could be referred to your unit-based quality assurance committee; or a task force of volunteers could meet and bring possible solutions to your staff meeting for decision and action. Some problems and suggested solutions can only be referred upward—by you. Even in this situation, however, your staff can help by gathering facts and suggestions so that you go to your boss with supporting data.

### Step Three: Plan for Change If Needed

Is there a discrepancy between the norm and the standard? Do you want to change it? "The purpose of control is to make the process go smoothly, properly, and according to high standards," says Drucker (1974, p. 218). The control system should maintain a process "within a permissible range of deviation with minimum effort." Is the work done on your unit within a permissible range of deviation? Is the effort expended minimal? Are your processes running smoothly and properly? Are your standards high?

We have looked at a variety of tools that measure a unit's functioning against the standards. In order to improve your unit's functioning, assess its current operation through audit and observation. Then compare this unit norm to the standards discussed in Step One. In Chapter 5, tasks were reviewed for fit with other system components. In this chapter, we add the variable of standards.

For each discrepancy, each difference between the reality and the standard, you need to make a judgment about any need for change. For example, you notice an increased number of incident reports on patient falls on your unit. Usually you have one or two; last month there were six. Why is the rate up? Is it acceptable? How can you lower it? Compare the current norm with the standard. Recognize any discrepancy. Decide whether or not change is needed to decrease the discrepancy. Of course, an absence of falls is desirable, but six is an unacceptable increase. Thus, a change is needed. Using the problem-solving techniques, you can work on this problem through your quality assurance committee or a unit task force. Complete failure to act is unacceptable.

You may find a discrepancy and decide that it is acceptable. For example, overtime has increased on your unit during the past two weeks. You realize it was because you had a sudden illness of one staff nurse and another nurse resigned on short notice to deal with an urgent personal matter. This created a staffing problem because yours is a small, very specialized renal dialysis unit, and overtime was the best solution at the time. You have since hired a new dialysis nurse, and your other nurse is back. You have chosen this discrepancy, overtime, as a "lesser of two evils" solution, and no further change is necessary.

If in the above scenario, however, the staff nurse had called in sick on a weekend after requesting and not receiving the weekend off, the need for action might have differed. In reviewing this nurse's attendance record, you find she is only "sick" on weekends and usually on weekends when her request to be off has not been honored. Further action is indicated. You may decide to handle weekend staffing the same way, with overtime. However, a counseling session is in order with this nurse (see Chapter 6).

If you decide the discrepancy between "what is" and "the standard" should not exist, you have two choices of how to bring them closer. The first is to improve the status quo; the second is to lower the standard. Although the latter is not usually desirable, you should consider this an option, especially in this era of increasing awareness of limited resources.

For example, your hospital may use a patient classification system that, considering various factors, predicts the number of staff needed for your next shift. Most evenings it calls for 3.5 registered nurses. If you always staff with 4 nurses, you will be grossly over budget for the year. Therefore, you make a judgment call on some evenings to staff with 3 and possibly to add an extra aide. Other situations in which your desired high standards may need to be compromised include:

- wanting primary nurses to answer all their own patient lights but finding that when they are busy, no one answers these lights with this rule in place
- preferring the intercom not to be used but knowing that on a busy night, timely intercom answering may be safer than long delays in light answering
- wishing all patient lights were answered within five minutes but, after observing and talking with staff and patients, accepting the average of ten minutes as realistic on your ambulatory care unit

We are not suggesting you lower all your standards. However, it is important to consider this a realistic option when standards and realities are not in congruence. Standards imposed by outside sources, such as state and federal laws, JCAH requirements, and union contract clauses, are not yours to change.

The other choice in bringing the reality and standards closer together is to improve the reality. This choice means some problem solving is necessary to plan a strategy that will reduce the discrepancy. The problem solving should involve your staff or your quality assurance committee. Some examples of problems needing solutions to comply with standards might include the following: the psychiatric unit, of which you are head nurse, has increasing numbers of against medical advice (AMA) leaves; you are head nurse on a surgical unit, and you learn that consent forms are not correctly stating the names of the procedures being done; or on your orthopedic unit, the narcotic count has been incorrect three times this week.

These discrepancies between the standards and the realities are typical of problems best solved by group input, with your approval of the final plan (see Chapter 3 for more about level of group participation in group problem solving. Problem solving is discussed in depth in Chapter 8).

The foregoing examples of discrepancies between realities and standards assumed that the realities were lower than the standards. Examples were shown for improving the reality and for lowering the standard. What about when the norm on a unit exceeds a standard? Your first reaction is probably "Great! It's terrific that we're exceeding the standard." While it is usually a positive sign to exceed a standard, there may be situations that should be changed. For example, what if your staff do diabetic patient teaching *so well* that patients leave the hospital knowing extensive pathophysiology, far beyond what is necessary for good self-care? We are not suggesting that holding extremely high standards, working for excellence, is undesirable. On the contrary, both patient compliance and staff satisfaction may rise because of this striving for excellence. However, it must be balanced on the economic principle of "opportunity cost." McConnell (1981) defines the opportunity cost of a good as "the amount of other products which must be forgone or sacrificed to obtain a unit of any given product" (p. 28). In this case, the resultant overtime or below-standard patient teaching of arthritic patients may be the opportunity cost of exceeding the diabetic teaching standard by such great lengths.

You may or may not want to decrease a discrepancy between the reality and the standard. This is especially true if striving for excellence is a job satisfier for your staff that decreases turnover, stress, and "down" time. One such discrepancy that you may decide to tolerate is longer coffee breaks because overall productivity is very high. These breaks seem to keep morale up in the intensive work environment of the burn unit. More positive tolerance of discrepancies is not permissible, of course, in those situations in which standards, such as JCAH requirements, are actually minimum or safe standards and could not actually be considered quality. In such situations, surpassing standards may actually be your goal as a unit standard.

Some tools that help you assess the norms on your unit and compare them to the various standards discussed above are the same tools that you can use to change discrepancies. These tools include performance appraisal, clinical ladder criteria, observations, audits—of patient care and charting (especially concurrently)—quality assurance tools, patient interviews during head nurse rounds, patient satisfaction surveys, incident reports, job satisfaction surveys, and pre-JCAH-visit surveys. Each of these tools is discussed below in relation to identifying discrepancies and planning needed change.

### Performance Appraisal

One of your most important functions as a manager is to develop your staff (see Chapter 6). Performance appraisal is the major process through which each individual receives your intensive attention for his or her development. This is not to say that your staff need coaching only at this one time each year. Coaching should be an ongoing event, so much so that performance appraisals yield no surprises for employees.

Performance appraisals should not include unmeasurable generalities such as attitudes, perceptions, appearance, and personality. "Although it is impossible for an evaluator to be completely objective, by limiting judgments to measurable behaviors, a greater degree of objectivity can be achieved" (del Bueno, 1977, p. 23). You need to review performance as related to preset standards using anecdotal records based on your observations of care given and audits of charting, care plans, and attendance records, as well as peer input from persons both you and the employee select. You need to use good listening and coaching skills and have the ability to solve problems and set goals. Be aware that critical comments usually demoralize staff, shifting the focus of the conference from learning to defending (Blansfield, 1966).

A study conducted at General Electric and reported in *Harvard Business Review* found that anecdotes were usually negative and that positive feedback was often stated in broad general terms. Praise was found to have little effect; criticism was found to have a negative effect and sometimes even produced inferior performance. The study also found that performance improved when specific goals were set, especially mutually set goals, with employee participation. The researchers recommended day-to-day coaching, not just annual appraisals (Meyer, Kay, & French, 1965).

Many forms are available for performance appraisals—from structured, detailed lists of questions with five-level, forced-choice answers to very sketchy guidelines merely mandating annual appraisals. Some hospitals use the same forms for everyone—from summer dietary help to professional registered nurses. Your employees need to be measured on all aspects of their job as stated in their job description, clinical ladder level, individual goals, and other standards related to the unit, the organization, and the profession. The tone should be open and positive, with shortcomings expressed as future goals.

Remember that improvement of job performance and staff development are primary performance appraisal goals. Metzger (1980) offers five methods to reach those goals:

1. Communicate specific standards to employees and gain acceptance of those standards.
2. Measure the employee's performance against the agreed upon standards.
3. Develop with the employee a plan of action to assist the employee in strengthening his or her capabilities.
4. Encourage reactions, facing and resolving differences, and reaching a mutual understanding of the implications of the review.
5. Offer constructive suggestions and tangible assistance toward personal development (p. 47).

It is your job to help your staff maintain standards.

### Dealing with Other Discrepancies

By now it is apparent that discrepancies between standards and realities on your unit are discovered only through a variety of sources. This is because of the complexity of health care. The data sources of discrepancies include quality assurance audits, patient interviews, observations, patient satisfaction surveys or interviews, job satisfaction surveys, and incident reports. Memos from superiors or other departments and letters from patients' families, doctors, and agencies can also bring discrepancies to your attention. You need to review these discrepancies and decide which ones need attention. Then you must decide how much group input is needed if change is desirable (see Chapter 3).

Two other important tools offer data on discrepancies on your unit: patient classification system reports and financial variance reports. They are discussed next.

## COST CONTROL

Many people consider budget as a tool to be used for *planning* rather than *controlling*. In reality, the budget is used for both. Budget is dollars and cents affixed to a plan. Every plan needs a cost consideration to be a valid plan. In evaluating an outcome, budget again plays an important role in serving as a measurement criterion.

As a manager, you are responsible for staying within your projected operating budget, which represents the financial goals for the year. The budget might be considered your unit's financial standard. Control of costs can be measured, maintained, and improved using the same three steps used for control of quality.

### Step One: Identify What the Standards Are in Relation to Cost

To understand money is your job as a nurse manager. And with the early eighties economic slump that resulted from efforts to curb inflation, health care gained the uncoveted reputation of being a great economic inflator—second only to defense. Even with severe economic recession, health care costs continued to climb at rates unequaled in other industries. Because of these increasing costs, government, private insurance companies, private industries that offer health care benefits, and consumers are pressuring hospitals to be more economically responsible, accountable, and competitive.

The finance departments of hospitals have used up most of their "tricks," cutting out the "fluff" in the systems. Cuts now require all levels to be knowledgeable, responsible, accountable, and creative, or hospitals will "go under," as many did in the early eighties.

One method of mandatory cutbacks introduced by the government is the diagnostic related group (D.R.G.) payment. This law states that hospitals will be reimbursed for Medicare patients based on each patient's specific illness (D.R.G.) regardless of the patient's length of stay. As the program expands to other third party payers, hospitals, beginning at the head nurse level, are challenged to be even more cost effective.

Your part in controlling unit finances, both material and human resources, is essential to total financial control in a hospital. As a first-line manager, you are there when disposable pads are wasted, spills are mopped up with linens, charge slips are ignored, and patients occupy hospital beds for hours after discharge orders because they are waiting for medications someone forgot to order.

Before getting into the details of resource management, let us look at the implications of not understanding it. Perhaps you feel that as a nurse you do not want to be bothered learning resource control. If you feel strongly about this, you should rethink taking a management position. In business the first-line manager is financially accountable. Health care is becoming more of a business each day. If you delegate this responsibility, you also give away much of your power to affect the care your unit provides.

For example, you will not know how to justify a second night nurse based on sustained increased disease acuteness, or how to justify primary care from a financial perspective, or how you may be able to lump the costs of two related pieces of equipment together to make them into one allowable capital expense when you realize that obtaining these needed items out of the operating budget is impossible. Unfortunately, nursing has a long history of giving away power. If nurse managers give this power away, they may not be able to regain it. The people who do understand and can talk in dollars will be able to make decisions that greatly affect clinical care on nursing units.

An annual budget is a plan for the upcoming year. It shows what you expect to earn (revenue) and what you expect to spend (expenditures). The primary revenue source for a hospital is from patients. Revenue, until recently, was not seen in the nursing budget. It was as if nurses "came with the room." Patient bills had no nursing charges, just room rates, even though other departments (for example, laboratory and x-ray) made charges. Therefore, for years, nursing appeared as a deficit (loss) on the hospital balance sheet (the balance sheet shows grand totals of money in and out). However, most patients are in the hospital for nursing care. If this were not true, all surgery could be done on an outpatient basis; only doctors' offices would be needed. But patients stay in the hospital primarily for 24-hour nursing care—monitoring, treatment, medication, teaching, and assistance with physical, physiological, emotional, and psychological problems given by nurses.

In the mid-seventies nurses became more verbal about not being recognized on balance sheets for contributions generating revenue. To change this, a unit of measure needed to be determined. Laboratory personnel charge so much per test; dietary charges so much per tray; physical therapy and respiratory therapy charge so much per treatment. After time/motion studies (watching what nurses do), it was decided that hours of care could be a measurable unit. Although some hospitals do not differentiate among levels of care, the unit of measure used to record revenue generation in the nursing budget (if revenue is in your nursing budget) is nursing care hours per patient day. The hours of care patients need are matched by the number of nurses needed to care for those patients. The number of nurses is expressed in "full-time equivalents" (F.T.E.'s) because some nurses work full-time and some work part-time.

You have an allotted number of F.T.E.'s for your unit based on the history of needed hours of nursing care. The revenue for your unit is thus the number of patient days (based on average occupancy) multiplied by your unit's room rate. These expenses include F.T.E.'s (salaries and benefits), called *manpower expenses*, and the costs of unit supplies, called *materials expenses*. Both are *direct expenses*. Indirect expenses, over which you usually have no control, include hospital administration, facilities, and so forth. (If you are in a medical center, the medical school increases the indirect charges substantially; thus, the room rate rises to generate more revenue for this added expense.)

Each year, a budget is planned. Many hospitals use a relatively simple budget format—"fixed" plus inflation or minus cutbacks. In other words, the percentage of expected inflation is added to last year's fixed budget or cutbacks are subtracted. Zero-based budgeting may be used in some hospitals for individual projects. That is, a new project has zero dollars last year and starts there each year, with new justifications for any budgeted monies for that project.

The budget year is called the *fiscal year*, which varies from one organization to another. Corporation hospitals often use the calendar year, like most industries.

Government hospitals often use July 1 to June 30. Medical centers follow the academic year—from September 1 to August 30. The budget will be your financial standard for your organization's fiscal year.

### Step Two: Compare the Reality or Status Quo to the Standards To Determine Any Discrepancies

Each month your hospital will compile a financial report that includes your unit. You need to be concerned about your unit's financial standard and should obtain a copy or summary of it. Each month review your unit's budget (planned expenditures) against its actual expenditures. Any discrepancies are called *variances*. Variances are expressed as positive or negative dollars or as percents. Compare revenue (based on your patient census) to expenses—indirect (you can do little about these) and direct (manpower and materials). Revenue minus expenses gives profit. Your primary concern on monthly reports is for the manpower and material budget. Each budget item—for example, linen—is represented by one line across the page. This is called a *line item* (see Exhibit 7–2).

*Operating Budget—Materials*

An example of a variance would be telephone expenses being double the monthly budgeted amount. Upon investigation, you may find that a resident has been talking long-distance to a sick patient's family trying to arrange discharge care. You explain this in your justification. On the other hand, perhaps you find someone using your long-distance code number to make a variety of long-distance calls. Your investigation does not track the caller, but in your justification you write that you plan to have that code number canceled and get a new one. Or perhaps you find a large positive variance on arterial lines; on investigation, you find that they are less expensive if purchased preassembled, as you have just begun to do. Next year you will budget less for this line item but for now will expect a monthly positive variance.

Another cause of negative variances, those of greatest concern, might be a special dietary line item. Upon investigation you find that expensive special feedings are being sent to your unit for a patient who no longer takes them. Your actions should include discontinuing the order with dietary, after a staff reminder, and checking the kitchen for additional food that can be returned and credited.

*Operating Budget—Manpower*

Besides line items or "things" in the budget (materials resources), the other major part of expenditures is for people, human resources. This also requires monitoring. The manpower budget needs to be reviewed for discrepancies between budgeted and actual expenditures. The primary item to review is over-

**Exhibit 7–2** Financial Statement for October 30, Fiscal Year to Date through September and October*

| | Current Month | | | | Year to Date | |
| Actual | Budgeted | Variance | | Actual | Budgeted | Variance |
|---|---|---|---|---|---|---|
| 7,025 | 5,311 | (1,714) | Transfer from Laundry 025-596 | 12,045 | 10,622 | (1,423) |

*Unfavorable variance is indicated by parentheses.

time, a great expense in hospitals. The overtime needs to be justified in terms of changes in the severity of patients' illness or in census (the number of patients). These factors are easily documented if you have a good patient classification system. A patient classification system itemizes elements of care and assigns amounts of time for each element. This number of minutes for all the patients on the unit translates into the number of hours of nursing care needed on your unit, or how many nurses are needed. It serves as the basis for the number of nurses and other patient care staff you have on a given shift (see Exhibit 7–3).

Hours of care needed are not a direct translation to F.T.E.'s or staff, because of nonproductive time. In other words, if you total on your patient classification system two tracheostomy suctionings, three IV medications, two bed baths, one diabetic teaching, and so forth, to equal eight hours, you will need more than one shift of one nurse (one F.T.E.) to accomplish these things. This is because the nurse has a coffee break and, over the year, vacation, sick days, holidays, and educational time. Formulas adjust for this nonproductive time when your staffing patterns are developed (see Exhibit 7–4). Variance reports are required in relation to manpower forms; you again justify variances—differences between budgeted and actual F.T.E.'s. You need to show why you used more float nurse time or overtime, and so forth.

### Capital Budget

We have been discussing *operating budget*—the day-to-day revenues and expenditures. Another type of budget is the *capital budget*. This is the budget that plans for "big ticket" items or "capital expenses." Each hospital has its own dollar definition of capital expense, but currently any amount exceeding $300 is usually considered a capital, not operating, expense.

---

**Exhibit 7–3** Hours of Patient Care Needed

| Unit South 3—PM Shift | R.N. | Other (N.A., L.V.N.) | Total |
|---|---|---|---|
| Total Hours | 22.9 | 10.1 | 33.0 |
| Total Staff | 2.8 | 1.3 | 4.1 |
| Total Patients—16 | | | |

Therefore the PM staff sent to South 3 on 11/15 was 3 R.N.'s and 1 N.A. for the 16 patients on this neurosurgical unit. This staffing was based on actual hours of care required by R.N. s and the N.A. to those specific 16 patients.

**Exhibit 7–4** Calculation of Staff Required To Fill a Single Full-Time Position Due to Nonproductive Time

---

Staffing for One R.N. Slot on 3 West for a Year (364 days)

I. Deduct days not worked, for total work days for an individual fulltime employee

    364 days (calculated at an "even" 52 weeks)
    − 104 days off (two days off per week × 52 weeks)

    260 days remaining
    − 10 paid holidays

    250 days remaining
    − 5 ill days (the institutional norm)

    245 days remaining
    − 5 paid inservice days (institutional norm)

    240 days remaining
    − 20 days paid vacation

II. Divide year by number of days worked by a full-time worker, to get number of full-time workers needed to fill the position

    220 days remaining = total work days

$$220 \overline{)364.00} \quad 1.65 = \text{RN workers to fill one job}$$

*Source:* Reprinted from *The Nurse as Executive* by B.J. Stevens with permission of Aspen Systems Corporation. © 1980.

---

Because of limited resources, the purchase of capital expense items is limited. You may need such items as a digital bed scale, atrial pacers, transducers, or IVAC machines. Your hospital probably has a special request form for such items. Again justification is required. As money continues to be tight in health care, only top-priority capital expense items are purchased. Some criteria according to which priorities are set on capital items include income generators (Will it make money for the hospital? Will it save money?), doctor preferences, replacement needs, JCAH or safety or legal requirements, patient aesthetics, and staff job satisfaction. These requests are usually weighed in relation to requests from the entire hospital; those items most needed for the good of the entire organization are the ones purchased.

### Step Three: Plan for Change If Needed

After identifying variances in your monthly financial reports, decide whether the discrepancy needs to be changed. Discuss it with your boss if you are unsure. Get ideas from your staff on how to lower negative variances.

Another important entity for regular review is the less easily measured relationship of cost to quality. This relationship is called *cost-effectiveness*. An example of cost-effectiveness is having a unit clerk note medical orders. Although the clerk is more cost-efficient to use, the quality needs to be maintained by an R.N. overseeing the task.

To enhance cost-effectiveness, cost containment measures are often essential. This might include conservation of linen, minimum but safe staffing, decreasing "loss" of supplies, and increasing compliance with charging systems.

## FULL CIRCLE

Your unit assessment comparison to standards allows you to discover discrepancies and have the data necessary for making changes if needed. This requires good planning. Good planning is essential if you are not to be a manager who is always putting out fires. Drucker (1973) says, "Work implies not only that somebody is supposed to do the job, but also accountability, a deadline, and finally the measurement of results, that is, feedback from results on the work and on the planning process itself" (p. 128).

We have come full circle: *planning, organizing, directing,* and *controlling,* with *controlling* output feeding back into a new *plan* (see Figure 7–1). And so the cycle of a manager's job goes, with things happening in various parts of the cycle

---

**Figure 7–1** The Cycle of Management Functions

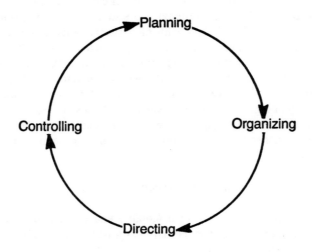

simultaneously. Daily problems, changes, and conflicts continually enter the cycle at any of the four phases. As a new manager, you may often find yourself needing tighter controls because of weaker planning skills and because your ability to tolerate ambiguities is not yet fully developed. As your experience increases, going through the cycle over and over, your skills and tolerance for ambiguity will increase. Your systems will improve, lessening gaps between desired norms and existing standards.

The input that will push you through this cycle many times a day comes from the rapid rate of change in today's society, increasing complexity, and subsequent problem solving and decision making on your part. Problem solving, like communication and leadership, is a learned skill. This skill, along with those to deal with change and conflict, are presented last, in Chapter 8, because these provide the key to help the manager many times daily through the four-function cycle.

## Activity 7:1

# Understanding and Monitoring Compliance with Joint Commission for Accreditation of Hospitals

Without accreditation by the Joint Commission for Accreditation of Hospitals (JCAH), your hospital is not eligible for any government funds (such as Medicare).

You have two major functions:

1. to know and understand JCAH requirements
2. to be sure your unit is in compliance with all of the standards

☐ Obtain a copy of the current JCAH requirements. Read the sections on nursing, quality assurance, and any other section cross-referenced under nursing in the index (also read special care units if applicable to you).

☐ Based on JCAH requirements, develop a checklist to use at least monthly on head nurse rounds (or delegate to staff to do regularly; you do random checks).

Be sure your survey includes:

- staffing and assignment requirements
- nursing process documentation requirements
- nursing care documentation requirements
- education and training program requirements
- policy and procedure requirements
- quality assurance requirements

# Activity 7:2

# Unit Environmental Control

Is your unit a safe working environment?

Find out your hospital's policies and services regarding:

- security _____
_____

- safety awareness _____
_____

- safety procedures _____
_____

- common safety hazards _____
_____

- electrical safety _____
_____

- fire procedures _____
_____

- employee T.B. testing _____
_____

- on-the-job injury procedure _____
_____

- infectious diseases _____
_____

- needle disposal _____
_____

- drug disposal _____
_____

- plaster disposal _____
_____

# Activity 7:3

# Assessing Patient Satisfaction

- Write an interview guide to ask patients about their care the day before discharge.

    —Keep questions open-ended and simple. For example: How did your hospitalization go for you? What would have improved your stay?
    —Do not ask more than seven questions.
    —Do survey orally, not written.
    —Use for one week; then refine interview tool to meet your specific unit's services.

- Share tool with staff, and have staff fill it out on all patients as discharge orders are written.
- Analyze (sort out) feedback and share with staff at a meeting. Ask for staff input on solving any problems raised, and be sure to share positive feedback.

# Activity 7:4

# Performance Appraisal of Staff

Think of a performance appraisal that went well for you in the past. What made it positive? _____

_____    _____

_____    _____

Think of a performance appraisal that did not go well for you in the past. What made it negative? _____

_____

_____

In order to have a performance appraisal session go well, some work prior to the session is essential. Modify the checklist below to meet your preferences in preparing for a performance appraisal.

☐ set up a system to know when performance appraisals are due

☐ notify the employee four weeks before due date to:

- set up a mutually agreeable time
- ask him or her to do a self-evaluation, including strengths and goals in relation to job description and present goals
- ask him or her to seek written peer input

☐ set a good tone

- meet in private setting
- hold telephone calls and other interruptions
- allow sufficient time
- be friendly
- be open

☐ listen to employee

- ask how the employee thinks he or she is doing
- listen to information from self-evaluation and peer input

**Activity 7:4** continued

☐ share your evaluation

- give positive feedback
- recognize areas where progress has been made
- use specific examples

☐ set goals together

- discuss any problem areas
- help set realistic, measurable goals to address these problems
- ask how you can be more supportive or helpful in these goals

☐ summarize

- review current status of work
- review goals
- schedule follow-up session if anything is left unresolved

# Activity 7:5

# Working with Your Union

Understanding your union contract is essential. As a manager, you represent one of the parties in the contract, and each union staff member represents the other party. You are responsible for managing in compliance with the contract.

Check your contract to find out:

- When, if ever, do you have to include a union representative when you conference people?

  _____

  _____

  _____

- What are your salary scales and criteria for promotion?

  _____

  _____

  _____

- Is there a seniority clause, and how does it affect your decision making as a manager?

  _____

  _____

  _____

- Read your contract and list key points on the left. For each point, write the subsequent implications for the manager.

| Union Contract Key Points | Implications for Manager |
|---|---|
| • | |
| • | |
| • | |
| • | |
| • | |
| • | |
| • | |
| • | |

- Review this page with your boss to validate your understanding.

# Activity 7:6

# Controlling Your Unit Budget

- Set a meeting with your boss or someone with budget expertise. For the meeting, obtain the monthly balance statement for your unit and various financial reports and manpower forms. During the meeting discuss the budget process and forms using the questions below as a guide.

**Part I.** Revenue

What are the sources of revenue for your hospital? _____
_____
_____

What is the unit charge for nursing services (hours of care, room rates, etc.)?
_____
_____

What is the cost to a patient for 24 hours of care? Does it vary with amount of care and type of care (ICU, for example)? _____
_____
_____

**Part II.** Expenses

Operating Budget—Materials

- Look at last month's financial statement for your unit. What is a line item?
_____
_____

- Select one line item. How much was budgeted for that item per month? ___
_____

How much was spent on it last month? _____

What is the variance (difference between amount budgeted and amount spent)? _____

Is the variance positive or negative? _____

Positive variance means you have spent less than allotted. Negative variance means that you have overspent. Find a line item with a large variance. What

**Activity 7:6** continued

are some reasons why this variance may be large? _____

_____

- Does your patient census or illness severity fluctuate by the season? By the day of the week? _____

  Does your F.T.E. allotment fluctuate accordingly? _____

  _____

- What is the relationship between your basic F.T.E. allotment and pre-shift staffing based on patient classification? _____

  _____

- Select one line item on your manpower budget (a line on a manpower budget is a person's name). Is overtime, nonproductive time, sick time, etc., recorded on this form? _____

  If not, where can you find this information? _____

  _____

- Can you change the F.T.E. allotment for your unit? _____

  How? _____

  _____

- Find an item with a large positive balance. Why might that be unspent? ___

  _____

- Look at your total variances. Is your unit over budget or under budget for the month? _____

  For year to date? _____

  _____

Operating Budget—Manpower

- How many F.T.E.'s are allotted to your unit? _____
- How was this number determined? _____

  _____

- How is the F.T.E. distribution planned (number of staff per shift, types of staff, etc.)? _____

  _____

- What percentage of an F.T.E. is nonproductive time in your hospital? ___

  _____

- What does nonproductive time include? _____

  _____

**Activity 7:6** continued

- What is the ratio and distribution of your staff on each shift (e.g., 2 R.N.s, 1 aide, nights; 7 R.N.s, 2 aides, 1 unit clerk, days)? _____

- If you disagree with the ratio and distribution, how can you change it? ___

Capital Budget

- What dollar amount defines a capital budget item in your organization? ___

- Who can request capital budget items? _____

- What are some examples of capital budget items recently purchased for your unit? _____

  For other units? _____

  For the hospital? _____
- What capital budget items does your unit currently need? _____

- What are the factors considered in your hospital in deciding which capital budget items to purchase? _____

- Who decides which capital budget items to purchase? _____

- How do you request a capital budget item? _____

**Part III.** Your Role in Budgeting

- What is the role of the head nurse in your hospital regarding budget? ____

- Regarding cost containment? _____

# Activity 7:7

# Controlling Quality of Care on Your Unit

Quality assurance programs must exist and be documented, and "each clinical discipline is responsible for identifying and resolving problems related to patient care" (JCAH, 1980, p. 153).

The form below integrates "the essential components of a sound quality assurance program."

- Use the form below to document *each* problem on which your unit quality assurance committee is working. Update form regularly (bimonthly).
- Compare your problems with other units at a departmental quality assurance meeting so you can identify and work on similar problems together.

---

Unit _____ Beginning date _____ Ending date _____

Problem ("Important or potential problems, related concerns in the care of patients"): _____

Objective assessment of the cause of the problem or concern:
_____
_____

Scope of the problem: _____

Priority of investigating and resolving problem:

☐ has (or has potential to have) grave adverse impact on patient care

☐ has (or has potential to have) moderate adverse impact on patient care

☐ has (or has potential to have) small or no adverse impact on patient care

---

**Activity 7:7** continued

| Date of Plan | Plan (state action to eliminate problem) | Implementation (include date and person responsible) | Outcome (if problem is not solved, proceed to line two) |
|---|---|---|---|
|  |  |  |  |
|  |  |  |  |
|  |  |  |  |
|  |  |  |  |

# Activity 7:8

# Knowing and Using Your Power Bases

*Power* is defined by Webster as the ability or capability to act. In order to perform the actions of a head nurse, you need a certain amount of power. Where do you get it?

French and Raven (1959) identify five sources of power. For each action you take as a head nurse, all five sources are available to you. Some have more positive results than others.

- For each type of power listed below, give an example of when you could use it and the predicted outcomes.
- Ask a peer to do this exercise and share results.

| Sources of Power | Describe a Situation Using this Power | Predicted Outcomes |
|---|---|---|
| *Reward Power* Manager has ability to reward (raise salary or promote) | | |
| *Coercive Power* Manager has ability to withhold a reward or punish (fire or demote) | | |
| *Expert Power* Manager has power based on his/her knowledge or skill (clinical expertise) | | |

**Activity 7:8** continued

| Sources of Power | Describe a Situation Using this Power | Predicted Outcomes |
|---|---|---|
| *Legitimate Power* Manager has power by virtue of his/her position (head nurse position) | | |
| *Referent Power* Manager has personal power or "charisma," idol or hero (attractive to followers) | | |

## CASE STUDY

While making head nurse rounds on your unit, you are appalled at overflowing wastebaskets and dust balls on the floors of patient rooms. For the past week your staff has been complaining about housekeeping services taking up to three hours to clean a bed after patients are discharged, resulting in patients waiting for several hours in the admitting office. Housekeeping is not working up to your standards.

You call the housekeeping supervisor, and he listens politely. He apologizes for the poor quality of work but explains that Jerry Brown, housekeeper, for your unit, is "kinda slow" but has worked here "forever." "Sorry," he says, "I just can't get Jerry to work any harder."

What do you do now?

## SOLUTION TO CASE STUDY

It is unacceptable to do nothing. You are responsible for the quality of the environment on your unit. It is also unacceptable to clean it yourself or to have your staff do the cleaning. (If you did decide to do the cleaning, you should negotiate with housekeeping for their F.T.E.!)

You need to document your telephone call to housekeeping, listing specific problems. Increase your calls to the housekeeping supervisor from weekly to daily. After one or two telephone calls and follow-up memos, send a letter to the housekeeping supervisor's boss and your boss with copies of prior problem-solving attempts attached to the memo.

## REFERENCES

American Nurses' Association. Standards of nursing practice. *The American Nurse*. July 1974, pp. 11–12.

Blansfield, M.G. *The professional nurse looks at appraisal of personnel: Leadership in nursing series*. Leadership Resources, 1966.

Committee for Recognition of Nursing Achievement (CRONA). Stanford Nurse's Contract. Stanford, Calif.: Stanford University Hospital, 1982.

del Bueno, D. Performance evaluation: When all is said and done, more is said than done. *Journal of Nursing Administration*, Dec. 1977, pp. 21–23.

Drucker, P. *Management: Tasks, responsibilities, practices*. New York: Harper & Row, 1974.

French, J.R., & Raven, B. The bases of social power. In D. Cartwright (Ed.), *Studies in social power*. Ann Arbor, Mich.: Institute for Social Research, 1959, pp. 150–163.

Joint Commission for Accreditation of Hospitals. *Accreditation manual for hospitals*. Chicago: JCAH Publications, 1980.

Levenstein, A. The art and science of supervision. *Supervisor Nurse*, July 1978, pp. 25; 28.

Mayers, M.G., Norby, R.B., & Watson, A.B. *Quality assurance for patient care*. New York: Appleton-Century-Crofts, 1977.

McConnell, C.R. *Economics: Principles, problems and policies*. New York: McGraw-Hill, 1981.

Metzger, N. *The health care supervisor's handbook*. Rockville, Md.: Aspen Systems, 1980.

Meyer, H., Kay, E., & French, J. Split roles in performance appraisal. *Harvard Business Review*, Jan.-Feb., 1965, p. 135.

Nehring, V., & Geach, B. Patients' evaluation of their care: Why don't they complain? *Nursing Outlook*, May 1973, *21*(5), 317–321.

Stanford Nursing. *After your heart surgery*. Stanford, Calif.: Stanford University Hospital, 1982.

Stanford Nursing. *Ophthalmology*. Stanford, Calif.: Stanford University Hospital, 1983.

Stanford University Hospital. Procedure for emergency external defibrillation, ICU & IICU. Policy and Procedure Manual for the ICU. Unpublished. Stanford University Medical Center: 1982.

Stanford University Hospital Policy and Procedure Manual for the ICU. *Statement of Policy: Intensive care and inter-mediate intensive care*. Unpublished, Stanford University Medical Center, 1983.

Stanford University Hospital, Department of Nursing Service. Staff nurse clinical performance criteria. In *Clinical Performance Monograph*, in press.

Walker, D.D. The clinical ladder: A tool for clinical excellence. *Nursing at Stanford*, 1983, *5*(4), 1; 8.

Weber, M. Bureaucracy. In J.M. Shafritz & P.H. Whitbeck (Eds.), *Classics of organization theory*. Oak Park, Ill.: Moore Publishing, 1978.

Weiss, C.H. *Evaluation research*. Englewood Cliffs, N.J.: Prentice-Hall, 1972.

Welches, L. (Quoted in M. Zalar.) Development of a unit-based nursing quality assurance program. *Nursing at Stanford*, 1982, *4*(5), 1; 3.

Zalar, M. Development of a unit based nursing quality assurance program. *Nursing at Stanford*, 1982, *4*(5), 1; 3; 4.

# Chapter 8

# Problem Solving

## OBJECTIVES

Upon completion of this chapter, including the activities, the new nurse manager will be able to:

- compare the nursing process to the problem-solving process
- use a problem-solving process to assess a situation, define the problem, plan and implement a solution, and evaluate the outcome
- establish criteria for solutions (conditions for solution) and weigh possible solutions against these criteria
- predict possible "ripples" from solutions or changes and adjust solutions accordingly
- explain the relationships between problem solving and change and between change and conflict
- use Kelly's (1980) nine critical steps of change to facilitate implementing a change
- explain the necessity of "unfreezing" the status quo before implementing a change
- recognize conflict as normal and healthy in a dynamic organization and explain negotiating principles to deal with it
- explain a variety of methods for dealing with interunit conflicts

## DEVELOPMENT OF THE NEW NURSE MANAGER™
1981

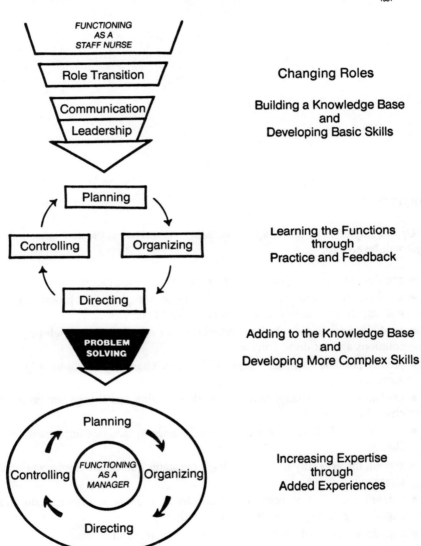

¶ As the nurse leader of the unit, you will be sought out often during the day by nursing staff, peers, physicians, administration, patients, patients' families, and persons from other departments regarding problems, needs, conflicts, and changes. As you improve your systems and develop your staff, the number of urgent problems reaching you should lessen. However, because of fast change and increasing complexity, you will continue to play a vital role in problem solving as a first-line manager.

In this chapter we look at a problem-solving model and how to use it. We also review who should problem solve—you, your staff, your boss, or some combination. Then we explore another part of problem solving, one that relates to how frequently you think a particular problem is likely to recur and how to set up systems to deal with recurring problems.

Next we explore one major problem source, change, and explain how to use a change model. Although change is not in itself a problem, changes—like problems—are questions needing solutions. And a change, like a problem, is best handled by good planning. Good planning for change will help prevent some future problems and lessen the number of urgent problems you must deal with each day. It is not desirable to prevent change. In fact, the emergence of greater problems is more likely without change.

Besides changes and problems confronting you as a first-line manager, conflicts will also offer you challenges. Conflicts relate to change and problem solving because change in one area affects someone or something in another area. This was explained in Chapter 5 as output from one system causing ripples in another system; so it is with change. Your change causes ripples into other people's units or departments. The ripples may be a source of conflict or a problem to these other parties.

Good problem-solving skills, planning skills, and negotiating skills are essential for dealing with the daily management challenges of planning changes, resolving conflicts, and solving problems. This is where it all comes together for you as a manager.

In this chapter are the tools to deal with the problems identified by other methods reviewed earlier. In this chapter you will find information about what to do right now and how to plan so that what you are doing right now is not largely of an urgent nature.

## PROBLEM SOLVING

Why do you need a problem-solving method? "Professional and administrative problems are inherent aspects of the supervisory nurse's role. The ability to handle problems early and effectively enables one to tackle the expected problems with greater vigor and thus the course of one's career will proceed in a smoother fashion," says Fain (1981, p. 62). Careful, rational, deliberate approaches to problems lead to more effective solutions. An orderly way to proceed offers guidelines for analyzing results and data for defensible decisions. Orderly ways to proceed can often "catch" what might otherwise have been a costly error. Structured problem solving "should enable nurses to be more effective and efficient in using the resources at their command in increasing judgmental skills, in defending the actions that have been taken, and in objectively evaluating the results" (Claus & Bailey, 1975, p. 17).

## How To Solve Problems

Many problem-solving and decision-making frameworks are available to assist you in reaching a good decision. We begin here with the model most familiar to you—the nursing process. Then we add perspective from other problem-solving models in both classic and current related literature to adapt this model for use in problem solving as a middle manager.

"The nursing process involves assessing, planning, implementing, and evaluating client situations, with the ultimate goal of preventing or resolving problematic situations" (Yura & Walsh, 1978, p. 20). Three kinds of skills are required to apply the nursing process—intellectual, interpersonal, and technical. Using this framework and these three skills, organized, systematic, and deliberate patient care can be delivered. The nursing process is "flexible and adaptable, adjustable to a number of variables, yet sufficiently structured so as to provide a base from which all systematic nursing actions can proceed" (Yura & Walsh, 1978, p. 2).

We explore problem solving through this model because of its flexibility and adaptability and because of your prior experience in using it. Besides, this model lends itself well to problem solving because it was designed to find answers to questions.

### Assess the Situation

"Assessing is the act of reviewing a situation for the purpose of diagnosing . . . problems" (Yura & Walsh, 1978, p. 27). How do you know there is a problem? Hints of a problem's existence come to you from various sources. Sometimes a few follow-up questions related to a grapevine rumor may lead you to discover a problem. Sometimes a problem enters no more subtly than a clap of thunder. To assess the problem, look at the situation and define what the problem is. You cannot usually define the problem well without asking some questions and gathering some information.

Carlisle (1975) suggests this might be done by stating the conditions for solution: "If you don't know what conditions have to be satisfied for a solution to be reached, how do you know when you have solved the problem" (p. 351)? You may want to divide the conditions into "musts" and "wants" (Kepner & Tregoe, 1965). Sometimes a problem is defined as a "lack of" something (Claus & Bailey, 1975) or a deviation from something that "should be" (Kepner & Tregoe, 1965).

Consider the following example: Several line items show increasing deficits in your unit's monthly financial report (see Chapter 7 for information on variance reports). Total negative variance in dollars is up from last month. Thus the percent of negative variance is up from last month. You know that the problem is due to staff not filling out charge slips when using certain supplies. Your staff complain they are too busy with patient care to stamp the charge slips.

In the preceding situation the problem might be defined as "my staff do not fill out all charge slips when using supplies." The problem might also be defined as a "lack of compliance by staff with the established system of charging the patient for use of supplies."

Another way to define the problem is to compare what is with what should be. This method of problem definition is similar to that used in Chapter 7, in which the status quo was compared to the standard in search of deviation. That deviation was the problem definition. In this situation, the answer to the question "What is?", simply stated, is "Staff don't fill out charge slips." The answer to the question "What should be?" is "Staff should fill out charge slips." Now consider the conditions for solution:

1. Staff will fill out charge slips.
2. Compliance will be voluntary, not policed.
3. Finance report will not show negative variances due to items used but not charged.
4. Solution will not be short-lived.
5. An easier charge system will be instituted.

You need to decide which of these conditions of solution are "musts" and which are "wants." If you decide the first and third conditions are "musts" and the second, fourth, and fifth are "wants," then you must take actions that will minimally meet the first and third criteria. The problem is not solved if you take some action and the staff still do not fill out charge slips (condition 1) or finance reports continue to show negative variances on line items because staff do not complete charge slips (condition 3).

## Plan a Solution

In step 2 you need to *plan* how to solve the problem. "Planning is the predetermination of what can be done . . . it involves setting goals, judging priorities, and designing methods to resolve problems" (Yura & Walsh, 1978,

p. 31). First, generate a list of possible solutions. Do the solutions meet the conditions listed in step 1—at least the "musts"? If a solution does not meet a "must," cross it out as a nonviable option. Consider what would happen, respectively, if you implemented each of the possible remaining solutions. Kepner and Tregoe (1965) call this playing "what if."

For the above situation, solutions might include the following:

1. Post a memo at the nurses' station requesting all staff to fill out charge slips.
2. Make an announcement at a staff meeting that people caught not filling out a charge slip will receive a written warning.
3. Assign someone on each shift to track down and fill out any charge slips at the end of that shift.
4. Ask nurses to drop slips in a box initialed with the patient's room number and have the unit clerk stamp them once per shift.
5. Write on your variance report justification column that your staff cannot always fill out slips because they are more concerned about patient care than money.

Alternative 5 is not viable because it does not meet the "must" conditions of staff compliance (condition 1) and decreased negative balance (condition 3). Cross out alternative 5.

Posting a memo has been tried in the past for other problems. You have found that few people seem to read such memos. Compliance on your unit is low for changes instituted through a one-way, nonverbal communiquè to the general staff. After about two days, the memo usually disappears. Cross out alternative 1.

This leaves three possible solutions: alternatives 2, 3, and 4. Compare these alternatives to your list of "wants." You want voluntary compliance, long-lived solutions, and an easier charge system. All three remaining alternatives are potentially long-lived. Only alternative 4 does not set up a policing system; rather, it makes compliance with the standard easier for staff who do not want to take the time from patient care. An easier charge system is beyond your realm of control, although you have talked to your boss about this problem. Other units are also concerned, and together you will work with purchasing for a long-range solution.

You need a more immediate solution, however, and alternative 4 looks best. It has all of the "musts" and more of the "wants" than any other alternative. The number of "wants" is not always as important as *which* "wants." You may need to set priorities on "wants."

"What if" also helps to look at this factor. To play "what if," you need to consider each alternative that meets "must" criteria in light of two factors. The first is staff satisfaction, which affects their compliance and job satisfaction and longer range issues such as morale and turnover. The second factor is the quality of the decision, including both quality care and cost.

"What if" you implemented solution 2—making the announcement and following up with written warnings for those who do not comply? This solution could have a high-quality result in terms of increased filling out of charge slips, but the level of staff satisfaction would be extremely low. This is true whenever you try using policed authoritarian systems with professionals who are used to practicing in a highly responsible, often autonomous, manner.

"What if" you implemented alternative 3, assigning someone to make charges at the end of each shift? This solution could also have high-quality results in terms of the number of charges made, but it still has implications of policing. This is a viable alternative if something better cannot be found.

"What if" you choose alternative 4, asking nurses simply to initial slips with the patient's room number and drop them in a box, having the unit clerk stamp all slips at the end of each shift? One of the implications of this alternative is the added task for your unit clerk. If you have unit clerks and can fit this into their schedules, this is more cost-effective than having nurses do this clerical task. It was on this rationale that the position of unit clerk came into existence 15 years ago. This alternative will probably have high-quality results in terms of compliance and also will produce high staff satisfaction because it lets nurses have more time for patients. It also shifts a clerical task to clerical personnel, yielding a good fit between task and individuals.

A good solution considers both the quality of the solution (time, expense, etc.) and the satisfaction level of the staff related to the solution. Sometimes one needs to be compromised for the other. Sometimes a new alternative, to balance the quality/satisfaction dilemma, can be generated that may be a combination of two or more alternatives. For example, you may like the alternative that utilizes unit clerks but do not have a unit clerk on the night shift. Perhaps you could combine this alternative with "assigning a staff nurse." Your solution becomes "Nurses put room number on charge slips and drop in a box for unit clerk to stamp except on night shifts, where a staff nurse is assigned to cover this function."

Generating a list of alternative solutions can often be done with your staff or a task force of interested staff members. This group process often yields more creative and acceptable solutions. Be sure you know what your "conditions for solution" are before seeking an alternative solution.

*Implement the Solution*

After you have decided on a solution, you need to decide how to implement this plan. "Implementation is the initiation and completion of the actions necessary to accomplish defined goals" (Yura & Walsh, 1978, p. 31). This may range from simply doing it yourself to performing a complex strategic path analysis—in which you plan the integration of a series of interrelated tasks and time frames. Whatever you plan, communication of that plan is vital, and your plan needs to "fit" with existing systems (see Chapter 5). Implementing the plan involves decisions about who will be responsible and when you will begin. It also involves making sure those affected are informed and defining what will happen.

In the charge slip situation, suppose you select alternative 4—having the unit clerk do the charge slips. The starting date needs to be established, allowing enough time for you to inform your unit staff. For clarity, the process should be written up as a procedure. Any training needed must be done first; in this case, none (or little) is needed. You should spend some time talking with your unit clerks, who probably already have a busy schedule. Listen to their concerns; help them to work out any potential snags. Because this plan predominantly involves unit clerks, seeking their input for the procedure is a good idea. Such participatory action will increase their support in helping make the plan work. They might have preferences about where the box should be located, whether patient room and bed numbers or patient last names would be easier referents, and so on.

### Evaluate the Solution

The last step of the process, evaluation, is very important; yet it is often forgotten. "Evaluation is the appraisal of the changes . . . as a result of the action" (Yura & Walsh, 1978, p. 33). Once the solution has been implemented, it is easy to forget about the problem unless the solution did not work, in which case the problem will resurface—and probably with greater impact. To avoid this, set a time frame within which to evaluate the solution. The standards by which you evaluate should be taken from the "conditions for solution." If the conditions for solution are satisfied within the allotted time frame, inform those people involved with the original situation. If the conditions for solution are not satisfied or have changed, this feedback can be used either to start the problem-solving process over with definition of the problem or to make adjustments to the solution to meet current conditions for solution.

Planned evaluation is also a way to get support for a plan. If staff know the solution will be tried for a specific time period and then evaluated, those who are hesitant about the solution often are willing to give it a try.

In the example of the charge slips, you evaluate the solution after three months, as decided at the time of implementation. At that time you review the conditions for solution with your current situation. Are the charge slips being filled out? Is compliance voluntary, or are you policing? Have finance reports shown decreased deficits in the offending line items? If you find all these conditions of solution met, are the conditions of solution still applicable? Finally, ask the people involved how the solution is working for them. Listen to options for revising or refining the solution. Evaluate again, in about the same amount of time, if you have instituted many changes. If you have left the solution essentially as is, your evaluation period may be lengthened to perhaps six months from this evaluation.

*Remember the Ripple*

Communication throughout this process must reach all those within the "ripple" (see Chapter 5). Other persons, units, and departments who will be affected by your decision may need to have input into development of your solution. Projecting the possibility of others' interests and/or reactions will surface as you try out your "what ifs."

For example, "what if" you decide to solve your charge slip problem by writing patient names on the slips and not stamping them with the patient stamp. You send the charges to materials management, and that department uses patient identification numbers, not names, for charging. Each charge slip will need to be tracked individually to charge the patient. This delays the process, and the charges are received by accounting so late that some patients' bills have already been processed. You can be sure you will hear from the materials management department and the accounting department, who will be quite upset about the ripple you threw into a working system. Thinking through and asking others about "what ifs" can avoid many such upsetting ripples.

## Problem-Solving Model

This problem-solving model based on the nursing process format is presented as a fill-in chart (Exhibit 8–1). It may be used in your daily problem solving. In using the form over and over, you will improve your problem-solving skills in several ways. You will see a pattern if you continually miss or give little attention to some particular step. For example, maybe you do not spend enough time or energy defining the problem. This may cause you to define the problem inaccurately. Then, of course, you develop a solution that solves the wrong problem or, worse, creates a new one. Perhaps you do not usually evaluate your solutions. Take some time to look around at past problem solving and see whether the original solutions still solve those problems. Evaluating your solutions elicits valuable information about your problem-solving skills and about what kinds of solutions work well with your staff.

Recording problems on these forms also provides you with a ready-made system for follow-up evaluation. After filling in the evaluation section of the form, file it in a folder for the month the evaluation is due, so it will surface automatically in your paperwork. If used regularly, this problem-solving framework will refine your problem-solving skills; it will eventually become "automatic" for you to define a problem, search for conditions of solutions (both "musts" and "wants"), generate solutions to compare with the conditions for solution, consider quality/satisfaction trade-offs, and try out your solutions in "what if" games. You will develop efficient plans more easily and systematically and will begin looking evaluatively at solutions in retrospect. Your problem-solving skills will continue to improve as you use the model for daily problem solving.

**Exhibit 8–1** Problem-Solving Sheet

---

I.  *Assess the Situation*

   A. *Describe the Situation*

   B. *Define the Problem*

   | • *Is* _____ | | • *Lack of* _____ |
   | _____ | | _____ |
   | • *Should be* _____ | OR | _____ |
   | _____ | | _____ |

   • *Conditions for Solution*                    *(Circle one for each condition.)*

   _____    must    want

   _____    must    want

   _____    must    want

   _____    must    want

   _____    must    want

II. *Plan a Solution*

   A. *Possible Solutions*
      • _____
      • _____
      • _____
      • _____
      • _____

   B. Cross out any that don't meet "must" criteria above.

   C. Play "what if" for any remaining viable solutions.

   D. Consider quality and satisfaction of the solutions left; can you combine any solutions to get higher quality and satisfaction?

   E. Select solution based on B, C, D.

**Exhibit 8–1** continued

III. *Implement the Solution*

   A. *Plan to Implement*
- Person responsible \_\_\_\_\_ _____
- Method of implementation _____
- Time frame _____
- Methods of communication to all without ripple _____

IV. *Evaluate the Solution*

   A. *Plan to Evaluate*
- Person responsible _____
- Method of evaluation _____
- Time frame _____
- Method of communication _____

- Standards for evaluation (taken from the "conditions for solutions") _____

*Using the Problem-Solving Model*

Some problems may seem rather small to put through this system. For example, you do not seem to get your telephone messages or your unit is short on IV poles. Use the model to think through your solution anyway and to increase your problem-solving skills. Maybe an abbreviated form will be adequate. For example:

1. *Assess Situation*

- *Problem definition:* Failure to receive messages; no system exists currently.
- *Condition for solution:* Must get messages.

2. *Plan Solution*

- Have messages put on a message pin located in nurses' station.

### 3. *Implement Solution*

- You will put up pin and inform staff.

### 4. *Evaluation*

- In two weeks, measure improvement and ask for feedback from others involved about how the system works for them.

Fain (1981) offers some additional ideas to improve problem solving, especially those useful to "speed the process" (p. 62). He suggests writing the facts in the fewest words possible to avoid getting bogged down. Do not let a problem become a "nagging" one. Put it away for a day or two, or get additional input. Ask for help from your boss or other "experts" on the subject in question. Be sure to have enough facts and figures; beginning with insufficient and/or erroneous data has a small chance of yielding a good solution. Do not reinvent the wheel. Has anyone else found a good solution for this problem? Break large problems down into approachable pieces, and solve the smaller parts. Finally, keep cost in mind in relation to all problems.

For some problems, shortcuts may not be the answer. You may have a problem that is quite complex and that requires a large amount of data, input from several units or departments, or even major changes in some policies and procedures. This model will still work and might be used as a guiding framework by a committee or task force charged with the problem. The model will guide the process of your task force while leaving the content open for the problem's uniqueness.

An example of a more complex problem-solving process using this model would be a change in the delivery room that promises to have an impact on other units. Suppose as head nurse in delivery, you decide it would be more cost-effective and more relaxing for new mothers to be sent to their postpartum rooms for recovery fifteen minutes after delivery. Currently, you are keeping these patients for two to three hours. Before instituting this solution to the problem of more cost-effective staffing, you decide to play "what if." You ask postpartum nurses, nursery nurses, and a few doctors what they think is good about this change and what problems they foresee. Based on their feedback, you may decide not to make any change or some better ideas may surface. If you decide to go ahead with this solution, you will have a better idea of the obstacles ahead and be able to plan to avoid or lessen them.

Some parts of this problem-solving model can be expanded for these complex problems; thus, the model adapts to particular types of problems. If you have a series of possible solutions that have large ripple effects—that is, the amount and type of change they generate may reach many people—you may want to expand the "what if" section into a survey by memo to get input from those people within the ripples.

For example, you are head nurse in the coronary care unit, and your unit sends one nurse to every "code" to lead cardiopulmonary resuscitation efforts. The hospital is about to purchase new crash carts and has asked your unit to select the cart and review the contents of current carts. You decide to solicit input from nursing units, pharmacy, purchasing, and selected physicians through a brief written survey before making decisions. You could also have approached this by sending out a memo stating that a task force was forming to look at crash cart changes and inviting interested persons to join the task force. Include the time, place, and date of the first meeting, and prepare an agenda that includes a clear statement of the purpose of the task force.

Whenever your possible solutions affect others, especially if they may perceive the effect as adverse, be sure to ask for their input. Expand your "what ifs" to a meeting or survey or a series of one-to-one conversations to get input from others within the ripple who will be most affected by your possible solutions.

## CHANGE

The relationship between problem solving and change is probably obvious at this point. Your solution initiates a change. There is a good chance your initial problem even resulted from someone else's change. Dealing with change is fast becoming the most important skill of today's manager.

How will change affect you as a manager? Odiorne (1961) says, "The fact of this changing world puts demands upon the skills and practices of management which promise to create a whole new breed of people in charge. The significant differences lie in the desire and ability to bring about change and improvement and to force innovation into the position of being a primary skill of the manager" (p. 19).

As a head nurse you must be able to manage change. This includes skill in diagnosing the need for change, then implementing and evaluating the changes. These skills in managing change are stated by Kelly (1980, p. 569), who gives a nine-step breakdown of the critical steps of change in three phases. The Diagnosis Phase, the Implementation Phase, and the Evaluation Phase are shown in Figure 8–1.

If this process looks familiar, that is because it essentially mirrors the steps of problem solving. Just as problem solving initiates a need for change, change initiates a need for problem solving. The change framework in Figure 8–1 illustrates how change may be handled through a framework similar to that used for problem solving. Consider the following example of change and its management through Kelly's nine critical steps of change.

**Figure 8–1** Stages of Change

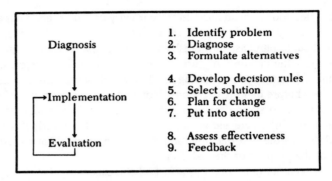

Diagnosis

Implementation

Evaluation

1. Identify problem
2. Diagnose
3. Formulate alternatives

4. Develop decision rules
5. Select solution
6. Plan for change
7. Put into action

8. Assess effectiveness
9. Feedback

*Source:* Reprinted from *Organizational Behavior: Its Data, First Principles, and Applications* (3rd Ed.) by Joe Kelly with permission of Richard D. Irwin, Inc., © 1980.

## Phase One: Diagnosis

### Step One—Identify the Problem

Nursing care on your unit seems disorganized and fragmented; accountability is low.

### Step Two—Diagnose

You look at what type of care delivery system you are currently using and what is available. According to Kron and Durbin (1981), three types of care delivery systems are currently in use in acute care settings. The first and oldest method is functional nursing. "In this method nursing care is divided into separate tasks. These are performed by varying levels of nursing personnel, depending upon the complexity of each task in terms of judgment and technical knowledge, and the preparation of the individual staff members. Each staff member is responsible for only the tasks done during a given tour of duty" (Kron & Durbin, 1981, p. 210). This type of nursing care sounds like what is currently in use on your unit.

The second method, according to Kron and Durbin (1981), is team nursing, which gained popularity in the 1960s. "This method utilizes a heterogeneous team of nursing personnel to deliver nursing care to a group of patients. The leader of the team is a registered nurse or, in some hospitals, a licensed practical nurse. The team leader is given the responsibility for planning, continuity and evaluation of the nursing care regimens of all patients cared for by the team, for supervising the team members in the implementation of nursing actions and for evaluating the results" (p. 210). This system will probably increase accountability but, basically, only for the team leader. Fragmentation of care will probably continue under team nursing.

Kron and Durbin (1981) describe the third type of care delivery system as primary nursing. "In this method of delivering nursing care, registered professional nurses are given total responsibility and authority for assessing, planning, implementing and evaluating the nursing care regimens of a specified number of patients within the health care facility. The primary nurse is responsible for the care of a patient 24 hours a day, from the time the patient is admitted to the nursing unit until the patient leaves it. An associate professional nurse carries out the nursing orders when the primary nurse is not on duty" (p. 210). This system seems to address both issues—accountability and fragmentation.

*Step Three—Formulate Alternatives*

- Alternative 1: Continue functional nursing care.
- Alternative 2: Change to team nursing.
- Alternative 3: Change to primary nursing.

**Phase Two: Implementation**

*Step Four—Develop Decision Rules*

This step is similar to formulating "conditions for solution" in the problem-solving process. For the nursing care delivery decision rules, consider such factors as quality of care, reducing fragmentation of care, increased accountability, staff availability, cost of staff, and so on.

*Step Five—Select Solution*

After gathering further information about the preceding factors and refining your decision rules, set priorities on them. Using the "musts" and "wants" system of problem solving discussed earlier will work well for this change situation. Based on your decision rules, you select one of the alternatives for your solution.

Suppose you select primary nursing using your decision rules. In looking at your initial problem definition, this would be your probable choice if primary nursing fits with other components of your organization well enough to enable its success.

Another necessary "fit" is between the system and your philosophy. Primary nursing is your first choice if you believe, for example, as Alfano et al. (1980, p. i) do, that: "the use of assistive, adjunctive, nonprofessional personnel rather than RNs to carry out personal services, treatments, other procedures and overall supervision of daily patient care has resulted in fragmentation of care, duplication of effort, lack of accountability, and more significantly, delayed recognition of changes in patient status.''

Alfano et al. (1980) also address cost: ''The cost of delivering nursing service is directly related to the number of people who give the care, which in turn is directly related to the degree of competency and skill each possesses'' (p. 1).

On the other side of the issue were eight nurse leaders who also support all-R.N. staffing but who, at a conference in 1978 under the auspices of *Nursing Digest*, explored not only the positive aspects of primary care but also the obstacles (Alfano, et al., 1980, p. 31). Some of these obstacles include:

- inadequacy of recruitment of R.N.s
- stability and tenure of aides and L.P.N.s
- power of organized labor within both nonprofessional and professional groups
- resistance to change by administration and physicians
- inadequate support services
- third party reimbursement
- lack of valid nursing standards
- political naiveté
- lack of tangible rewards

If you hold to the preceding philosophy, these obstacles should not thwart your efforts toward primary nursing. However, in selecting your solution, these issues will need to be addressed.

### Step Six—Plan for Change

An addition to the problem-solving framework that is useful to consider when dealing with change is Lewin's change model (1936). Lewin refers to three phases of change: unfreezing, moving, and refreezing (see Figure 8–2).

This framework is useful within the planning and implementing phases of the problem-solving format. *Unfreezing* means to take the current situation (frozen in status quo) and start melting it. You need to plan and implement steps to unfreeze the status quo and to begin preparing people for the change. Let those within the ripple effect know why things are not acceptable as they are. The more time allowed to prepare people for a change, the easier it is to make the change.

Unfreezing is where managers earn their bucks (Labovitz, 1975). To unfreeze a situation, motivation is the key. An old adage about a man trying to move a donkey forward reduces motivating mechanisms to a carrot, a symbol of tempting the

**Figure 8–2** Phases of Change

Unfreeze————————▶Move————————▶Refreeze

donkey forward, or a stick, to whack it on the other end. This reward or punishment theme is common in motivation literature. These externally applied motivators, tempting or pushing someone forward, often have short-lived results. If, however, you present the rationale for needed change and bring the staff along by involving them in the planning of change, slowly you begin to melt the current situation to the point that people are actually ready for, if not anticipating, the change. This melting involves changing the current state of harmony that exists between what is and what is desired. The lack of harmony you wish to create is called cognitive dissonance (Festinger, 1957) and comes about with shared information, involvement of staff, and time. With a state of cognitive dissonance created, the staff are ready to move forward. In other words, once people are made uncomfortable in their current situations, they change more easily. If you effectively "unfreeze" the current situation by creating cognitive dissonance, the "move" (the change itself) will go much more smoothly.

For example, you might circulate a very positive article on primary care, such as, "With Primary Nursing We Have it All Together" (Dahlen, 1980). Visiting a unit or hospital with some of your staff where primary care is working well and reporting back to staff might be helpful. Or bring in an expert speaker or consultant on primary care, such as Maria Manthey, the originator of primary care nursing.

Bringing to light the current problems may help; the best way to do this is to brainstorm as a group.

One major difference between managing change and solving problems is that in problem solving, the status quo is not acceptable; there is a perceived need for change. This often makes the "move" easier. In change, the need for moving or the reason to alter the status quo may be unclear. You need to spend some time and energy planning the change and getting people to "buy in" to your solution—especially if they do not see a problem.

What happens if you just "move" without "unfreezing" or preparing for the change? For example, suppose you announce, "We will begin primary care next month." Chances are, you will move alone. Without getting a commitment from those within the ripple, your change will need to be "policed" or things will revert back to the status quo. The same problem occurs if you move too fast. The more time allowed for unfreezing, the easier the move.

Poorly planned change, unmanaged change, or too rapid change causes frozen status quo situations to remain frozen. These are changes that are not likely to produce desired results. You will see definite differences in the success of primary nursing on your unit depending on whether it is introduced as a well-planned change, an unmanaged change, a poorly planned change, or too rapid a change. Well-managed unfreezing for change saves much work later. Sometimes a failure due to poor strategy in planning may kill an idea forever. You may never get a second chance. Even if you do get another chance, you will start from a much more difficult status quo. Staff who do not want the change will "dig-in" against it, with lines like: "Oh, we tried that before. . . . It will never work because. . . ."

Planning your change is of vital importance and is directly related to its success. In a complex change, such as instituting primary nursing, a task force is helpful in considering the multiple facets of the change. In "Applied Organization Change in Industry: Structured, Technical and Human Approaches," Leavitt (1965) named four variables useful in approaching change. These may be helpful in planning your change and organizing the work of your task force.

The four variables are task, structure, technology, and actors. The *task* refers to the service offered. The *structure* refers to systems of communication, authority, and work flow. By *technology,* Leavitt means technical tools such as problem solving and work measurement. *Actors* are, of course, the people concerned. Using these variables to help plan your change will reduce chances of major items falling "between the cracks."

### Step Seven—Put into Action

After developing a good plan and "unfreezing," you will find this step less difficult than it would have been without good planning. Be ready to problem solve snags. Ask your staff to help you. If your plans clearly state who, what, where, when, and how much, and if your staff helped design the plans, your implementation should go smoothly. This step is what Lewin calls the move (1936).

## Phase Three: Evaluation

### Step Eight—Assess Effectiveness

Kelly (1980) suggests: "When change agents are allocating resources to the three major stages of change, they should budget a little extra for the follow up. Once the change is underway, there is a real danger of slacking off in terms of effort. Did the plans work out? To what extent were the objectives [conditions for solution] reached? What dysfunctions were generated? Assessment may require the employment of fairly sophisticated statistical experimental designs with control groups to ascertain if a real change took place. At least the opinions of participants should be polled" (p. 572).

*Step Nine—Feedback*

Information gained through evaluations should be fed back to revise the plans and refine the change.

The problem-solving model is thus easily adapted for dealing with change by emphasizing unfreezing when planning a solution. The model can also be adapted to be more specific to management of change if, when you are diagnosing, you include the following questions to help formulate conditions for solution:

- Will any new attitudes, skills, knowledge, or costs be needed for any tasks related to this change?
- What persons, units, and/or departments fall within the ripple, and what will help them to "buy in" to the change?
- What resistance can be anticipated, and how might it be overcome?
- What is a realistic time frame for implementation, including time for unfreezing?
- What degree of change is necessary? What is desired? What is ideal?

Why all this emphasis on change? In the words of Burach and Torda (1979): "The function of a manager is to manage. And if change is the order of the day, then the function of the manager is to manage that change" (p. 3). Managing change is a skill challenged daily in the manager. Solving problems is an equally necessary survival skill for today's manager because of increasingly complex, specialized, and highly technical organizations. Even managers with both problem-solving and change management skills will find themselves face to face with conflict. This is unavoidable in a dynamic organization.

## CONFLICT

"Conflict is not only a natural, but an important part of organizational life. If dealt with . . . it can be a powerful catapult. If ignored or mishandled, it can create major problems" (Burach & Torda, 1979, p. 100). If you are managing a dynamic environment, change is a healthy norm and a necessity in keeping your organization up-to-date. Change is no longer an exceptional occurrence in an organization; routine change is essential to an organization's survival. With so much change along with the ripples from those changes, conflict is inevitable. A dynamic organization implies constant motion, and that explains a predictable number of collisions. Collisions are conflicts

Conflict, then, is normal and healthy and should be dealt with as you would deal with any everyday problem, using problem-solving skills in combination with good negotiating skills.

The problem definition phase of conflict resolution, using the problem-solving model, would include understanding each person's priority. A need by each person is essential to the trade involved in negotiation. These identified needs become the two primary "conditions for solution." Most of the negotiation process then becomes planning the solution.

Fisher and Ury (1981) define negotiation as "back and forth communication designed to reach an agreement when you and the other side have some interests that are shared and others that are opposed" (p. xi). If you and the other person use active listening skills, the problem-solving model, and a commitment to the negotiation process, resolution is likely. The solution must meet both persons' primary "conditions for solution" or it is not likely to last.

If both people do not attempt negotiation openly, with a desire to satisfy each other's concerns, good problem solving is not likely to occur. Thomas (1976) describes conflict-handling orientations by plotting "a person's desire to satisfy the other's concern" (uncooperative to cooperative) against "a person's desire to satisfy own concern" (unassertive to assertive). The five resultant behaviors (see Figure 8–3) are:

- Avoidant (neglect)—uncooperative, unassertive
- Accommodative (appeasement)—cooperative, unassertive
- Competitive (domination)—uncooperative, assertive
- Sharing (compromise)—somewhat cooperative, somewhat assertive
- Collaborative (integration)—cooperative, assertive

In evaluating the complicated problem solving, you should evaluate your own and the other person's behaviors and determine how each helped or hindered the negotiation process. Examples of how one situation might be handled with varying amounts of concern follow.

Imagine yourself as the head nurse on a surgical unit. Perhaps you have a staff nurse who avoids starting IVs on patients. Because most of your patients have an IV at some time during their hospitalization, this nurse needs to gain this skill. If this person has little desire to satisfy your concern and has little concern for the task itself, the behavior you will see is avoidant. She will neglect the task. If you become dominant, the situation will become competitive, and your staff nurse will probably accommodate your desire in an appeasement fashion. This is a dangerous situation, as this nurse will resent the situation and you. But if you can work out a compromise through sharing information, a more positive relationship will result. This might happen through your listening to her concerns about starting IVs. Perhaps she needs more training or feedback. Or maybe you will find that she does not want to go on evening shift but knows she will have to as soon as she gains this particular skill. An even better resolution of the conflict would be to collaborate, reaching a solution that meets both of your needs and integrates both of your ideas.

**Figure 8–3** Five Conflict-Handling Orientations, Plotted According to a Person's Desire to Satisfy His or Her Own and the Other Person's Concern

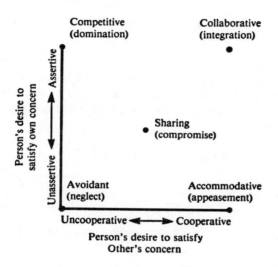

*Source:* Reprinted with permission from Handbook of Industrial and Organizational Psychology, M.D. Dunette, Ed. Copyright 1976 by John Wiley & Sons, Inc.

Negotiating, conflict resolution, and managing change are all problem-solving skills that are essential to your daily functioning as a nurse manager. You work in a dynamic environment requiring continual decision making. These are the skills required for that daily unit management.

Good solutions coexist with or complement existing systems. This is good planning. Thus, problem solving initiates planning, organizing, directing, and controlling—your functions as a manager. Good problem solving initiates the cycle many times daily. Each time through the cycle gives you more experience as a manager. Using good tools as you go through the cycle repeatedly will help you grow and develop as a nurse manager.

# Should You Solve This Problem?

If a problem exists on the unit where you are head nurse, it is your problem. But are you alone? Does anyone else have this problem? If all head nurses have the same problem, it is not good use of resources for each of you to solve it individually. By joining together you can save time and energy while increasing the size and scope of your power base.

- Think of three current problems on your unit.

  1. _____
  2. _____
  3. _____

- Put each problem through the flow diagram below to decide if you should solve it.

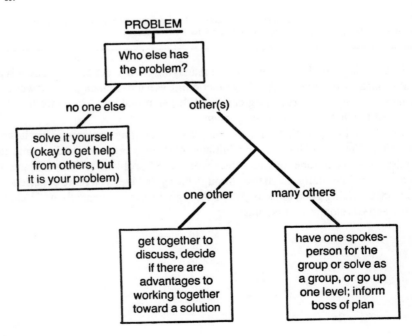

# Activity 8:2

# Problem-Solving Practice

- Select a problem on your unit
- Use the problem-solving framework below to work through the four steps of the problem-solving process.

Problem-Solving Sheet

I. *Assess the Situation*

    A. *Describe the Situation*

    B. *Define the Problem*

| | | |
|---|---|---|
| • *Is* _____ <br><br> • *Should be* _____ | OR | • *Lack of* _____ <br><br> _____ <br><br> _____ |

    • *Conditions for Solution*           *(Circle one for each condition.)*

| | | |
|---|---|---|
| _____ | must | want |
| _____ | must | want |
| _____ | must | want |
| _____ | must | want |
| _____ | must | want |

289

**Activity 8:2** continued

II. *Plan a Solution*

A. *Possible Solutions*
- _____
- _____
- _____
- _____
- _____

B. Cross out any that don't meet "must" criteria above.

C. Play "what if" for any remaining viable solutions.

D. Consider quality and satisfaction of the solutions left; can you combine any solutions to get higher quality and satisfaction?

E. Select solution based on B, C, D.

III. *Implement the Solution*

A. *Plan to Implement*
- Person responsible _____
- Method of implementation _____
- Time frame _____
- Methods of communication to all without ripple _____

IV. *Evaluate the Solution*

A. *Plan to Evaluate*
- Person responsible _____
- Method of evaluation _____
- Time frame _____
- Method of communication _____

- Standards for evaluation (taken from the "conditions for solutions")

# Activity 8:3

# Reacting to Change

"Our general experience is that the answer to 'Do I want to change?' is more often than not negative" (Burach & Torda, 1979, p. 32). Yet personal and professional growth is retarded without change. Your experiences with change and subsequent attitudes about change will affect how you deal with change on your unit.

- Answer the following questions to assess your attitude about change.

|  | Disagree | Agree |
|---|---|---|
| 1. I prefer a face watch to a digital watch. | | |
| 2. Promotions should be based solely on seniority. | | |
| 3. Nurses should wear white hose. | | |
| 4. Hospital pharmacies should be centrally, not unit, based. | | |
| 5. Nurses, not ward clerks, should note doctors' orders. | | |
| 6. Head nurses should take AM report daily. | | |
| 7. Only physicians should defibrillate patients. | | |
| 8. Robots delivering medications will increase medication errors. | | |
| 9. Computers are dehumanizing health care. | | |
| 10. TV patient education should not be part of a hospital system. | | |

if you agree with more than three statements above, you may have enough resistance to change to warrant some coaching from your boss when planning your next unit change

## Activity 8:4

# Promoting Change

Using Lewin's (1936) framework for change, analyze a change that happened within the past year.

- What was done to "unfreeze" the situation:

_____
_____
_____
_____
_____

- What was done to "move" to the new situation?

_____
_____
_____
_____
_____

- What was done to "refreeze" the new situation?

_____
_____
_____
_____
_____

- Did the change go well?

_____

- Was there sufficient unfreezing?

_____

- How might this change have gone better?

_____
_____
_____
_____
_____

# Activity 8:5

# Diagnosing and Managing Your Conflict Style

Answer the following questions with a *yes* or a *no*.

1. Most trouble in business arises from shop stewards, radicals, or prima donnas.
   Yes _____ No _____
2. Most work problems would vanish if people just followed exactly their job descriptions.
   Yes _____ No _____
3. Managers have abdicated their leader role.
   Yes _____ No _____
4. Conflict is basically bad, injurious to mental health, and counter-productive.
   Yes _____ No _____
5. Conflict is caused by poor communications.
   Yes _____ No _____
6. Conflict is spread by stereotyping (e.g., He is an Uncle Tom, a Captain Quigg, a troublemaker, etc.)
   Yes _____ No _____
7. When people start talking to each other instead of at each other, problems will start to go away.
   Yes _____ No _____
8. What most people need is a week in an encounter group (or T group or EST group or Gestalt therapy group, etc.)
   Yes _____ No _____
9. At the bottom of every problem you will find the wrong information in the wrong hands at the wrong time.
   Yes _____ No _____
10. When the workers can read printouts on production, marketing, and finance, everything is going to be OK.
    Yes _____ No _____

*Source:* Reprinted from *Organizational Behavior: Its Data, First Principles, and Applications* (3rd Ed.) by Joe Kelly with permission of Richard D. Irwin. Inc.. © 1980.

**Activity 8:5** continued

11. There is an institutional information gap between sales and production. What we need is a SOLD (sales organization liaison department)
    Yes _____ No _____
12. To get good government in the United States, what we need is a set of telex machines in the basement of the Oval office to copy everything going into the Pentagon, State Department, CIA, and FBI.
    Yes _____ No _____
13. Conflict is good for you.
    Yes _____ No _____
14. Most conflicts arise from the powerful trying to deprive the poor, the weak, the ethnics, the less powerful of their rights.
    Yes _____ No _____
15. What we need is a true meeting of minds. Then we can avoid zero-sum compromises (you win, I lose).
    Yes _____ No _____
16. Small is beautiful.
    Yes _____ No _____

Answers: A yes to Questions 1 through 4 indicates a classical orientation to conflict; a yes to Questions 5 through 8 suggests a basic human relations view of conflict; a yes to Questions 9 through 12 reveals a preoccupation with the information aspects of systems; a yes to Questions 13 through 16 reveals a true existential spirit.

How did you score? What is the correct position? The answer is the old contingency one, "It all depends . . ."

# Activity 8:6

# Handling Interunit Conflicts

Carnarius (1976) suggests 11 methods of handling conflicts between units.

| Methods to Handle Inter Unit Conflicts | Advantages | Disadvantages | Check Usable Strategies |
|---|---|---|---|
| • Focus on the task to be done, not on the dynamics of the group process | | | |
| • Depersonalize the issue; Concentrate on solving the issue not rejecting persons. | | | |
| • Catch the problem early before it spreads to broader issues | | | |
| • Enlist a third party on neutral ground to work with the groups | | | |
| • Seek some basis of cooperation | | | |
| • Review for actual overlap and duplication of work | | | |
| • Cut down areas of contact if no other way opens | | | |
| • Overcome a win/lose psychology by finding some way both units come out winning. (win/win) | | | |
| • Determine why others might wish to maintain practices you dislike. | | | |

**Activity 8:6** continued

| | | | |
|---|---|---|---|
| ● Try to explain how what you want can be helpful to them. | | | |
| ● Analyze the forces than encourage and inhibit change. | | | |

- Consider the advantages and disadvantages of each method
- Put a check next to any of these alternatives you would select to handle interunit conflict.

## Activity 8:7

# Moving to Win/Win Positions

Changing a win/lose situation to a win/win situation requires creativity on your part. A staff nurse comes to you on Thursday requesting the coming weekend off for a special event. She didn't know about this event earlier. She seldom requests special days off. You have a policy to submit requests one month prior to date(s) wanted. You have the power and the right to refuse this request (*you win/she loses*).

● How could you change this situation to *win/win*?

_____
_____
_____
_____
_____
_____
_____
_____
_____
_____
_____

## Activity 8:8

# Negotiating Strategies

To be able to negotiate you must be willing to give something away to get something.

- In the situation below, could you give something away? What?

  * A staff nurse files a grievance about the performance appraisal you wrote. She comes to you to try to work it out.

  _____
  _____
  _____
  _____

- Negotiation also involves getting something. In the situation below, is there something you could request? What?

  * The emergency department head nurse wants you to take patients who are ready for admission sooner (often your PM staff goes to dinner and gets the patient on the way back).

  _____
  _____
  _____
  _____

## CASE STUDY

Your staff do not like to come to monthly staff meetings. They say the meetings are dull and boring and only reiterate information posted on the bulletin board. Your boss notices that attendance is low and suggests you improve the turnout.

What do you do?

## SOLUTION TO CASE STUDY

*Problem*   Lack of attendance at staff meeting.

*Conditions for Solutions*

    A. Seventy-five percent of staff attend meetings. (must)
    B. Staff want to attend meetings. (want)
    C. Meetings are interesting to staff. (want)
    D. Staff contribute to meetings. (want)

*Possible Solutions*

    1. Mandate staff attendance.
    2. Ask staff for input to improve meetings.
    3. Cancel staff meetings.

*Solution Analysis*

    Solution 1: Will meet condition A but probably not B, C, or D. "What if" you chose A? You may have problems with your union or overtime issues; better check about this.

    Solution 3: You decide this is the easiest. 'What if" you do? You discuss the possibility with your boss, who says you must hold staff meetings.

    Solution 2: This may meet condition A; and B, C, and D are also likely to happen. Try this solution.

    Ask your staff, "Why don't you want to come to staff meetings? What would improve the meetings?" Use their input to improve your meetings.

    Be sure to take the time to develop a meaningful agenda. Development of a good staff meeting agenda is an ongoing process. In the back of your calendar, keep an ongoing list of potential agenda items, including announcements, discussion items, items on which you need staff input, reminders of new policies, and procedures they need to read. Collect these items during your meeting with your boss, reading your mail, head nurse meetings, etc. Provide a page in your communication book or on your bulletin board for staff input to agendas.

    Make announcements and one-way communications at staff meetings brief. Use the time for decision making and some team building. Keep the meeting moving and begin and end on time. Evaluate quarterly.

## REFERENCES

Alfano, G., Burt, M., Christman, L., Brown, B., Werner, J., McClure, M., Donaho, B., & Carlson, S. Reports of the work group identifying obstacles of the all-R.N. nursing staff. In G. Alfano (Ed.), *All-R.N. Nursing Staff*. Wakefield, Mass.: Nursing Resources, 1980.

Burach, E.H., & Torda, F. *Manager's guide to change*. Belmont, Calif.: Lifetime Learning Publications, 1979.

Carlisle, A.E. *Organizational dynamics*. New York: AMACOM Division of American Management Associations, 1975.

Carnarius, S. *Management problems and solutions*. Reading, Mass.: Addison-Wesley, 1976.

Claus, K., & Bailey, J. *Decision making in nursing*. St. Louis, Mo.: C.V. Mosby, 1975.

Dahlen, A. With primary nursing we have it all together. In G. Alfano (Ed.), *All-R.N. nursing staff*. Wakefield, Mass.: Nursing Resources, 1980.

Fain, E. Shortcuts to problem solving. *Supervisor Nurse*, April 1981, p. 62.

Fetsinger, L. *A theory of cognitive dissonance*. Stanford: Stanford University Press, 1957, pp. 260–266.

Fisher, R., & Ury, W. *Getting to yes: Negotiating agreement without giving in*. New York: Penguin Books, 1981.

Kelly, J. *Organizational behavior*. Homewood, Ill.: Irwin, 1980.

Kepner, C.H., & Tregoe, B.V. *The rational manager*. New York: McGraw-Hill, 1965.

Kron, T., & Durbin, E. *The management of patient care*. Philadelphia: Saunders, 1981.

Labovitz, G. *Motivational dynamics*. Minneapolis, Minn.: Control Data Corporation, 1975.

Leavitt, H.J. Applied organization change in industry: Structured, technical and human approaches. In J.G. March (Ed.), *Handbook of organizations*. Chicago: Rand-McNally, 1965.

Lewin, K. Concepts in topological psychology. *Principles of topological psychology*. New York: McGraw-Hill, 1936, pp. 215–217.

Odiorne, G.S. *How managers make things happen*. Englewood Cliffs, N.J.: Prentice-Hall, 1961.

Thomas, K. Conflict and conflict management. In M.D. Dunnette (Ed.), *Handbook of industrial and organizational psychology*. Chicago: Rand-McNally, 1976.

Yura, H., & Walsh, M.B. *The nursing process*. New York: Appleton-Century-Crofts, 1978.

# Index